THE COMPLETE POETRY OF ROBERT LOUIS STEVENSON

A Digireads.com Book
Digireads.com Publishing

The Complete Poetry of Robert Louis Stevenson
By Robert Louis Stevenson
ISBN 10: 1-4209-4139-9
ISBN 13: 978-1-4209-4139-5

This edition copyright © 2011

Please visit *www.digireads.com*

CONTENTS

I. A CHILD'S GARDEN OF VERSES

DEDICATION: TO ALISON CUNNINGHAM, p. 13

I. Bed in Summer, p. 13
II. A Thought, p. 14
III. At the Sea-Side, p. 14
IV. Young Night-Thought, p. 14
V. Whole Duty of Children, p. 15
VI. Rain, p. 15
VII. Pirate Story, p. 15
VIII. Foreign Lands, p. 15
IX. Windy Nights, p. 16
X. Travel, p. 17
XI. Singing, p. 18
XII. Looking Forward, p. 18
XIII. A Good Play, p. 18
XIV. Where Go the Boats?, p. 19
XV. Auntie's Skirts, p. 19
XVI. The Land of Counterpane, p. 19
XVII. The Land of Nod, p. 20
XVIII. My Shadow, p. 20
XIX. System, p. 21
XX. A Good Boy, p. 21
XXI. Escape at Bedtime, p. 22
XXII. Marching Song, p. 22
XXIII. The Cow, p. 23
XXIV. The Happy Thought, p. 23
XXV. The Wind, p. 23
XXVI. Keepsake Mill, p. 24
XXVII. Good and Bad Children, p. 25
XXVIII. Foreign Children, p. 25
XXIX. The Sun Travels, p. 26
XXX. The Lamplighter, p. 26
XXXI. My Bed is a Boat, p. 27
XXXII. The Moon, p. 27
XXXIII. The Swing, p. 28
XXXIV. Time to Rise, p. 28
XXXV. Looking-Glass River, p. 28
XXXVI. Fairy Bread, p. 29
XXXVII. From a Railway Carriage, p. 29
XXXVIII. Winter-Time, p. 30
XXXIX. The Hayloft, p. 30
XL. Farewell to the Farm, p. 31
XLI. North-West Passage, p. 32

1. Good-Night, p. 32
2. Shadow March, p. 32
3. In Port, p. 33

THE CHILD ALONE

I. The Unseen Playmate, p. 33
II. My Ship and I, p. 34
III. My Kingdom, p. 34
IV. Picture-Books in Winter, p. 35
V. My Treasures, p. 36
VI. Block City, p. 36
VII. The Land of Story-Books, p. 37
VIII. Armies in the Fire, p. 38
IX. The Little Land, p. 39

GARDEN DAYS

I. Night and Day, p. 40
II. Nest Eggs, p. 42
III. The Flowers, p. 43
IV. Summer Sun, p. 43
V. The Dumb Soldier, p. 44
VI. Autumn Fires, p. 45
VII. The Gardener, p. 45
VIII. Historical Associations, p. 46

ENVOYS

I. To Willie and Henrietta, p. 46
II. To My Mother, p. 47
III. To Auntie, p. 47
IV. To Minnie, p. 48
V. To My Name-Child, p. 49
VI. To Any Reader, p. 50

II. UNDERWOODS

BOOK I

IN ENGLISH

I. Envoy, p. 52
II. A Song of the Road, p. 52
III. The Canoe Speaks, p. 53
IV. It is the season now to go, p. 54
V. The House Beautiful, p. 54
VI. A Visit from the Sea, p. 55

VII. To a Gardener, p. 56
VIII. To Minnie, p. 57
IX. To K. de M., p. 57
X. To N. V. de G. S., p. 58
XI. To Will H. Low, p. 58
XII. To Mrs. Will H. Low, p. 59
XIII. To H. F. Brown, p. 60
XIV. To Andrew Lang, p. 61
XV. Et Tu In Arcadia Vixisti, p. 61
XVI. To W. E. Henley, p. 63
XVII. Henry James, p. 64
XVIII. The Mirror Speaks, p. 64
XIX. Katharine, p. 65
XX. To F. J. S., p. 65
XXI. Requiem, p. 66
XXII. The Celestial Surgeon, p. 66
XXIII. Our Lady of the Snows, p. 66
XXIV. Not yet, my soul, these friendly fields desert, p. 68
XXV. It is not yours, O mother, to complain, p. 69
XXVI. The Sick Child, p. 70
XXVII. In Memoriam F. A. S., p. 71
XXVIII. To My Father, p. 71
XXIX. In the States, p. 72
XXX. A Portrait ., p. 73
XXXI. Sing clearlier, Muse, or evermore be still, p. 73
XXXII. A Camp, p. 73
XXXIII. The Country of the Camisards, p. 74
XXXIV. Skerryvore, p. 74
XXXV. Skerryvore: the Parallel, p. 74
XXXVI. *My house*, I say. But hark to the sunny doves, p. 75
XXXVII. My body which my dungeon is, p. 75
XXXVIII. Say not of me that weakly I declined, p. 76
XXXIX. Dedicatory Poem, p. 76

BOOK II

IN SCOTS

I. The Maker to Posterity, p. 79
II. Ille Terrarum, p. 79
III. When aince Aprile has fairly come, p. 80
IV. A Mile an' a Bittock, p. 83
V. A Lowden Sabbath Morn, p. 83
VI. The Spaewife, p. 87
VII. The Blast—1875, p. 88
VIII. The Counterblast—1886, p. 89
IX. The Counterblast Ironical, p. 91
X. Their Laureate to an Academy Class Dinner Club, p. 92

XI. Embro Hie Kirk, p. 93
XII. The Scotsman's Return from Abroad, p. 95
XIII. Late in the nicht in bed I lay, p. 98
XIV. My Conscience!, p. 100
XV. To Doctor John Brown, p. 101
XVI. It's an owercome sooth for age an' youth, p. 103

III. SONGS OF TRAVEL AND OTHER VERSES

I. The Vagabond, p. 105
II. Youth and Love—I, p. 105
III. Youth and Love—II, p. 106
IV. The Unforgotten—I, p. 106
V. The Unforgotten—II, p. 107
VI. The infinite shining heavens, p. 107
VII. Plain as the glistering planets shine, p. 107
VIII. To you, let snow and roses, p. 108
IX. Let Beauty awake in the morn from beautiful dreams, p. 109
X. I know not how it is with you, p. 109
XI. I will make you brooches and toys for your delight, p. 109
XII. We Have Loved of Yore, p. 110
XIII. Ditty, p. 111
XIV. Mater Triumphans, p. 111
XV. Bright is the ring of words, p. 111
XVI. In the highlands, in the country places, p. 112
XVII. Home no more home to me, whither must I wander, p. 113
XVIII. To Dr. Hake, p. 113
XIX. To—, p. 114
XX. The morning drum-call on my eager ear, p. 115
XXI. I have trod the upward and the downward slope, p. 115
XXII. He hears with gladdened heart the thunder, p. 115
XXIII. The Lost Occasion, p. 115
XXIV. If This Were Faith, p. 116
XXV. My Wife, p. 117
XXVI. Winter, p. 117
XXVII. The stormy evening closes now in vain, p. 117
XXVIII. To an Island Princess, p. 118
XXIX. To Kalakaua, p. 119
XXX. To Princess Kaiulani, p. 120
XXXI. To Mother Maryanne, p. 120
XXXII. In Memoriam, E. H., p. 120
XXXIII. To My Wife, p. 121
XXXIV. To the Muse, p. 122
XXXV. To My Old Familiars, p. 122
XXXVI. The tropics vanish, and meseems that I, p. 123
XXXVII. To S. C., p. 124
XXXVIII. The House of Tembinoka, p. 125
XXXIX. The Woodman, p. 128

XL. Tropic Rain, p. 131
XLI. An End of Travel, p. 132
XLII. We uncommiserate pass into the night, p. 132
XLIII. The Last Sight, p. 133
XLIV. Sing me a song of a lad that is gone, p. 133
XLV. To S. R. Crockett, p. 134
XLVI. Evensong, p. 134

IV. BALLADS

THE SONG OF RAHERO: A LEGEND OF TAHITI

DEDICATION: TO ORI A ORI, p. 135

I. The Slaying of Támatéa, p. 135
II. The Venging of Támatéa, p. 141
III. Rahéro, p. 146

THE FEAST OF FAMINE: MARQUESAN MANNERS

I. The Priest's Vigil, p. 151
II. The Lovers, p. 153
III. The Feast, p. 156
IV. The Raid, p. 159

TICONDEROGA: A LEGEND OF THE WEST HIGHLANDS

I. The Saying of the Name, p. 162
II. The Seeking of the Name, p. 166
III. The Place of the Name, p. 168

HEATHER ALE: A GALLOWAY LEGEND

Heather Ale: A Galloway Legend, p. 170

CHRISTMAS AT SEA

Christmas at Sea, p. 172

V. NEW POEMS

I. Summer Night, p. 175
II. I sit up here at midnight, p. 175
III. Lo! in thine honest eyes I read, p. 176
IV. Though deep indifference should drowse, p. 176
V. My heart, when first the blackbird sings, p. 177
VI. I dreamed of forest alleys fair, p. 177
VII. Verses Written in 1872, p. 179

VIII. To H. C. Bunner, p. 180
IX. From Wishing-land, p. 180
X. The Well-head, p. 181
XI. The Mill-house, p. 182
XII. St. Martin's Summer, p. 184
XIII. All influences were in vain, p. 185
XIV. The old world moans and topes, p. 186
XV. I am like one that has sat alone, p. 187
XVI. The whole day thro', in contempt and pity, p. 188
XVII. The old Chimaeras, old receipts, p. 188
XVIII. Dedication, p. 189
XIX. Prelude, p. 190
XX. The Vanquished Knight, p. 190
XXI. Auld Reekie, p. 191
XXII. Athole Brose, p. 191
XXIII. Over the Water wi' Charlie, p. 192
XXIV. To the Commissioners of Northern Lights, p. 193
XXV. After reading "Antony and Cleopatra", p. 194
XXVI. The relic taken, what avails the shrine?, p. 194
XXVII. About the sheltered garden ground, p. 195
XXVIII. I know not how, but as I count, p. 195
XXIX. Take not my hand as mine alone, p. 196
XXX. The angler rose, he took his rod, p. 196
XXXI. Spring-Song, p. 196
XXXII. Thou strainest through the mountain fern, p. 197
XXXIII. The summer sun shone round me, p. 197
XXXIV. You looked so tempting in the pew, p. 197
XXXV. Love's Vicissitudes, p. 198
XXXVI. The moon is sinking-the tempestuous weather, p. 198
XXXVII. Death, p. 199
XXXVIII. Duddingstone, p. 200
XXXIX. Stout marches lead to certain ends, p. 200
XL. Away with funeral music, p. 201
XLI. To Sydney, p. 201
XLII. Had I the power that have the will, p. 203
XLIII. O, dull cold northern sky, p. 203
XLIV. Apologetic postscript of a year later, p. 204
XLV. To Marcus, p. 205
XLVI. To Ottilie, p. 206
XLVII. This gloomy, northern day, p. 206
XLVIII. To a Youth, p. 207
XLIX. John Cavalier, p. 208
L. Praise and Prayer, p. 209
LI. Hopes, p. 209
LII. I have a friend: I have a story, p. 210
LIII. Link your arm in mine, my lad, p. 211
LIV. The wind is without there and howls in the trees, p. 212
LV. A Valentine's Song, p. 213

LVI. Hail! Childish slaves of social rules, p. 214
LVII. Swallows travel to and fro, p. 216
LVIII. To Mesdames Zassetsky and Garschine, p. 217
LIX. To Madame Garschine, p. 218
LX. Music at the Villa Marina, p. 218
LXI. Fear not, dear friend, but freely live your days, p. 219
LXII. Let love go, if go 'she will, p. 219
LXIII. I do not fear to own me kin, p. 220
LXIV. I am like one that for long days had sate, p. 221
LXV. Sit doon by me, my canty freend, p. 221
LXVI. Here he comes, big with statistics, p. 222
LXVII. Voluntary, p. 222
LXVIII. O now, although the year be done, p. 223
LXIX. Ad Se Ipsum, p. 224
LXX. In the green and gallant spring, p. 224
LXXI. Death, to the dead forevermore, p. 224
LXXII. To Charles Baxter, p. 225
LXXIII. The look of death is both severe and mild, p. 227
LXXIV. Her name is as a word of old romance, p. 227
LXXV. In autumn when the woods are red, p. 228
LXXVI. Light as my heart was long ago, p. 228
LXXVII. Gather ye roses while ye may, p. 228
LXXVIII. Poem for a Class Re-union, p. 229
LXXIX. I saw red evening through the rain, p. 230
LXXX. Last night we had a thunderstorm in style, p. 231
LXXXI. O lady fair and sweet, p. 231
LXXXII. If I had wings, my lady, like a dove, p. 232
LXXXIII. Rondels, p. 232
LXXXIV. Eh, man Henley, you're a don, p. 234
LXXXV. All night through, raves or broods, p. 234
LXXXVI. The rain is over and done, p. 234
LXXXVII. There where the land of love, p. 235
LXXVIII. Love is the very heart of spring, p. 235
LXXXIX. On His Pitiable Transformation, p. 236
XC. I, who all the winter through, p. 236
XCI. Love-what is love?, p. 236
XCII. Soon our friends perish, p. 237
XCIII. As one who having wandered all night long, p. 237
XCIV. Strange are the ways of men, p. 237
XCV. The wind blew shrill and smart, p. 238
XCVI. Man sails the deep a while, p. 239
XCVII. The cock's clear voice into the clearer air, p. 240
XCVIII. Now when the number of my years, p. 241
XCIX. What man may learn, what man may do, p. 241
C. The Susquehanna and the Delaware, p. 242
CI. If I could arise and travel away, p. 242
CII. Good old ale, mild or pale, p. 243
CIII. Nay, but I fancy somehow, year by year, p. 243

CIV. My wife and I, in one romantic cot, p. 244
CV. At morning on the garden seat, p. 244
CVI. Small is the trust when love is green, p. 244
CVII. Know you the river near to Grez, p. 245
CVIII. It's forth across the roaring foam, p. 246
CIX. Dedication, p. 246
CX. Farewell, p. 247
CXI. The Fine Pacific Islands, p. 247
CXII. Topical Song, p. 248
CXIII. Student Song, p. 249
CXIV. An English Breeze, p. 250
CXV. To Miss Cornish, p. 251
CXVI. To Rosabelle, p. 251
CXVII. As in their flight the birds of song, p. 252
CXVIII. Prayer, p. 253
CXIX. The Piper, p. 254
CXX. Epistle to Albert Dew-Smith, p. 254
CXXI. Of schooners, islands, and maroons, p. 256
CXXII. To Mrs. Macmarland, p. 257
CXXIII. Yes, I remember, and still remember wailing, p. 258
CXXIV. Tales of Arabia, p. 258
CXXV. Behold, as goblins dark of mien, p. 259
CXXVI. Still I love to rhyme, and still more, rhyming, to wander, p. 260
CXXVII. Long time I lay m little ease, p. 260
CXXVIII. Flower God, God of the spring, beautiful, bountiful, p. 261
CXXIX. Come, my beloved, hear from me, p. 261
CXXX. Since years ago forevermore, p. 262
CXXXI. For Richmond's Garden Wall, p. 263
CXXXII. Here Lies Erotion, p. 263
CXXXIII. To Priapus, p. 263
CXXXIV. Aye mon, it's true; I'm no' that weel, p. 264
CXXXV. Hail, guest, and enter freely!, p. 264
CXXXVI. Lo, now, my guest, if aught amiss were said, p. 264
CXXXVII. So live, so love, so use that fragile hour, p. 264
CXXXVIII. Before this little gift was come, p. 265
CXXXIX. Go, little book-the ancient phrase, p. 265
CXL. My love was warm: for that I crossed, p. 266
CXLI. Come, my little children, here are songs for you!, p. 266
CXLII. Home from the daisied meadows, where you linger yet, p. 267
CXLIII. Early in the morning I hear on your piano, p. 267
CXLIV. Fair isle at sea-thy lovely name, p. 267
CXLV. Loud and low in the chimney, p. 267
CXLVI. I love to be warm by the red fireside, p. 268
CXLVII. Mine eyes were swift to know thee, p. 268
CXLVIII. Fixed is the doom: and to the last of years, p. 269
CXLIX. Men are heaven's piers, they evermore, p. 269
CL. Spring Carol, p. 270
CLI. To what shall I compare her, p. 271

CLII. When the sun comes after rain, p. 271
CLIII. Late, O miller, p. 272
CLIV. To friends at home, the lone, the admired, the lost, p. 272
CLV. I, whom Apollo sometimes visited, p. 272
CLVI. The Far-farers, p. 273
CLVII. Far over seas an island is, p. 273
CLVIII. On the gorgeous hills of morning, p. 273
CLIX. Rivers and winds among the twisted hills, p. 274
CLX. Tempest tossed and sore afflicted, p. 274
CLXI. I, now, O friend, whom noiselessly the snows, p. 275
CLXII. Since thou hast given me this good hope, O God, p. 277
CLXIII. God gave to me a child in part, p. 277
CLXIV. Over the land is April, p. 278
CLXV. Light as a linnet on my way I start, p. 278
CLXVI. Come, here is adieu to the city, p. 278
CLXVII. It blows a snowing gale in the winter of the year, p. 279
CLXVIII. Ne Sit Ancillae Tibi Amor Pudori, p. 279
CLXIX. To all that love the far and blue, p. 280
CLXX. Now bare to the beholder's eye, p. 280
CLXXI. The Bour-Tree Den, p. 281
CLXXII. Sonnets, p. 284
CLXXIII. The Family, p. 289
CLXXIV. Air of Diabelli's, p. 295
CLXXV. De Erotio Puella, p. 298
CLXXVI. I look across the ocean, p. 298
CLXXVII. I am a hunchback, yellow faced, p. 298
CLXXVIII. Song, p. 299
CLXXIX. The New House, p. 299
CLXXX. Men marvel at the works of man, p. 300
CLXXXI. To Master Andrew Lang, p. 301
CLXXXII. To the Stormy Petrel, p. 301
CLXXXIII. The indefensible impulse of my blood, p. 302
CLXXXIV. Who would think, herein to look, p. 302
CLXXXV. Epistle to Charles Baxter, p. 303
CLXXXVI. Ad Martialem, p. 304
CLXXXVII. De M. Antonio, p. 305
CLXXXVIII. Not roses to the rose, I trow, p. 305
CLXXXIX. To a Little Girl, p. 306
CXC. To Miss Rawlinson, p. 306
CXCI. The pleasant river gushes, p. 306
CXCII. To H. F. Brown, p. 307
CXCIII. To W. E. Henley, p. 308
CXCIV. O, Henley, in my hours of ease, p. 309
CXCV. All things on earth and sea, p. 309
CXCVI. On Some Ghostly Companions at a Spa, p. 310
CXCVII. To Charles Baxter, p. 310
CXCVIII. To Henry James, p. 312
CXCIX. Here you rest among the valleys, maiden known to but a few, p. 313

CC. And thorns, but did the sculptor spare, p. 313
CCI. My brain swims, empty and light, p. 314
CCII. The Light-Keeper, p. 315
CCIII. The Daughter of Herodias, p. 317
CCIV. The Cruel Mistress, p. 318
CCV. Storm, p. 319
CCVI. Stormy Nights, p. 320
CCVII. Song at Dawn, p. 322
CCVIII. Sole scholar of your college I appear, p. 323
CCIX. Dark Women, p. 324
CCX. A Valentine, p. 325
CCXI. To a Midshipman, p. 326
CCXII. The faces and forms of yore, p. 327
CCXIII. The Consecration of Braille, p. 327
CCXIV. Burlesque Sonnet, p. 328
CCXV. To Teuila, p. 328
CCXVI. To Ko Ung, p. 329
CCXVII. To Ko Ung, the Goddess, p. 330
CCVIII. In Lupum, p. 330
CCXIX. In Charidemum, p. 331
CCXX. Ad Nepotem, p. 331
CCXXI. Epitaphium Erotii, p. 332
CCXXII. Ad Quintilianum, p. 332
CCXXIII. De Hortis Julii Martialis, p. 332
CCXXIV. In Maximum, p. 333
CCXXV. Ad Olum, p. 333
CCXXVI. De Coenatione Micae, p. 334
CCXXVII. Ad Piscatorem, p. 334

I. A CHILD'S GARDEN OF VERSES

To
Alison Cunningham
From Her Boy

For the long nights you lay awake
And watched for my unworthy sake:
For your most comfortable hand
That led me through the uneven land:
For all the story-books you read:
For all the pains you comforted:

For all you pitied, all you bore,
In sad and happy days of yore:—
My second Mother, my first Wife,
The angel of my infant life—
From the sick child, now well and old,
Take, nurse, the little book you hold!

And grant it, Heaven, that all who read
May find as dear a nurse at need,
And every child who lists my rhyme,
In the bright, fireside, nursery clime,
May hear it in as kind a voice
As made my childish days rejoice!
                                R. L. S.

I

BED IN SUMMER

In winter I get up at night
And dress by yellow candle-light.
In summer quite the other way,
I have to go to bed by day.

I have to go to bed and see
The birds still hopping on the tree,
Or hear the grown-up people's feet
Still going past me in the street.

And does it not seem hard to you,
When all the sky is clear and blue,
And I should like so much to play,
To have to go to bed by day?

II

A THOUGHT

It is very nice to think
The world is full of meat and drink,
With little children saying grace
In every Christian kind of place.

III

AT THE SEA-SIDE

When I was down beside the sea
A wooden spade they gave to me
   To dig the sandy shore.

My holes were empty like a cup.
In every hole the sea came up,
   Till it could come no more.

IV

YOUNG NIGHT-THOUGHT

All night long and every night,
When my mama puts out the light,
I see the people marching by,
As plain as day before my eye.

Armies and emperor and kings,
All carrying different kinds of things,
And marching in so grand a way,
You never saw the like by day.

So fine a show was never seen
At the great circus on the green;
For every kind of beast and man
Is marching in that caravan.

As first they move a little slow,
But still the faster on they go,
And still beside me close I keep
Until we reach the town of Sleep.

V

WHOLE DUTY OF CHILDREN

A child should always say what's true
And speak when he is spoken to,
And behave mannerly at table;
At least as far as he is able.

VI

RAIN

The rain is falling all around,
   It falls on field and tree,
It rains on the umbrellas here,
   And on the ships at sea.

VII

PIRATE STORY

Three of us afloat in the meadow by the swing,
   Three of us abroad in the basket on the lea.
Winds are in the air, they are blowing in the spring,
   And waves are on the meadow like the waves there are at sea.

Where shall we adventure, to-day that we're afloat,
   Wary of the weather and steering by a star?
Shall it be to Africa, a-steering of the boat,
   To Providence, or Babylon or off to Malabar?

Hi! but here's a squadron a-rowing on the sea—
   Cattle on the meadow a-charging with a roar!
Quick, and we'll escape them, they're as mad as they can be,
   The wicket is the harbour and the garden is the shore.

VIII

FOREIGN LANDS

Up into the cherry tree
Who should climb but little me?
I held the trunk with both my hands
And looked abroad in foreign lands.

I saw the next door garden lie,
Adorned with flowers, before my eye,
And many pleasant places more
That I had never seen before.

I saw the dimpling river pass
And be the sky's blue looking-glass;
The dusty roads go up and down
With people tramping in to town.

If I could find a higher tree
Farther and farther I should see,
To where the grown-up river slips
Into the sea among the ships,

To where the roads on either hand
Lead onward into fairy land,
Where all the children dine at five,
And all the playthings come alive.

IX

WINDY NIGHTS

Whenever the moon and stars are set,
   Whenever the wind is high,
All night long in the dark and wet,
   A man goes riding by.
Late in the night when the fires are out,
Why does he gallop and gallop about?

Whenever the trees are crying aloud,
   And ships are tossed at sea,
By, on the highway, low and loud,
   By at the gallop goes he.
By at the gallop he goes, and then
By he comes back at the gallop again.

X

TRAVEL

I should like to rise and go
Where the golden apples grow;—
Where below another sky
Parrot islands anchored lie,
And, watched by cockatoos and goats,
Lonely Crusoes building boats;—
Where in sunshine reaching out
Eastern cities, miles about,
Are with mosque and minaret
Among sandy gardens set,
And the rich goods from near and far
Hang for sale in the bazaar;—
Where the Great Wall round China goes,
And on one side the desert blows,
And with the voice and bell and drum,
Cities on the other hum;—
Where are forests hot as fire,
Wide as England, tall as a spire,
Full of apes and cocoa-nuts
And the negro hunters' huts;—
Where the knotty crocodile
Lies and blinks in the Nile,
And the red flamingo flies
Hunting fish before his eyes;—
Where in jungles near and far,
Man-devouring tigers are,
Lying close and giving ear
Lest the hunt be drawing near,
Or a comer-by be seen
Swinging in the palanquin;—
Where among the desert sands
Some deserted city stands,
All its children, sweep and prince,
Grown to manhood ages since,
Not a foot in street or house,
Not a stir of child or mouse,
And when kindly falls the night,
In all the town no spark of light.
There I'll come when I'm a man
With a camel caravan;
Light a fire in the gloom
Of some dusty dining room;
See the pictures on the walls,

Heroes, fights and festivals;
And in a corner find the toys
Of the old Egyptian boys.

XI

SINGING

Of speckled eggs the birdie sings
   And nests among the trees;
The sailor sings of ropes and things
   In ships upon the seas.

The children sing in far Japan,
   The children sing in Spain;
The organ with the organ man
   Is singing in the rain.

XII

LOOKING FORWARD

When I am grown to man's estate
I shall be very proud and great,
And tell the other girls and boys
Not to meddle with my toys.

XIII

A GOOD PLAY

We built a ship upon the stairs
All made of the back-bedroom chairs,
And filled it full of sofa pillows
To go a-sailing on the billows.

We took a saw and several nails,
And water in the nursery pails;
And Tom said, "Let us also take
An apple and a slice of cake;"—
Which was enough for Tom and me
To go a-sailing on, till tea.

We sailed along for days and days,
And had the very best of plays;
But Tom fell out and hurt his knee,
So there was no one left but me.

XIV

WHERE GO THE BOATS?

Dark brown is the river,
   Golden is the sand.
It flows along for ever,
   With trees on either hand.

Green leaves a-floating,
   Castles of the foam,
Boats of mine a-boating—
   Where will all come home?

On goes the river
   And out past the mill,
Away down the valley,
   Away down the hill.

Away down the river,
   A hundred miles or more,
Other little children
   Shall bring my boats ashore.

XV

AUNTIE'S SKIRTS

Whenever Auntie moves around,
   Her dresses make a curious sound,
They trail behind her up the floor,
   And trundle after through the door.

XVI

THE LAND OF COUNTERPANE

When I was sick and lay a-bed,
I had two pillows at my head,
And all my toys beside me lay,
To keep me happy all the day.

And sometimes for an hour or so
I watched my leaden soldiers go,
With different uniforms and drills,
Among the bed-clothes, through the hills;

And sometimes sent my ships in fleets
All up and down among the sheets;
Or brought my trees and houses out,
And planted cities all about.

I was the giant great and still
That sits upon the pillow-hill,
And sees before him, dale and plain,
The pleasant land of counterpane.

XVII

THE LAND OF NOD

From breakfast on through all the day
At home among my friends I stay,
But every night I go abroad
Afar into the land of Nod.

All by myself I have to go,
With none to tell me what to do—
All alone beside the streams
And up the mountain-sides of dreams.

The strangest things are these for me,
Both things to eat and things to see,
And many frightening sights abroad
Till morning in the land of Nod.

Try as I like to find the way,
I never can get back by day,
Nor can remember plain and clear
The curious music that I hear.

XVIII

MY SHADOW

I have a little shadow that goes in and out with me,
And what can be the use of him is more than I can see.
He is very, very like me from the heels up to the head;
And I see him jump before me, when I jump into my bed.

The funniest thing about him is the way he likes to grow—
Not at all like proper children, which is always very slow;
For he sometimes shoots up taller like an india-rubber ball,
And he sometimes goes so little that there's none of him at all.

He hasn't got a notion of how children ought to play,
And can only make a fool of me in every sort of way.
He stays so close behind me, he's a coward you can see;
I'd think shame to stick to nursie as that shadow sticks to me!

One morning, very early, before the sun was up,
I rose and found the shining dew on every buttercup;
But my lazy little shadow, like an arrant sleepy-head,
Had stayed at home behind me and was fast asleep in bed.

XIX

SYSTEM

Every night my prayers I say,
And get my dinner every day;
And every day that I've been good,
I get an orange after food.

The child that is not clean and neat,
With lots of toys and things to eat,
He is a naughty child, I'm sure—
Or else his dear papa is poor.

XX

A GOOD BOY

I woke before the morning, I was happy all the day,
I never said an ugly word, but smiled and stuck to play.

And now at last the sun is going down behind the wood,
And I am very happy, for I know that I've been good.

My bed is waiting cool and fresh, with linen smooth and fair,
And I must be off to sleepsin-by, and not forget my prayer.

I know that, till to-morrow I shall see the sun arise,
No ugly dream shall fright my mind, no ugly sight my eyes.

But slumber hold me tightly till I waken in the dawn,
And hear the thrushes singing in the lilacs round the lawn.

XXI

ESCAPE AT BEDTIME

The lights from the parlour and kitchen shone out
    Through the blinds and the windows and bars;
And high overhead and all moving about,
    There were thousands of millions of stars.
There ne'er were such thousands of leaves on a tree,
    Nor of people in church or the Park,
As the crowds of the stars that looked down upon me,
    And that glittered and winked in the dark.

The Dog, and the Plough, and the Hunter, and all,
    And the star of the sailor, and Mars,
These shown in the sky, and the pail by the wall
    Would be half full of water and stars.
They saw me at last, and they chased me with cries,
    And they soon had me packed into bed;
But the glory kept shining and bright in my eyes,
    And the stars going round in my head.

XXII

MARCHING SONG

Bring the comb and play upon it!
    Marching, here we come!
Willie cocks his highland bonnet,
    Johnnie beats the drum.

Mary Jane commands the party,
    Peter leads the rear;
Feet in time, alert and hearty,
    Each a Grenadier!

All in the most martial manner
    Marching double-quick;
While the napkin, like a banner,
    Waves upon the stick!

Here's enough of fame and pillage,
    Great commander Jane!
Now that we've been round the village,
    Let's go home again.

XXIII

THE COW

The friendly cow all red and white,
   I love with all my heart:
She gives me cream with all her might,
   To eat with apple-tart.

She wanders lowing here and there,
   And yet she cannot stray,
All in the pleasant open air,
   The pleasant light of day;

And blown by all the winds that pass
   And wet with all the showers,
She walks among the meadow grass
   And eats the meadow flowers.

XXIV

HAPPY THOUGHT

The world is so full of a number of things,
I'm sure we should all be as happy as kings.

XXV

THE WIND

I saw you toss the kites on high
And blow the birds about the sky;
And all around I heard you pass,
Like ladies' skirts across the grass—
   O wind, a-blowing all day long,
   O wind, that sings so loud a song!

I saw the different things you did,
But always you yourself you hid.
I felt you push, I heard you call,
I could not see yourself at all—
   O wind, a-blowing all day long,
   O wind, that sings so loud a song!

O you that are so strong and cold,
O blower, are you young or old?
Are you a beast of field and tree,
Or just a stronger child than me?
    O wind, a-blowing all day long,
    O wind, that sings so loud a song!

XXVI

KEEPSAKE MILL

Over the borders, a sin without pardon,
    Breaking the branches and crawling below,
Out through the breach in the wall of the garden,
    Down by the banks of the river we go.

Here is a mill with the humming of thunder,
    Here is the weir with the wonder of foam,
Here is the sluice with the race running under—
    Marvellous places, though handy to home!

Sounds of the village grow stiller and stiller,
    Stiller the note of the birds on the hill;
Dusty and dim are the eyes of the miller,
    Deaf are his ears with the moil of the mill.

Years may go by, and the wheel in the river
    Wheel as it wheels for us, children, to-day,
Wheel and keep roaring and foaming for ever
    Long after all of the boys are away.

Home for the Indies and home from the ocean,
    Heroes and soldiers we all will come home;
Still we shall find the old mill wheel in motion,
    Turning and churning that river to foam.

You with the bean that I gave when we quarrelled,
    I with your marble of Saturday last,
Honoured and old and all gaily apparelled,
    Here we shall meet and remember the past.

XXVII

GOOD AND BAD CHILDREN

Children, you are very little,
And your bones are very brittle;
If you would grow great and stately,
You must try to walk sedately.

You must still be bright and quiet,
And content with simple diet;
And remain, through all bewild'ring,
Innocent and honest children.

Happy hearts and happy faces,
Happy play in grassy places—
That was how in ancient ages,
Children grew to kings and sages.

But the unkind and the unruly,
And the sort who eat unduly,
They must never hope for glory—
Theirs is quite a different story!

Cruel children, crying babies,
All grow up as geese and gabies,
Hated, as their age increases,
By their nephews and their nieces.

XXVIII

FOREIGN CHILDREN

Little Indian, Sioux, or Crow,
Little frosty Eskimo,
Little Turk or Japanee,
Oh! don't you wish that you were me?

You have seen the scarlet trees
And the lions over seas;
You have eaten ostrich eggs,
And turned the turtles off their legs.

Such a life is very fine,
But it's not so nice as mine:
You must often as you trod,
Have wearied *not* to be abroad.

You have curious things to eat,
I am fed on proper meat;
You must dwell upon the foam,
But I am safe and live at home.
Little Indian, Sioux or Crow,
Little frosty Eskimo,
Little Turk or Japanee,
Oh! don't you wish that you were me?

XXIX

THE SUN TRAVELS

The sun is not a-bed, when I
At night upon my pillow lie;
Still round the earth his way he takes,
And morning after morning makes.

While here at home, in shining day,
We round the sunny garden play,
Each little Indian sleepy-head
Is being kissed and put to bed.

And when at eve I rise from tea,
Day dawns beyond the Atlantic Sea;
And all the children in the west
Are getting up and being dressed.

XXX

THE LAMPLIGHTER

My tea is nearly ready and the sun has left the sky.
It's time to take the window to see Leerie going by;
For every night at teatime and before you take your seat,
With lantern and with ladder he comes posting up the street.

Now Tom would be a driver and Maria go to sea,
And my papa's a banker and as rich as he can be;
But I, when I am stronger and can choose what I'm to do,
O Leerie, I'll go round at night and light the lamps with you!

For we are very lucky, with a lamp before the door,
And Leerie stops to light it as he lights so many more;
And oh! before you hurry by with ladder and with light;
O Leerie, see a little child and nod to him to-night!

XXXI

MY BED IS A BOAT

My bed is like a little boat;
   Nurse helps me in when I embark;
She girds me in my sailor's coat
   And starts me in the dark.

At night I go on board and say
   Good-night to all my friends on shore;
I shut my eyes and sail away
   And see and hear no more.

And sometimes things to bed I take,
   As prudent sailors have to do;
Perhaps a slice of wedding-cake,
   Perhaps a toy or two.

All night across the dark we steer;
   But when the day returns at last,
Safe in my room beside the pier,
   I find my vessel fast.

XXXII

THE MOON

The moon has a face like the clock in the hall;
She shines on thieves on the garden wall,
On streets and fields and harbour quays,
And birdies asleep in the forks of the trees.

The squalling cat and the squeaking mouse,
The howling dog by the door of the house,
The bat that lies in bed at noon,
All love to be out by the light of the moon.

But all of the things that belong to the day
Cuddle to sleep to be out of her way;
And flowers and children close their eyes
Till up in the morning the sun shall arise.

XXXIII

THE SWING

How do you like to go up in a swing,
   Up in the air so blue?
Oh, I do think it the pleasantest thing
   Ever a child can do!

Up in the air and over the wall,
   Till I can see so wide,
River and trees and cattle and all
   Over the countryside—

Till I look down on the garden green,
   Down on the roof so brown—
Up in the air I go flying again,
   Up in the air and down!

XXXIV

TIME TO RISE

A birdie with a yellow bill
Hopped upon my window sill,
Cocked his shining eye and said:
"Ain't you 'shamed, you sleepy-head!"

XXXV

LOOKING-GLASS RIVER

Smooth it glides upon its travel,
    Here a wimple, there a gleam—
      O the clean gravel!
      O the smooth stream!

Sailing blossoms, silver fishes,
    Paven pools as clear as air—
      How a child wishes
      To live down there!

We can see our colored faces
    Floating on the shaken pool
      Down in cool places,
      Dim and very cool;

Till a wind or water wrinkle,
     Dipping marten, plumping trout,
         Spreads in a twinkle
         And blots all out.

See the rings pursue each other;
     All below grows black as night,
         Just as if mother
         Had blown out the light!

Patience, children, just a minute—
     See the spreading circles die;
         The stream and all in it
         Will clear by-and-by.

XXXVI

FAIRY BREAD

Come up here, O dusty feet!
   Here is fairy bread to eat.
Here in my retiring room,
   Children, you may dine
On the golden smell of broom
   And the shade of pine;
And when you have eaten well,
Fairy stories hear and tell.

XXXVII

FROM A RAILWAY CARRIAGE

Faster than fairies, faster than witches,
Bridges and houses, hedges and ditches;
And charging along like troops in a battle
All through the meadows the horses and cattle:
All of the sights of the hill and the plain
Fly as thick as driving rain;
And ever again, in the wink of an eye,
Painted stations whistle by.

Here is a child who clambers and scrambles,
All by himself and gathering brambles;
Here is a tramp who stands and gazes;
And here is the green for stringing the daisies!
Here is a cart run away in the road
Lumping along with man and load;
And here is a mill, and there is a river:
Each a glimpse and gone forever!

XXXVIII

WINTER-TIME

Late lies the wintry sun a-bed,
A frosty, fiery sleepy-head;
Blinks but an hour or two; and then,
A blood-red orange, sets again.

Before the stars have left the skies,
At morning in the dark I rise;
And shivering in my nakedness,
By the cold candle, bathe and dress.

Close by the jolly fire I sit
To warm my frozen bones a bit;
Or with a reindeer-sled, explore
The colder countries round the door.

When to go out, my nurse doth wrap
Me in my comforter and cap;
The cold wind burns my face, and blows
Its frosty pepper up my nose.

Black are my steps on silver sod;
Thick blows my frosty breath abroad;
And tree and house, and hill and lake,
Are frosted like a wedding cake.

XXXIX

THE HAYLOFT

Through all the pleasant meadow-side
  The grass grew shoulder-high,
Till the shining scythes went far and wide
  And cut it down to dry.

Those green and sweetly smelling crops
    They led in wagons home;
And they piled them here in mountain tops
    For mountaineers to roam.

Here is Mount Clear, Mount Rusty-Nail,
    Mount Eagle and Mount High;—
The mice that in these mountains dwell,
    No happier are than I!

Oh, what a joy to clamber there,
    Oh, what a place for play,
With the sweet, the dim, the dusty air,
    The happy hills of hay!

XL

FAREWELL TO THE FARM

The coach is at the door at last;
The eager children, mounting fast
And kissing hands, in chorus sing:
Good-bye, good-bye, to everything!

To house and garden, field and lawn,
The meadow-gates we swang upon,
To pump and stable, tree and swing,
Good-bye, good-bye, to everything!

And fare you well for evermore,
O ladder at the hayloft door,
O hayloft where the cobwebs cling,
Good-bye, good-bye, to everything!

Crack goes the whip, and off we go;
The trees and houses smaller grow;
Last, round the woody turn we sing:
Good-bye, good-bye, to everything!

XLI

NORTH-WEST PASSAGE

1. GOOD-NIGHT

When the bright lamp is carried in,
The sunless hours again begin;
O'er all without, in field and lane,
The haunted night returns again.

Now we behold the embers flee
About the firelit hearth; and see
Our faces painted as we pass,
Like pictures, on the window glass.

Must we to bed indeed? Well then,
Let us arise and go like men,
And face with an undaunted tread
The long black passage up to bed.

Farewell, O brother, sister, sire!
O pleasant party round the fire!
The songs you sing, the tales you tell,
Till far to-morrow, fare you well!

2. SHADOW MARCH

All around the house is the jet-black night;
   It stares through the window-pane;
It crawls in the corners, hiding from the light,
   And it moves with the moving flame.

Now my little heart goes a beating like a drum,
   With the breath of the Bogies in my hair;
And all around the candle the crooked shadows come,
   And go marching along up the stair.

The shadow of the balusters, the shadow of the lamp,
   The shadow of the child that goes to bed—
All the wicked shadows coming tramp, tramp, tramp,
   With the black night overhead.

3. IN PORT

Last, to the chamber where I lie
My fearful footsteps patter nigh,
And come out from the cold and gloom
Into my warm and cheerful room.

There, safe arrived, we turn about
To keep the coming shadows out,
And close the happy door at last
On all the perils that we past.

Then, when mamma goes by to bed,
She shall come in with tip-toe tread,
And see me lying warm and fast
And in the land of Nod at last.

THE CHILD ALONE

I

THE UNSEEN PLAYMATE

When children are playing alone on the green,
In comes the playmate that never was seen.
When children are happy and lonely and good,
The Friend of the Children comes out of the wood.

Nobody heard him, and nobody saw,
His is a picture you never could draw,
But he's sure to be present, abroad or at home,
When children are happy and playing alone.

He lies in the laurels, he runs on the grass,
He sings when you tinkle the musical glass;
Whene'er you are happy and cannot tell why,
The Friend of the Children is sure to be by!

He loves to be little, he hates to be big,
'Tis he that inhabits the caves that you dig;
'Tis he when you play with your soldiers of tin
That sides with the Frenchmen and never can win.

'Tis he, when at night you go off to your bed,
Bids you go to sleep and not trouble your head;
For wherever they're lying, in cupboard or shelf,
'Tis he will take care of your playthings himself!

II

MY SHIP AND I

O it's I that am the captain of a tidy little ship,
   Of a ship that goes a sailing on the pond;
And my ship it keeps a-turning all around and all about;
But when I'm a little older, I shall find the secret out
   How to send my vessel sailing on beyond.

For I mean to grow as little as the dolly at the helm,
   And the dolly I intend to come alive;
And with him beside to help me, it's a-sailing I shall go,
It's a-sailing on the water, when the jolly breezes blow
   And the vessel goes a divie-divie-dive.

O it's then you'll see me sailing through the rushes and the reeds,
   And you'll hear the water singing at the prow;
For beside the dolly sailor, I'm to voyage and explore,
To land upon the island where no dolly was before,
   And to fire the penny cannon in the bow.

III

MY KINGDOM

Down by a shining water well
I found a very little dell,
   No higher than my head.
The heather and the gorse about
In summer bloom were coming out,
   Some yellow and some red.

I called the little pool a sea;
The little hills were big to me;
   For I am very small.
I made a boat, I made a town,
I searched the caverns up and down,
   And named them one and all.

And all about was mine, I said,
The little sparrows overhead,
   The little minnows too.
This was the world and I was king;
For me the bees came by to sing,
   For me the swallows flew.

I played there were no deeper seas,
Nor any wider plains than these,
    Nor other kings than me.
At last I heard my mother call
Out from the house at evenfall,
    To call me home to tea.

And I must rise and leave my dell,
And leave my dimpled water well,
    And leave my heather blooms.
Alas! and as my home I neared,
How very big my nurse appeared.
    How great and cool the rooms!

IV

PICTURE-BOOKS IN WINTER

Summer fading, winter comes—
Frosty mornings, tingling thumbs,
Window robins, winter rooks,
And the picture story-books.

Water now is turned to stone
Nurse and I can walk upon;
Still we find the flowing brooks
In the picture story-books.

All the pretty things put by,
Wait upon the children's eye,
Sheep and shepherds, trees and crooks,
In the picture story-books.

We may see how all things are
Seas and cities, near and far,
And the flying fairies' looks,
In the picture story-books.

How am I to sing your praise,
Happy chimney-corner days,
Sitting safe in nursery nooks,
Reading picture story-books?

V

MY TREASURES

These nuts, that I keep in the back of the nest,
Where all my tin soldiers are lying at rest,
Were gathered in Autumn by nursie and me
In a wood with a well by the side of the sea.

This whistle we made (and how clearly it sounds!)
By the side of a field at the end of the grounds.
Of a branch of a plane, with a knife of my own,
It was nursie who made it, and nursie alone!

The stone, with the white and the yellow and grey,
We discovered I cannot tell *how* far away;
And I carried it back although weary and cold,
For though father denies it, I'm sure it is gold.

But of all my treasures the last is the king,
For there's very few children possess such a thing;
And that is a chisel, both handle and blade,
Which a man who was really a carpenter made.

VI

BLOCK CITY

What are you able to build with your blocks?
Castles and palaces, temples and docks.
Rain may keep raining, and others go roam,
But I can be happy and building at home.

Let the sofa be mountains, the carpet be sea,
There I'll establish a city for me:
A kirk and a mill and a palace beside,
And a harbour as well where my vessels may ride.

Great is the palace with pillar and wall,
A sort of a tower on the top of it all,
And steps coming down in an orderly way
To where my toy vessels lie safe in the bay.

This one is sailing and that one is moored:
Hark to the song of the sailors aboard!
And see, on the steps of my palace, the kings
Coming and going with presents and things!

Now I have done with it, down let it go!
All in a moment the town is laid low.
Block upon block lying scattered and free,
What is there left of my town by the sea?

Yet as I saw it, I see it again,
The kirk and the palace, the ships and the men,
And as long as I live and where'er I may be,
I'll always remember my town by the sea.

VII

THE LAND OF STORY-BOOKS

At evening when the lamp is lit,
Around the fire my parents sit;
They sit at home and talk and sing,
And do not play at anything.

Now, with my little gun, I crawl
All in the dark along the wall,
And follow round the forest track
Away behind the sofa back.

There, in the night, where none can spy,
All in my hunter's camp I lie,
And play at books that I have read
Till it is time to go to bed.

These are the hills, these are the woods,
These are my starry solitudes;
And there the river by whose brink
The roaring lions come to drink.

I see the others far away
As if in firelit camp they lay,
And I, like to an Indian scout,
Around their party prowled about.

So when my nurse comes in for me,
Home I return across the sea,
And go to bed with backward looks
At my dear land of Story-books.

VIII

ARMIES IN THE FIRE

The lamps now glitter down the street;
Faintly sound the falling feet;
And the blue even slowly falls
About the garden trees and walls.

Now in the falling of the gloom
The red fire paints the empty room:
And warmly on the roof it looks,
And flickers on the back of books.

Armies march by tower and spire
Of cities blazing, in the fire;—
Till as I gaze with staring eyes,
The armies fade, the lustre dies.

Then once again the glow returns;
Again the phantom city burns;
And down the red-hot valley, lo!
The phantom armies marching go!

Blinking embers, tell me true
Where are those armies marching to,
And what the burning city is
That crumbles in your furnaces!

IX

THE LITTLE LAND

When at home alone I sit
And am very tired of it,
I have just to shut my eyes
To go sailing through the skies—
To go sailing far away
To the pleasant Land of Play;
To the fairy land afar
Where the Little People are;
Where the clover-tops are trees,
And the rain-pools are the seas,
And the leaves, like little ships,
Sail about on tiny trips;
And above the Daisy tree
    Through the grasses,
High o'erhead the Bumble Bee
    Hums and passes.

In that forest to and fro
I can wander, I can go;
See the spider and the fly,
And the ants go marching by,
Carrying parcels with their feet
Down the green and grassy street.
I can in the sorrel sit
Where the ladybird alit.
I can climb the jointed grass
    And on high
See the greater swallows pass
    In the sky,
And the round sun rolling by
Heeding no such things as I.

Through that forest I can pass
Till, as in a looking-glass,
Humming fly and daisy tree
And my tiny self I see,
Painted very clear and neat
On the rain-pool at my feet.
Should a leaflet come to land
Drifting near to where I stand,
Straight I'll board that tiny boat
Round the rain-pool sea to float.

Little thoughtful creatures sit
On the grassy coasts of it;
Little things with lovely eyes
See me sailing with surprise.
Some are clad in armour green—
(These have sure to battle been!)—
Some are pied with ev'ry hue,
Black and crimson, gold and blue;
Some have wings and swift are gone;—
But they all look kindly on.

When my eyes I once again
Open, and see all things plain:
High bare walls, great bare floor;
Great big knobs on drawer and door;
Great big people perched on chairs,
Stitching tucks and mending tears,
Each a hill that I could climb,
And talking nonsense all the time—
    O dear me,
    That I could be
A sailor on a the rain-pool sea,
A climber in the clover tree,
And just come back a sleepy-head,
Late at night to go to bed.

GARDEN DAYS

I

NIGHT AND DAY

When the golden day is done,
    Through the closing portal,
Child and garden, flower and sun,
    Vanish all things mortal.

As the building shadows fall
    As the rays diminish,
Under evening's cloak they all
    Roll away and vanish.

Garden darkened, daisy shut,
    Child in bed, they slumber—
Glow-worm in the hallway rut,
    Mice among the lumber.

In the darkness houses shine,
  Parents move the candles;
Till on all the night divine
  Turns the bedroom handles.

Till at last the day begins
  In the east a-breaking,
In the hedges and the whins
  Sleeping birds a-waking.

In the darkness shapes of things,
  Houses, trees and hedges,
Clearer grow; and sparrow's wings
  Beat on window ledges.

These shall wake the yawning maid;
  She the door shall open—
Finding dew on garden glade
  And the morning broken.

There my garden grows again
  Green and rosy painted,
As at eve behind the pane
  From my eyes it fainted.

Just as it was shut away,
  Toy-like, in the even,
Here I see it glow with day
  Under glowing heaven.

Every path and every plot,
  Every blush of roses,
Every blue forget-me-not
  Where the dew reposes,

"Up!" they cry, "the day is come
  On the smiling valleys:
We have beat the morning drum;
  Playmate, join your allies!"

II

NEST EGGS

Birds all the sunny day
   Flutter and quarrel
Here in the arbour-like
   Tent of the laurel.

Here in the fork
   The brown nest is seated;
Four little blue eggs
   The mother keeps heated.

While we stand watching her
   Staring like gabies,
Safe in each egg are the
   Bird's little babies.

Soon the frail eggs they shall
   Chip, and upspringing
Make all the April woods
   Merry with singing.

Younger than we are,
   O children, and frailer,
Soon in the blue air they'll be,
   Singer and sailor.

We, so much older,
   Taller and stronger,
We shall look down on the
   Birdies no longer.

They shall go flying
   With musical speeches
High overhead in the
   Tops of the beeches.

In spite of our wisdom
   And sensible talking,
We on our feet must go
   Plodding and walking.

III

THE FLOWERS

All the names I know from nurse:
Gardener's garters, Shepherd's purse,
Bachelor's buttons, Lady's smock,
And the Lady Hollyhock.

Fairy places, fairy things,
Fairy woods where the wild bee wings,
Tiny trees for tiny dames—
These must all be fairy names!

Tiny woods below whose boughs
Shady fairies weave a house;
Tiny tree-tops, rose or thyme,
Where the braver fairies climb!

Fair are grown-up people's trees,
But the fairest woods are these;
Where, if I were not so tall,
I should live for good and all.

IV

SUMMER SUN

Great is the sun, and wide he goes
Through empty heaven with repose;
And in the blue and glowing days
More thick than rain he showers his rays.

Though closer still the blinds we pull
To keep the shady parlour cool,
Yet he will find a chink or two
To slip his golden fingers through.

The dusty attic spider-clad
He, through the keyhole, maketh glad;
And through the broken edge of tiles
Into the laddered hay-loft smiles.

Meantime his golden face around
He bares to all the garden ground,
And sheds a warm and glittering look
Among the ivy's inmost nook.

Above the hills, along the blue,
Round the bright air with footing true,
To please the child, to paint the rose,
The gardener of the World, he goes.

V

THE DUMB SOLDIER

When the grass was closely mown,
Walking on the lawn alone,
In the turf a hole I found,
And hid a soldier underground.

Spring and daisies came apace;
Grasses hide my hiding place;
Grasses run like a green sea
O'er the lawn up to my knee.

Under grass alone he lies,
Looking up with leaden eyes,
Scarlet coat and pointed gun,
To the stars and to the sun.

When the grass is ripe like grain,
When the scythe is stoned again,
When the lawn is shaven clear,
Then my hole shall reappear.

I shall find him, never fear,
I shall find my grenadier;
But for all that's gone and come,
I shall find my soldier dumb.

He has lived, a little thing,
In the grassy woods of spring;
Done, if he could tell me true,
Just as I should like to do.

He has seen the starry hours
And the springing of the flowers;
And the fairy things that pass
In the forests of the grass.

In the silence he has heard
Talking bee and ladybird,
And the butterfly has flown
O'er him as he lay alone.

Not a word will he disclose,
Not a word of all he knows.
I must lay him on the shelf,
And make up the tale myself.

VI

AUTUMN FIRES

In the other gardens
   And all up the vale,
From the autumn bonfires
   See the smoke trail!

Pleasant summer over
   And all the summer flowers,
The red fire blazes,
   The grey smoke towers.

Sing a song of seasons!
   Something bright in all!
Flowers in the summer,
   Fires in the fall!

VII

THE GARDENER

The gardener does not love to talk.
He makes me keep the gravel walk;
And when he puts his tools away,
He locks the door and takes the key.

Away behind the currant row,
Where no one else but cook may go,
Far in the plots, I see him dig,
Old and serious, brown and big.

He digs the flowers, green, red, and blue,
Nor wishes to be spoken to.
He digs the flowers and cuts the hay,
And never seems to want to play.

Silly gardener! summer goes,
And winter comes with pinching toes,
When in the garden bare and brown
You must lay your barrow down.

Well now, and while the summer stays,
To profit by these garden days
O how much wiser you would be
To play at Indian wars with me!

VIII

HISTORICAL ASSOCIATIONS

Dear Uncle Jim, this garden ground
That now you smoke your pipe around,
Has seen immortal actions done
And valiant battles lost and won.

Here we had best on tip-toe tread,
While I for safety march ahead,
For this is that enchanted ground
Where all who loiter slumber sound.

Here is the sea, here is the sand,
Here is simple Shepherd's Land,
Here are the fairy hollyhocks,
And there are Ali Baba's rocks.

But yonder, see! apart and high,
Frozen Siberia lies; where I,
With Robert Bruce and William Tell,
Was bound by an enchanter's spell.

ENVOYS

I

TO WILLIE AND HENRIETTA

If two may read aright
These rhymes of old delight
And house and garden play,
You two, my cousins, and you only, may.

  You in a garden green
  With me were king and queen,
  Were hunter, soldier, tar,
And all the thousand things that children are.

  Now in the elders' seat
  We rest with quiet feet,
  And from the window-bay
We watch the children, our successors, play.

  "Time was," the golden head
  Irrevocably said;
  But time which one can bind,
While flowing fast away, leaves love behind.

II

TO MY MOTHER

You too, my mother, read my rhymes
For love of unforgotten times,
And you may chance to hear once more
The little feet along the floor.

III

TO AUNTIE

"Chief *of our aunts*"—not only I,
But all your dozen of nurselings cry—
*"What did the other children do?
And what were childhood, wanting you?"*

IV

TO MINNIE

The red room with the giant bed
Where none but elders laid their head;
The little room where you and I
Did for awhile together lie
And, simple suitor, I your hand
In decent marriage did demand;
The great day nursery, best of all,
With pictures pasted on the wall
And leaves upon the blind—
A pleasant room wherein to wake
And hear the leafy garden shake
And rustle in the wind—
And pleasant there to lie in bed
And see the pictures overhead—
The wars about Sebastopol,
The grinning guns along the wall,
The daring escalade,
The plunging ships, the bleating sheep,
The happy children ankle-deep
And laughing as they wade:

All these are vanished clean away,
And the old manse is changed to-day;
It wears an altered face
And shields a stranger race.
The river, on from mill to mill,
Flows past our childhood's garden still;
But ah! we children never more
Shall watch it from the water-door!
Below the yew—it still is there—
Our phantom voices haunt the air
As we were still at play,
And I can hear them call and say:
"How far is it to Babylon?"

Ah, far enough, my dear,
Far, far enough from here—
Yet you have farther gone!
"Can I get there by candlelight?"
So goes the old refrain.
I do not know—perchance you might—
But only, children, hear it right,
Ah, never to return again!
The eternal dawn, beyond a doubt,
Shall break on hill and plain,
And put all stars and candles out
Ere we be young again.

To you in distant India, these
I send across the seas,
Nor count it far across.
For which of us forgets
The Indian cabinets,
The bones of antelope, the wings of albatross,
The pied and painted birds and beans,
The junks and bangles, beads and screens,
The gods and sacred bells,
And the loud-humming, twisted shells!
The level of the parlour floor
Was honest, homely, Scottish shore;
But when we climbed upon a chair,
Behold the gorgeous East was there!
Be this a fable; and behold
Me in the parlour as of old,
And Minnie just above me set
In the quaint Indian cabinet!
Smiling and kind, you grace a shelf
Too high for me to reach myself.
Reach down a hand, my dear, and take
These rhymes for old acquaintance' sake!

V

TO MY NAME-CHILD

1

Some day soon this rhyming volume, if you learn with proper speed,
Little Louis Sanchez, will be given you to read.
Then you shall discover, that your name was printed down
By the English printers, long before, in London town.

In the great and busy city where the East and West are met,
All the little letters did the English printer set;
While you thought of nothing, and were still too young to play,
Foreign people thought of you in places far away.

Ay, and when you slept, a baby, over all the English lands
Other little children took the volume in their hands;
Other children questioned, in their homes across the seas:
Who was little Louis, won't you tell us, mother, please?

2

Now that you have spelt your lesson, lay it down and go and play,
Seeking shells and seaweed on the sands of Monterey,
Watching all the mighty whalebones, lying buried by the breeze,
Tiny sandy-pipers, and the huge Pacific seas.

And remember in your playing, as the sea-fog rolls to you,
Long ere you could read it, how I told you what to do;
And that while you thought of no one, nearly half the world away
Some one thought of Louis on the beach of Monterey!

VI

TO ANY READER

As from the house your mother sees
You playing round the garden trees,
So you may see, if you will look
Through the windows of this book,
Another child, far, far away,
And in another garden, play.
But do not think you can at all,
By knocking on the window, call
That child to hear you. He intent
Is all on his play-business bent.
He does not hear, he will not look,
Nor yet be lured out of this book.
For, long ago, the truth to say,
He has grown up and gone away,
And it is but a child of air
That lingers in the garden there.

II. UNDERWOODS

Of all my verse, like not a single line;
But like my title, for it is not mine.
That title from a better man I stole:
Ah, how much better, had I stol'n the whole!

DEDICATION

There are men and classes of men that stand above the common herd: the soldier, the sailor and the shepherd not unfrequently; the artist rarely; rarely still, the clergyman; the physician almost as a rule. He is the flower (such as it is) of our civilisation; and when that stage of man is done with, and only remembered to be marvelled at in history, he will be thought to have shared as little as any in the defects of the period, and most notably exhibited the virtues of the race. Generosity he has, such as is possible to those who practise an art, never to those who drive a trade; discretion, tested by a hundred secrets; tact, tried in a thousand embarrassments; and what are more important, Heraclean cheerfulness and courage. So it is that he brings air and cheer into the sickroom, and often enough, though not so often as he wishes, brings healing.

Gratitude is but a lame sentiment; thanks, when they are expressed, are often more embarrassing than welcome; and yet I must set forth mine to a few out of many doctors who have brought me comfort and help: to Dr. Willey of San Francisco, whose kindness to a stranger it must be as grateful to him, as it is touching to me, to remember; to Dr. Karl Ruedi of Davos, the good genius of the English in his frosty mountains; to Dr. Herbert of Paris, whom I knew only for a week, and to Dr. Caissot of Montpellier, whom I knew only for ten days, and who have yet written their names deeply in my memory; to Dr. Brandt of Royat; to Dr. Wakefield of Nice; to Dr. Chepmell, whose visits make it a pleasure to be ill; to Dr. Horace Dobell, so wise in counsel; to Sir Andrew Clark, so unwearied in kindness and to that wise youth, my uncle, Dr. Balfour.

I forget as many as I remember; and I ask both to pardon me, these for silence, those for inadequate speech. But one name I have kept on purpose to the last, because it is a household word with me, and because if I had not received favours from so many hands and in so many quarters of the world, it should have stood upon this page alone: that of my friend Thomas Bodley Scott of Bournemouth. Will he accept this, although shared among so many, for a dedication to himself? and when next my ill-fortune (which has thus its pleasant side) brings him hurrying to me when he would fain sit down to meat or lie down to rest, will he care to remember that he takes this trouble for one who is not fool enough to be ungrateful?

R. L. S.

Skerryvore,
   Bournemouth.

BOOK I.

IN ENGLISH

I—ENVOY

Go, little book, and wish to all
Flowers in the garden, meat in the hall,
A bin of wine, a spice of wit,
A house with lawns enclosing it,
A living river by the door,
A nightingale in the sycamore!

II—A SONG OF THE ROAD

The gauger walked with willing foot,
And aye the gauger played the flute;
And what should Master Gauger play
But *Over the hills and far away?*

Whene'er I buckle on my pack
And foot it gaily in the track,
O pleasant gauger, long since dead,
I hear you fluting on ahead.

You go with me the self-same way—
The self-same air for me you play;
For I do think and so do you
It is the tune to travel to.

For who would gravely set his face
To go to this or t'other place?
There's nothing under Heav'n so blue
That's fairly worth the travelling to.

On every hand the roads begin,
And people walk with zeal therein;
But wheresoe'er the highways tend,
Be sure there's nothing at the end.

Then follow you, wherever hie
The travelling mountains of the sky.
Or let the streams in civil mode
Direct your choice upon a road;

For one and all, or high or low,
Will lead you where you wish to go;
And one and all go night and day
Over the hills and far away!

FOREST OF MONTARGIS, 1878.

III—THE CANOE SPEAKS

On the great streams the ships may go
About men's business to and fro.
But I, the egg-shell pinnace, sleep
On crystal waters ankle-deep:
I, whose diminutive design,
Of sweeter cedar, pithier pine,
Is fashioned on so frail a mould,
A hand may launch, a hand withhold:
I, rather, with the leaping trout
Wind, among lilies, in and out;
I, the unnamed, inviolate,
Green, rustic rivers, navigate;
My dipping paddle scarcely shakes
The berry in the bramble-brakes;
Still forth on my green way I wend
Beside the cottage garden-end;
And by the nested angler fare,
And take the lovers unaware.
By willow wood and water-wheel
Speedily fleets my touching keel;
By all retired and shady spots
Where prosper dim forget-me-nots;
By meadows where at afternoon
The growing maidens troop in June
To loose their girdles on the grass.
Ah! speedier than before the glass
The backward toilet goes; and swift
As swallows quiver, robe and shift
And the rough country stockings lie
Around each young divinity.
When, following the recondite brook,
Sudden upon this scene I look,
And light with unfamiliar face
On chaste Diana's bathing-place,
Loud ring the hills about and all
The shallows are abandoned. . . .

IV

It is the season now to go
About the country high and low,
Among the lilacs hand in hand,
And two by two in fairy land.

The brooding boy, the sighing maid,
Wholly fain and half afraid,
Now meet along the hazel'd brook
To pass and linger, pause and look.

A year ago, and blithely paired,
Their rough-and-tumble play they shared;
They kissed and quarrelled, laughed and cried,
A year ago at Eastertide.

With bursting heart, with fiery face,
She strove against him in the race;
He unabashed her garter saw,
That now would touch her skirts with awe.

Now by the stile ablaze she stops,
And his demurer eyes he drops;
Now they exchange averted sighs
Or stand and marry silent eyes.

And he to her a hero is
And sweeter she than primroses;
Their common silence dearer far
Than nightingale and mavis are.

Now when they sever wedded hands,
Joy trembles in their bosom-strands
And lovely laughter leaps and falls
Upon their lips in madrigals.

V—THE HOUSE BEAUTIFUL

A naked house, a naked moor,
A shivering pool before the door,
A garden bare of flowers and fruit
And poplars at the garden foot:
Such is the place that I live in,
Bleak without and bare within.

Yet shall your ragged moor receive
The incomparable pomp of eve,
And the cold glories of the dawn
Behind your shivering trees be drawn;
And when the wind front place to place
Doth the unmoored cloud-galleons chase,
Your garden gloom and gleam again,
With leaping sun, with glancing rain.
Here shall the wizard moon ascend
The heavens, in the crimson end
Of day's declining splendour; here
The army of the stars appear.
The neighbour hollows dry or wet,
Spring shall with tender flowers beset;
And oft the morning muser see
Larks rising from the broomy lea,
And every fairy wheel and thread
Of cobweb dew-bediamonded.
When daisies go, shall winter time
Silver the simple grass with rime;
Autumnal frosts enchant the pool
And make the cart-ruts beautiful;
And when snow-bright the moor expands,
How shall your children clap their hands!
To make this earth our hermitage,
A cheerful and a changeful page,
God's bright and intricate device
Of days and seasons doth suffice.

VI—A VISIT FROM THE SEA

Far from the loud sea beaches
　Where he goes fishing and crying,
Here in the inland garden
　Why is the sea-gull flying?

Here are no fish to dive for;
　Here is the corn and lea;
Here are the green trees rustling.
　Hie away home to sea!

Fresh is the river water
　And quiet among the rushes;
This is no home for the sea-gull
　But for the rooks and thrushes.

Pity the bird that has wandered!
   Pity the sailor ashore!
Hurry him home to the ocean,
   Let him come here no more!

High on the sea-cliff ledges
   The white gulls are trooping and crying,
Here among the rooks and roses,
   Why is the sea-gull flying?

VII—TO A GARDENER

Friend, in my mountain-side demesne
My plain-beholding, rosy, green
And linnet-haunted garden-ground,
Let still the esculents abound.
Let first the onion flourish there,
Rose among roots, the maiden-fair,
Wine-scented and poetic soul
Of the capacious salad bowl.
Let thyme the mountaineer (to dress
The tinier birds) and wading cress,
The lover of the shallow brook,
From all my plots and borders look.

Nor crisp and ruddy radish, nor
Pease-cods for the child's pinafore
Be lacking; nor of salad clan
The last and least that ever ran
About great nature's garden-beds.
Nor thence be missed the speary heads
Of artichoke; nor thence the bean
That gathered innocent and green
Outsavours the belauded pea.

These tend, I prithee; and for me,
Thy most long-suffering master, bring
In April, when the linnets sing
And the days lengthen more and more
At sundown to the garden door.
And I, being provided thus.
Shall, with superb asparagus,
A book, a taper, and a cup
Of country wine, divinely sup.

LA SOLITUDE, HYÈRES

VIII—TO MINNIE

(WITH A HAND-GLASS)

A picture-frame for you to fill,
   A paltry setting for your face,
A thing that has no worth until
   You lend it something of your grace

I send (unhappy I that sing
   Laid by awhile upon the shelf)
Because I would not send a thing
   Less charming than you are yourself.

And happier than I, alas!
   (Dumb thing, I envy its delight)
'Twill wish you well, the looking-glass,
   And look you in the face to-night.

IX—TO K. DE M.

A lover, of the moorland bare
And honest country winds, you were;
The silver-skimming rain you took;
And loved the floodings of the brook,
Dew, frost and mountains, fire and seas,
Tumultuary silences,
Winds that in darkness fifed a tune,
And the high-riding, virgin moon.

And as the berry, pale and sharp,
Springs on some ditch's counterscarp
In our ungenial, native north—
You put your frosted wildings forth,
And on the heath, afar from man,
A strong and bitter virgin ran.

The berry ripened keeps the rude
And racy flavour of the wood.
And you that loved the empty plain
All redolent of wind and rain,
Around you still the curlew sings—
The freshness of the weather clings—
The maiden jewels of the rain
Sit in your dabbled locks again.

X—TO N. V. DE G. S.

The unfathomable sea, and time, and tears,
The deeds of heroes and the crimes of kings
Dispart us; and the river of events
Has, for an age of years, to east and west
More widely borne our cradles. Thou to me
Art foreign, as when seamen at the dawn
Descry a land far off and know not which.
So I approach uncertain; so I cruise
Round thy mysterious islet, and behold
Surf and great mountains and loud river-bars,
And from the shore hear inland voices call.
Strange is the seaman's heart; he hopes, he fears;
Draws closer and sweeps wider from that coast;
Last, his rent sail refits, and to the deep
His shattered prow uncomforted puts back.
Yet as he goes he ponders at the helm
Of that bright island; where he feared to touch,
His spirit readventures; and for years,
Where by his wife he slumbers safe at home,
Thoughts of that land revisit him; he sees
The eternal mountains beckon, and awakes
Yearning for that far home that might have been.

XI—TO WILL. H. LOW

Youth now flees on feathered foot
Faint and fainter sounds the flute,
Rarer songs of gods; and still
Somewhere on the sunny hill,
Or along the winding stream,
Through the willows, flits a dream;
Flits but shows a smiling face,
Flees but with so quaint a grace,
None can choose to stay at home,
All must follow, all must roam.

This is unborn beauty: she
Now in air floats high and free,
Takes the sun and breaks the blue;—
Late with stooping pinion flew
Raking hedgerow trees, and wet
Her wing in silver streams, and set
Shining foot on temple roof:
Now again she flies aloof,
Coasting mountain clouds and kiss't
By the evening's amethyst.

In wet wood and miry lane,
Still we pant and pound in vain;
Still with leaden foot we chase
Waning pinion, fainting face;
Still with gray hair we stumble on,
Till, behold, the vision gone!

Where hath fleeting beauty led?
To the doorway of the dead.
Life is over, life was gay:
We have come the primrose way.

XII—TO MRS. WILL. H. LOW

Even in the bluest noonday of July,
There could not run the smallest breath of wind
But all the quarter sounded like a wood;
And in the chequered silence and above
The hum of city cabs that sought the Bois,
Suburban ashes shivered into song.
A patter and a chatter and a chirp
And a long dying hiss—it was as though
Starched old brocaded dames through all the house
Had trailed a strident skirt, or the whole sky
Even in a wink had over-brimmed in rain.
Hark, in these shady parlours, how it talks
Of the near Autumn, how the smitten ash
Trembles and augurs floods! O not too long
In these inconstant latitudes delay,
O not too late from the unbeloved north
Trim your escape! For soon shall this low roof
Resound indeed with rain, soon shall your eyes
Search the foul garden, search the darkened rooms,
Nor find one jewel but the blazing log.

12 RUE VERNIER, PARIS.

XIII—TO H. F. BROWN

(WRITTEN DURING A DANGEROUS SICKNESS.)

I sit and wait a pair of oars
On cis-Elysian river-shores.
Where the immortal dead have sate,
'Tis mine to sit and meditate;
To re-ascend life's rivulet,
Without remorse, without regret;
And sing my *Alma Genetrix*
Among the willows of the Styx.

And lo, as my serener soul
Did these unhappy shores patrol,
And wait with an attentive ear
The coming of the gondolier,
Your fire-surviving roll I took,
Your spirited and happy book; [1]
Whereon, despite my frowning fate,
It did my soul so recreate
That all my fancies fled away
On a Venetian holiday.

[1] *Light on the Lagoons*, by H. F. Brown, originally burned in the fire at Messrs. Kegan Paul, Trench. and Co.'s.

Now, thanks to your triumphant care,
Your pages clear as April air,
The sails, the bells, the birds, I know,
And the far-off Friulan snow;
The land and sea, the sun and shade,
And the blue even lamp-inlaid.

For this, for these, for all, O friend,
For your whole book from end to end—
For Paron Piero's mutton-ham—
I your defaulting debtor am.

Perchance, reviving, yet may I
To your sea-paven city hie,
And in *felze*, some day yet
Light at your pipe my cigarette.

XIV—TO ANDREW LANG

Dear Andrew, with the brindled hair,
Who glory to have thrown in air,
High over arm, the trembling reed,
By Ale and Kail, by Till and Tweed:
An equal craft of band you show
The pen to guide, the fly to throw:
I count you happy starred; for God,
When He with inkpot and with rod
Endowed you, bade your fortune lead
Forever by the crooks of Tweed,
Forever by the woods of song
And lands that to the Muse belong;
Or if in peopled streets, or in
The abhorred pedantic sanhedrin,
It should be yours to wander, still
Airs of the morn, airs of the hill,
The plovery Forest and the seas
That break about the Hebrides,
Should follow over field and plain
And find you at the window pane;
And you again see hill and peel,
And the bright springs gush at your heel.
So went the fiat forth, and so
Garrulous like a brook you go,
With sound of happy mirth and sheen
Of daylight—whether by the green
You fare that moment, or the gray;
Whether you dwell in March or May;
Or whether treat of reels and rods
Or of the old unhappy gods:
Still like a brook your page has shone,
And your ink sings of Helicon.

XV—ET TU IN ARCADIA VIXISTI

(TO R. A. M. S. [2])

[2] Stevenson's cousin, Robert A. M. Stevenson.

In ancient tales, O friend, thy spirit dwelt;
There, from of old, thy childhood passed; and there
High expectation, high delights and deeds,
Thy fluttering heart with hope and terror moved.
And thou hast heard of yore the Blatant Beast,
And Roland's horn, and that war-scattering shout

Of all-unarmed Achilles, aegis-crowned
And perilous lands thou sawest, sounding shores
And seas and forests drear, island and dale
And mountain dark. For thou with Tristram rod'st
Or Bedevere, in farthest Lyonesse.
Thou hadst a booth in Samarcand, whereat
Side-looking Magians trafficked; thence, by night,
An Afreet snatched thee, and with wings upbore
Beyond the Aral mount; or, hoping gain,
Thou, with a jar of money, didst embark,
For Balsorah, by sea. But chiefly thou
In that clear air took'st life; in Arcady
The haunted, land of song; and by the wells
Where most the gods frequent. There Chiron old,
In the Pelethronian antre, taught thee lore:
The plants, he taught, and by the shining stars
In forests dim to steer. There hast thou seen
Immortal Pan dance secret in a glade,
And, dancing, roll his eyes; these, where they fell,
Shed glee, and through the congregated oaks
A flying horror winged; while all the earth
To the god's pregnant footing thrilled within.
Or whiles, beside the sobbing stream, he breathed,
In his clutched pipe unformed and wizard strains
Divine yet brutal; which the forest heard,
And thou, with awe; and far upon the plain
The unthinking ploughman started and gave ear.
Now things there are that, upon him who sees,
A strong vocation lay; and strains there are
That whoso hears shall hear for evermore.
For evermore thou hear'st immortal Pan
And those melodious godheads, ever young
And ever quiring, on the mountains old.
What was this earth, child of the gods, to thee?
Forth from thy dreamland thou, a dreamer, cam'st
And in thine ears the olden music rang,
And in thy mind the doings of the dead,
And those heroic ages long forgot.
To a so fallen earth, alas! too late,
Alas! in evil days, thy steps return,
To list at noon for nightingales, to grow
A dweller on the beach till Argo come
That came long since, a lingerer by the pool
Where that desired angel bathes no more.

As when the Indian to Dakota comes,
Or farthest Idaho, and where he dwelt,
He with his clan, a humming city finds;
Thereon awhile, amazed, he stares, and then
To right and leftward, like a questing dog,
Seeks first the ancestral altars, then the hearth
Long cold with rains, and where old terror lodged,
And where the dead. So thee undying Hope,
With all her pack, hunts screaming through the years:
Here, there, thou fleeëst; but nor here nor there
The pleasant gods abide, the glory dwells.
That, that was not Apollo, not the god.
This was not Venus, though she Venus seemed
A moment. And though fair yon river move,
She, all the way, from disenchanted fount
To seas unhallowed runs; the gods forsook
Long since her trembling rushes; from her plains
Disconsolate, long since adventure fled;
And now although the inviting river flows,
And every poplared cape, and every bend
Or willowy islet, win upon thy soul
And to thy hopeful shallop whisper speed;
Yet hope not thou at all; hope is no more;
And O, long since the golden groves are dead
The faëry cities vanished from the land!

XVI—TO W. E. HENLEY

The year runs through her phases; rain and sun,
Springtime and summer pass; winter succeeds;
But one pale season rules the house of death.
Cold falls the imprisoned daylight; fell disease
By each lean pallet squats, and pain and sleep
Toss gaping on the pillows.

        But O thou!
Uprise and take thy pipe. Bid music flow,
Strains by good thoughts attended, like the spring
The swallows follow over land and sea.
Pain sleeps at once; at once, with open eyes,
Dozing despair awakes. The shepherd sees
His flock come bleating home; the seaman hears
Once more the cordage rattle. Airs of home!
Youth, love and roses blossom; the gaunt ward
Dislimns and disappears, and, opening out,
Shows brooks and forests, and the blue beyond
Of mountains.

                    Small the pipe; but oh! do thou,
Peak-faced and suffering piper, blow therein
The dirge of heroes dead; and to these sick,
These dying, sound the triumph over death.
Behold! each greatly breathes; each tastes a joy
Unknown before, in dying; for each knows
A hero dies with him—though unfulfilled,
Yet conquering truly—and not dies in vain.

So is pain cheered, death comforted; the house
Of sorrow smiles to listen. Once again—
O thou, Orpheus and Heracles, the bard
And the deliverer, touch the stops again!

XVII—HENRY JAMES

Who comes to-night? We ope the doors in vain.
Who comes? My bursting walls, can you contain
The presences that now together throng
Your narrow entry, as with flowers and song,
As with the air of life, the breath of talk?
Lo, how these fair immaculate women walk
Behind their jocund maker; and we see
Slighted *De Mauves*, and that far different she,
GRESSIE, the trivial sphynx; and to our feast
Daisy and *Barb* and *Chancellor* (she not least!)
With all their silken, all their airy kin,
Do like unbidden angels enter in.
But he, attended by these shining names,
Comes (best of all) himself—our welcome James.

XVIII—THE MIRROR SPEAKS

Where the bells peal far at sea
Cunning fingers fashioned me.
There on palace walls I hung
While that Consuelo sung;
But I heard, though I listened well,
Never a note, never a trill,
Never a beat of the chiming bell.
There I hung and looked, and there
In my gray face, faces fair
Shone from under shining hair.
Well I saw the poising head,
But the lips moved and nothing said;
And when lights were in the hall,
Silent moved the dancers all.

So awhile I glowed, and then
Fell on dusty days and men;
Long I slumbered packed in straw,
Long I none but dealers saw;
Till before my silent eye
One that sees came passing by.

Now with an outlandish grace,
To the sparkling fire I face
In the blue room at Skerryvore;
Where I wait until the door
Open, and the Prince of Men,
Henry James, shall come again.

XIX—KATHARINE

We see you as we see a face
That trembles in a forest place
Upon the mirror of a pool
Forever quiet, clear and cool;
And in the wayward glass, appears
To hover between smiles and tears,
Elfin and human, airy and true,
And backed by the reflected blue.

XX—TO F. J. S.

I read, dear friend, in your dear face
Your life's tale told with perfect grace;
The river of your life, I trace
Up the sun-chequered, devious bed
To the far-distant fountain-head.

Not one quick beat of your warm heart,
Nor thought that came to you apart,
Pleasure nor pity, love nor pain
Nor sorrow, has gone by in vain;

But as some lone, wood-wandering child
Brings home with him at evening mild
The thorns and flowers of all the wild,
From your whole life, O fair and true
Your flowers and thorns you bring with you!

XXI—REQUIEM

Under the wide and starry sky,
   Dig the grave and let me lie.
Glad did I live and gladly die,
   And I laid me down with a will.

This be the verse you grave for me:
Here he lies where he longed to be,
Home is the sailor, home from sea,
   And the hunter home from the hill.

XXII—THE CELESTIAL SURGEON

If I have faltered more or less
In my great task of happiness;
If I have moved among my race
And shown no glorious morning face;
If beams from happy human eyes
Have moved me not; if morning skies,
Books, and my food, and summer rain
Knocked on my sullen heart in vain:-
Lord, thy most pointed pleasure take
And stab my spirit broad awake;
Or, Lord, if too obdurate I,
Choose thou, before that spirit die,
A piercing pain, a killing sin,
And to my dead heart run them in!

XXIII—OUR LADY OF THE SNOWS

Out of the sun, out of the blast,
Out of the world, alone I passed
Across the moor and through the wood
To where the monastery stood.
There neither lute nor breathing fife,
Nor rumour of the world of life,
Nor confidences low and dear,
Shall strike the meditative ear.
Aloof, unhelpful, and unkind,
The prisoners of the iron mind,
Where nothing speaks except the hell
The unfraternal brothers dwell.

Poor passionate men, still clothed afresh
With agonising folds of flesh;
Whom the clear eyes solicit still
To some bold output of the will,
While fairy Fancy far before
And musing Memory-Hold-the-door
Now to heroic death invite
And now uncurtain fresh delight:
O, little boots it thus to dwell
On the remote unneighboured hill!

O to be up and doing, O
Unfearing and unshamed to go
In all the uproar and the press
About my human business!
My undissuaded heart I hear
Whisper courage in my ear.
With voiceless calls, the ancient earth
Summons me to a daily birth,
Thou, O my love, ye, O my friends—
The gist of life, the end of ends—
To laugh, to love, to live, to die,
Ye call me by the ear and eye!

Forth from the casemate, on the plain
Where honour has the world to gain,
Pour forth and bravely do your part,
O knights of the unshielded heart!
Forth and forever forward!—out
From prudent turret and redoubt,
And in the mellay charge amain,
To fall but yet to rise again!
Captive? ah, still, to honour bright,
A captive soldier of the right!
Or free and fighting, good with ill?
Unconquering but unconquered still!

And ye, O brethren, what if God,
When from Heav'n's top he spies abroad,
And sees on this tormented stage
The noble war of mankind rage:
What if his vivifying eye,
O monks, should pass your corner by?
For still the Lord is Lord of might;
In deeds, in deeds, he takes delight;
The plough, the spear, the laden barks,
The field, the founded city, marks;

He marks the smiler of the streets,
The singer upon garden seats;
He sees the climber in the rocks:
To him, the shepherd folds his flocks.
For those he loves that underprop
With daily virtues Heaven's top,
And bear the falling sky with ease,
Unfrowning caryatides.
Those he approves that ply the trade,
That rock the child, that wed the maid,
That with weak virtues, weaker hands,
Sow gladness on the peopled lands,
And still with laughter, song and shout,
Spin the great wheel of earth about.

But ye?—O ye who linger still
Here in your fortress on the hill,
With placid face, with tranquil breath,
The unsought volunteers of death,
Our cheerful General on high
With careless looks may pass you by.

XXIV

Not yet, my soul, these friendly fields desert,
Where thou with grass, and rivers, and the breeze,
And the bright face of day, thy dalliance hadst;
Where to thine ear first sang the enraptured birds;
Where love and thou that lasting bargain made.
The ship rides trimmed, and from the eternal shore
Thou hearest airy voices; but not yet
Depart, my soul, not yet awhile depart.

Freedom is far, rest far. Thou art with life
Too closely woven, nerve with nerve entwined;
Service still craving service, love for love,
Love for dear love, still suppliant with tears.
Alas, not yet thy human task is done!
A bond at birth is forged; a debt doth lie
Immortal on mortality. It grows—
By vast rebound it grows, unceasing growth;
Gift upon gift, alms upon alms, upreared,
From man, from God, from nature, till the soul
At that so huge indulgence stands amazed.

Leave not, my soul, the unfoughten field, nor leave
Thy debts dishonoured, nor thy place desert
Without due service rendered. For thy life,
Up, spirit, and defend that fort of clay,
Thy body, now beleaguered; whether soon
Or late she fall; whether to-day thy friends
Bewail thee dead, or, after years, a man
Grown old in honour and the friend of peace.
Contend, my soul, for moments and for hours;
Each is with service pregnant; each reclaimed
Is as a kingdom conquered, where to reign.

As when a captain rallies to the fight
His scattered legions, and beats ruin back,
He, on the field, encamps, well pleased in mind.
Yet surely him shall fortune overtake,
Him smite in turn, headlong his ensigns drive;
And that dear land, now safe, to-morrow fall.
But he, unthinking, in the present good
Solely delights, and all the camps rejoice.

XXV

It is not yours, O mother, to complain,
   Not, mother, yours to weep,
Though nevermore your son again
   Shall to your bosom creep,
   Though nevermore again you watch your baby sleep.

Though in the greener paths of earth,
   Mother and child, no more
We wander; and no more the birth
   Of me whom once you bore,
   Seems still the brave reward that once it seemed of yore;

Though as all passes, day and night,
   The seasons and the years,
From you, O mother, this delight,
   This also disappears—
   Some profit yet survives of all your pangs and tears.

The child, the seed, the grain of corn,
   The acorn on the hill,
Each for some separate end is born
   In season fit, and still
   Each must in strength arise to work the almighty will.

So from the hearth the children flee,
  By that almighty hand
Austerely led; so one by sea
  Goes forth, and one by land;
    Nor aught of all man's sons escapes from that command

So from the sally each obeys
  The unseen almighty nod;
So till the ending all their ways
  Blindfolded loth have trod:
    Nor knew their task at all, but were the tools of God.

And as the fervent smith of yore
  Beat out the glowing blade,
Nor wielded in the front of war
  The weapons that he made,
    But in the tower at home still plied his ringing trade;

So like a sword the son shall roam
  On nobler missions sent;
And as the smith remained at home
  In peaceful turret pent,
    So sits the while at home the mother well content.

XXVI—THE SICK CHILD

Child.   O Mother, lay your hand on my brow!
        O mother, mother, where am I now?
        Why is the room so gaunt and great?
        Why am I lying awake so late?

Mother. Fear not at all: the night is still.
        Nothing is here that means you ill—
        Nothing but lamps the whole town through,
        And never a child awake but you.

Child.   Mother, mother, speak low in my ear,
        Some of the things are so great and near,
        Some are so small and far away,
        I have a fear that I cannot say,
        What have I done, and what do I fear,
        And why are you crying, mother dear?

Mother. Out in the city, sounds begin
        Thank the kind God, the carts come in!
        An hour or two more, and God is so kind,
        The day shall be blue in the window-blind,
        Then shall my child go sweetly asleep,
        And dream of the birds and the hills of sheep.

XXVII—IN MEMORIAM F. A. S.

Yet, O stricken heart, remember, O remember
  How of human days he lived the better part.
April came to bloom and never dim December
  Breathed its killing chills upon the head or heart.

Doomed to know not Winter, only Spring, a being
  Trod the flowery April blithely for a while,
Took his fill of music, joy of thought and seeing,
  Came and stayed and went, nor ever ceased to smile.

Came and stayed and went, and now when all is finished,
  You alone have crossed the melancholy stream,
Yours the pang, but his, O his, the undiminished
  Undecaying gladness, undeparted dream.

All that life contains of torture, toil, and treason,
  Shame, dishonour, death, to him were but a name.
Here, a boy, he dwelt through all the singing season
  And ere the day of sorrow departed as he came.

DAVOS, 1881.

XXVIII—TO MY FATHER

Peace and her huge invasion to these shores
Puts daily home; innumerable sails
Dawn on the far horizon and draw near;
Innumerable loves, uncounted hopes
To our wild coasts, not darkling now, approach:
Not now obscure, since thou and thine are there,
And bright on the lone isle, the foundered reef,
The long, resounding foreland, Pharos stands.

These are thy works, O father, these thy crown;
Whether on high the air be pure, they shine
Along the yellowing sunset, and all night
Among the unnumbered stars of God they shine;
Or whether fogs arise and far and wide
The low sea-level drown—each finds a tongue
And all night long the tolling bell resounds:
So shine, so toll, till night be overpast,
Till the stars vanish, till the sun return,
And in the haven rides the fleet secure.

In the first hour, the seaman in his skiff
Moves through the unmoving bay, to where the town
Its earliest smoke into the air upbreathes
And the rough hazels climb along the beach.
To the tugg'd oar the distant echo speaks.
The ship lies resting, where by reef and roost
Thou and thy lights have led her like a child.

This hast thou done, and I—can I be base?
I must arise, O father, and to port
Some lost, complaining seaman pilot home.

XXIX—IN THE STATES

With half a heart I wander here
   As from an age gone by
A brother—yet though young in years.
   An elder brother, I.

You speak another tongue than mine,
   Though both were English born.
I towards the night of time decline,
   You mount into the morn.

Youth shall grow great and strong and free,
   But age must still decay:
To-morrow for the States—for me,
   England and Yesterday.

SAN FRANCISCO.

XXX—A PORTRAIT

I am a kind of farthing dip,
   Unfriendly to the nose and eyes;
A blue-behinded ape, I skip
   Upon the trees of Paradise.

At mankind's feast, I take my place
   In solemn, sanctimonious state,
And have the air of saying grace
   While I defile the dinner plate.

I am "the smiler with the knife,"
   The battener upon garbage, I—
Dear Heaven, with such a rancid life,
   Were it not better far to die?

Yet still, about the human pale,
   I love to scamper, love to race,
To swing by my irreverent tail
   All over the most holy place;

And when at length, some golden day,
   The unfailing sportsman, aiming at,
Shall bag, me—all the world shall say:
Thank God, and there's an end of that!

XXXI

Sing clearlier, Muse, or evermore be still,
Sing truer or no longer sing!
No more the voice of melancholy Jacques
To wake a weeping echo in the hill;
But as the boy, the pirate of the spring,
From the green elm a living linnet takes,
One natural verse recapture—then be still.

XXXII—A CAMP [3]

The bed was made, the room was fit,
By punctual eve the stars were lit;
The air was still, the water ran,
No need was there for maid or man,
When we put up, my ass and I,
At God's green caravanserai.

[3] From *Travels with a Donkey*

XXXIII—THE COUNTRY OF THE CAMISARDS [4]

We travelled in the print of olden wars,
Yet all the land was green,
And love we found, and peace,
Where fire and war had been.

They pass and smile, the children of the sword—
   No more the sword they wield;
   And O, how deep the corn
   Along the battlefield!

[4] From *Travels with a Donkey*

XXXIV—SKERRYVORE

For love of lovely words, and for the sake
Of those, my kinsmen and my countrymen,
Who early and late in the windy ocean toiled
To plant a star for seamen, where was then
The surfy haunt of seals and cormorants:
I, on the lintel of this cot, inscribe
The name of a strong tower.

XXXV—SKERRYVORE: THE PARALLEL

Here all is sunny, and when the truant gull
Skims the green level of the lawn, his wing
Dispetals roses; here the house is framed
Of kneaded brick and the plumed mountain pine,
Such clay as artists fashion and such wood
As the tree-climbing urchin breaks. But there
Eternal granite hewn from the living isle
And dowelled with brute iron, rears a tower
That from its wet foundation to its crown
Of glittering glass, stands, in the sweep of winds,
Immovable, immortal, eminent.

XXXVI

My house, I say. But hark to the sunny doves
That make my roof the arena of their loves,
That gyre about the gable all day long
And fill the chimneys with their murmurous song:
Our house, they say; and MINE, the cat declares
And spreads his golden fleece upon the chairs;
And *mine* the dog, and rises stiff with wrath
If any alien foot profane the path.
So too the buck that trimmed my terraces,
Our whilome gardener, called the garden his;
Who now, deposed, surveys my plain abode
And his late kingdom, only from the road.

XXXVII

My body which my dungeon is,
And yet my parks and palaces:-
Which is so great that there I go
All the day long to and fro,
And when the night begins to fall
Throw down my bed and sleep, while all
The building hums with wakefulness—
Even as a child of savages
When evening takes her on her way,
(She having roamed a summer's day
Along the mountain-sides and scalp)
Sleeps in an antre of that alp:-
Which is so broad and high that there,
As in the topless fields of air,
My fancy soars like to a kite
And faints in the blue infinite:-
   Which is so strong, my strongest throes
And the rough world's besieging blows
Not break it, and so weak withal,
Death ebbs and flows in its loose wall
As the green sea in fishers' nets,
And tops its topmost parapets:-
   Which is so wholly mine that I
Can wield its whole artillery,
And mine so little, that my soul
Dwells in perpetual control,
And I but think and speak and do
As my dead fathers move me to:-
   If this born body of my bones
The beggared soul so barely owns,

What money passed from hand to hand,
What creeping custom of the land,
What deed of author or assign,
Can make a house a thing of mine?

XXXVIII

Say not of me that weakly I declined
The labours of my sires, and fled the sea,
The towers we founded and the lamps we lit,
To play at some with paper like a child.
But rather say: *In the afternoon of time*
A strenuous family dusted from its hands
The sand of granite, and beholding far
Along the sounding coast its pyramids
And tall memorials catch the dying sun,
Smiled well content, and to this childish task
Around the fire addressed its evening hours.

XXXIX—DEDICATORY POEM

To her, for I must still regard her
As feminine in her degree,
Who has been my unkind bombarder
Year after year, in grief and glee,
Year after year, with oaken tree;
And yet betweenwhiles my laudator
In terms astonishing to me—
To the Right Reverend The Spectator
I here, a humble dedicator,
Bring the last apples from my tree.

In tones of love, in tones of warning,
She hailed me through my brief career;
And kiss and buffet, night and morning,
Told me my grandmamma was near;
Whether she praised me high and clear
Through her unrivalled circulation,
Or, sanctimonious insincere,
She damned me with a misquotation—
A chequered but a sweet relation,
Say, was it not, my granny dear?

Believe me, granny, altogether
Yours, though perhaps to your surprise.
Oft have you spruced my wounded feather,
Oft brought a light into my eyes—
For notice still the writer cries.
In any civil age or nation,
The book that is not talked of dies.
So that shall be my termination:
Whether in praise or execration,
Still, if you love me, criticise!

BOOK II.

IN SCOTS

NOTE

 THE human conscience has fled of late the troublesome domain of conduct for what I should have supposed to be the less congenial field of art: there she may now be said to rage, and with special severity in all that touches dialect; so that in every novel the letters of the alphabet are tortured, and the reader wearied, to commemorate shades of mispronunciation. Now spelling is an art of great difficulty in my eyes, and I am inclined to lean upon the printer, even in common practice, rather than to venture abroad upon new quests. And the Scots tongue has an orthography of its own, lacking neither "authority nor author." Yet the temptation is great to lend a little guidance to the bewildered Englishman. Some simple phonetic artifice might defend your verses from barbarous mishandling, and yet not injure any vested interest. So it seems at first; but there are rocks ahead. Thus, if I wish the diphthong OU to have its proper value, I may write OOR instead of OUR; many have done so and lived, and the pillars of the universe remained unshaken. But if I did so, and came presently to DOUN, which is the classical Scots spelling of the English DOWN, I should begin to feel uneasy; and if I went on a little farther, and came to a classical Scots word, like STOUR or DOUR or CLOUR, I should know precisely where I was—that is to say, that I was out of sight of land on those high seas of spelling reform in which so many strong swimmers have toiled vainly. To some the situation is exhilarating; as for me, I give one bubbling cry and sink. The compromise at which I have arrived is indefensible, and I have no thought of trying to defend it. As I have stuck for the most part to the proper spelling, I append a table of some common vowel sounds which no one need consult; and just to prove that I belong to my age and have in me the stuff of a reformer, I have used modification marks throughout. Thus I can tell myself, not without pride, that I have added a fresh stumbling-block for English readers, and to a page of print in my native tongue, have lent a new uncouthness. SED NON NOBIS.

 I note again, that among our new dialecticians, the local habitat of every dialect is given to the square mile. I could not emulate this nicety if I desired; for I simply wrote my Scots as well as I was able, not caring if it hailed from Lauderdale or Angus, from the Mearns or Galloway; if I had ever heard a good word, I used it without shame; and when Scots was lacking, or the rhyme jibbed, I was glad (like my betters) to fall back on

English. For all that, I own to a friendly feeling for the tongue of Fergusson and of Sir Walter, both Edinburgh men; and I confess that Burns has always sounded in my ear like something partly foreign. And indeed I am from the Lothians myself; it is there I heard the language spoken about my childhood; and it is in the drawling Lothian voice that I repeat it to myself. Let the precisians call my speech that of the Lothians. And if it be not pure, alas! what matters it? The day draws near when this illustrious and malleable tongue shall be quite forgotten; and Burn's Ayrshire, and Dr. Macdonald's Aberdeen-awa', and Scott's brave, metropolitan utterance will be all equally the ghosts of speech. Till then I would love to have my hour as a native Maker, and be read by my own countryfolk in our own dying language: an ambition surely rather of the heart than of the head, so restricted as it is in prospect of endurance, so parochial in bounds of space.

TABLE OF COMMON SCOTTISH VOWEL SOUNDS

ae, ai } = open A as in *rare*.

a', au, aw } = AW as in *law*.

ea = open E as in *mere*, but this with exceptions, as *heather* = *heather, wean=wain, lear=lair*.

ee, ei, ie } = open E as in *mere*.

oa = open O as in *more*.
ou = doubled O as in *poor*.
ow = OW as in *bower*.
u = doubled O as in *poor*.
ui or u-umlaut before R = (say roughly) open A as in *rare*.
ui or u-umlaut before any other consonant = (say roughly) close I as in *grin*.
y = open I as in *kite*.
i = pretty nearly what you please, much as in English, Heaven guide the reader through that labyrinth! But in Scots it dodges usually from the short I, as in *grin*, to the open E, as in *mere*. Find the *blind*, I may remark, are pronounced to rhyme with the preterite of *grin*.

UNDERWOODS

I—THE MAKER TO POSTERITY

Far 'yont amang the years to be
   When a' we think, an' a' we see,
An' a' we luve, 's been dung ajee
   By time's rouch shouther,
An' what was richt and wrang for me
   Lies mangled throu'ther,

It's possible—it's hardly mair—
That some ane, ripin' after lear—
Some auld professor or young heir,
   If still there's either—
May find an' read me, an' be sair
   Perplexed, puir brither!

"What tongue does your auld bookie speak?"
He'll spier; an' I, his mou to steik:
"No bein' fit to write in Greek,
   I write in Lallan,
Dear to my heart as the peat reek,
   Auld as Tantallon.

"Few spak it then, an' noo there's nane.
My puir auld sangs lie a' their lane,
Their sense, that aince was braw an' plain,
   Tint a'thegether,
Like runes upon a standin' stane
   Amang the heather.

"But think not you the brae to speel;
You, tae, maun chow the bitter peel;
For a' your lear, for a' your skeel,
   Ye're nane sae lucky;
An' things are mebbe waur than weel
   For you, my buckie.

"The hale concern (baith hens an' eggs,
Baith books an' writers, stars an' clegs)
Noo stachers upon lowsent legs
   An' wears awa';
The tack o' mankind, near the dregs,
   Rins unco law.

"Your book, that in some braw new tongue,
Ye wrote or prentit, preached or sung,
Will still be just a bairn, an' young
   In fame an' years,
Whan the hale planet's guts are dung
   About your ears;

"An' you, sair gruppin' to a spar
Or whammled wi' some bleezin' star,
Cryin' to ken whaur deil ye are,
   Hame, France, or Flanders—
Whang sindry like a railway car
   An' flie in danders."

II—ILLE TERRARUM

Frae nirly, nippin', Eas'lan' breeze,
Frae Norlan' snaw, an' haar o' seas,
Weel happit in your gairden trees,
   A bonny bit,
Atween the muckle Pentland's knees,
   Secure ye sit.

Beeches an' aiks entwine their theek,
An' firs, a stench, auld-farrant clique.
A' simmer day, your chimleys reek,
   Couthy and bien;
An' here an' there your windies keek
   Amang the green.

A pickle plats an' paths an' posies,
A wheen auld gillyflowers an' roses:
A ring o' wa's the hale encloses
   Frae sheep or men;
An' there the auld housie beeks an' dozes,
   A' by her lane.

The gairdner crooks his weary back
A' day in the pitaty-track,
Or mebbe stops awhile to crack
   Wi' Jane the cook,
Or at some buss, worm-eaten-black,
   To gie a look.

Frae the high hills the curlew ca's;
The sheep gang baaing by the wa's;
Or whiles a clan o' roosty craws
    Cangle thegether;
The wild bees seek the gairden raws,
    Weariet wi' heather.

Or in the gloamin' douce an' gray
The sweet-throat mavis tunes her lay;
The herd comes linkin' doun the brae;
    An' by degrees
The muckle siller mune maks way
    Amang the trees.

Here aft hae I, wi' sober heart,
For meditation sat apairt,
When orra loves or kittle art
    Perplexed my mind;
Here socht a balm for ilka smart
    O' humankind.

Here aft, weel neukit by my lane,
Wi' Horace, or perhaps Montaigne,
The mornin' hours hae come an' gane
    Abüne my heid—
I wadnae gi'en a chucky-stane
    For a' I'd read.

But noo the auld city, street by street,
An' winter fu' o' snaw an' sleet,
Awhile shut in my gangrel feet
    An' goavin' mettle;
Noo is the soopit ingle sweet,
    An' liltin' kettle.

An' noo the winter winds complain;
Cauld lies the glaur in ilka lane;
On draigled hizzie, tautit wean
    An' drucken lads,
In the mirk nicht, the winter rain
    Dribbles an' blads.

Whan bugles frae the Castle rock,
An' beaten drums wi' dowie shock,
Wauken, at cauld-rife sax o'clock,
   My chitterin' frame,
I mind me on the kintry cock,
   The kintry hame.

I mind me on yon bonny bield;
An' Fancy traivels far afield
To gaither a' that gairdens yield
   O' sun an' Simmer:
To hearten up a dowie chield,
   Fancy's the limmer!

III

When aince Aprile has fairly come,
An' birds may bigg in winter's lum,
An' pleisure's spreid for a' and some
   O' whatna state,
Love, wi' her auld recruitin' drum,
   Than taks the gate.

The heart plays dunt wi' main an' micht;
The lasses' een are a' sae bricht,
Their dresses are sae braw an' ticht,
   The bonny birdies!-
Puir winter virtue at the sicht
   Gangs heels ower hurdies.

An' aye as love frae land to land
Tirls the drum wi' eident hand,
A' men collect at her command,
   Toun-bred or land'art,
An' follow in a denty band
   Her gaucy standart.

An' I, wha sang o' rain an' snaw,
An' weary winter weel awa',
Noo busk me in a jacket braw,
   An' tak my place
I' the ram-stam, harum-scarum raw,
   Wi' smilin' face.

IV—A MILE AN' A BITTOCK

A mile an' a bittock, a mile or twa,
Abune the burn, ayont the law,
Davie an' Donal' an' Cherlie an' a',
   An' the müne was shinin' clearly!

Ane went hame wi' the ither, an' then
The ither went hame wi' the ither twa men,
An' baith wad return him the service again,
   An' the müne was shinin' clearly!

The clocks were chappin' in house an' ha',
Eleeven, twal an' ane an' twa;
An' the guidman's face was turnt to the wa',
   An' the müne was shinin' clearly!

A wind got up frae affa the sea,
It blew the stars as clear's could be,
It blew in the een of a' o' the three,
   An' the müne was shinin' clearly!

Noo, Davie was first to get sleep in his head,
"The best o' frien's maun twine," he said;
"I'm weariet, an' here I'm awa' to my bed."
   An' the müne was shinin' clearly!

Twa o' them walkin' an' crackin' their lane,
The mornin' licht cam gray an' plain,
An' the birds they yammert on stick an' stane,
   An' the müne was shinin' clearly!

O years ayont, O years awa',
My lads, ye'll mind whate'er befa'-
My lads, ye'll mind on the bield o' the law,
   When the müne was shinin' clearly.

V—A LOWDEN SABBATH MORN

The clinkum-clank o' Sabbath bells
Noo to the hoastin' rookery swells,
Noo faintin' laigh in shady dells,
   Sounds far an' near,
An' through the simmer kintry tells
   Its tale o' cheer.

An' noo, to that melodious play,
A' deidly awn the quiet sway—
A' ken their solemn holiday,
   Bestial an' human,
The singin' lintie on the brae,
   The restin' plou'man,

He, mair than a' the lave o' men,
His week completit joys to ken;
Half-dressed, he daunders out an' in,
   Perplext wi' leisure;
An' his raxt limbs he'll rax again
   Wi' painfü' pleesure.

The steerin' mither strang afit
Noo shoos the bairnies but a bit;
Noo cries them ben [5], their Sinday shüit
   To scart upon them,
Or sweeties in their pouch to pit,
   Wi' blessin's on them.

[5] "But"—the outer room, "ben"—the inner room of a two-roomed cottage.

The lasses, clean frae tap to taes,
Are busked in crunklin' underclaes;
The gartened hose, the weel-filled stays,
   The nakit shift,
A' bleached on bonny greens for days,
   An' white's the drift.

An' noo to face the kirkward mile:
The guidman's hat o' dacent style,
The blackit shoon, we noo maun fyle
   As white's the miller:
A waefü' peety tae, to spile
The warth o' siller.

Our Marg'et, aye sae keen to crack,
Douce-stappin' in the stoury track,
Her emeralt goun a' kiltit back
   Frae snawy coats,
White-ankled, leads the kirkward pack
   Wi' Dauvit Groats.

A thocht ahint, in runkled breeks,
A' spiled wi' lyin' by for weeks,
The guidman follows closs, an' cleiks
   The sonsie missis;
His sarious face at aince bespeaks
   The day that this is.

And aye an' while we nearer draw
To whaur the kirkton lies alaw,
Mair neebours, comin' saft an' slaw
   Frae here an' there,
The thicker thrang the gate an' caw
   The stour in air.

But hark! the bells frae nearer clang;
To rowst the slaw, their sides they bang;
An' see! black coats a'ready thrang
   The green kirkyaird;
And at the yett, the chestnuts spang
   That brocht the laird.

The solemn elders at the plate
Stand drinkin' deep the pride o' state:
The practised hands as gash an' great
   As Lords o' Session;
The later named, a wee thing blate
   In their expression.

The prentit stanes that mark the deid,
Wi' lengthened lip, the sarious read;
Syne wag a moraleesin' heid,
   An' then an' there
Their hirplin' practice an' their creed
   Try hard to square.

It's here our Merren lang has lain,
A wee bewast the table-stane;
An' yon's the grave o' Sandy Blane;
   An' further ower,
The mither's brithers, dacent men!
   Lie a' the fower.

Here the guidman sall bide awee
To dwall amang the deid; to see
Auld faces clear in fancy's e'e;
   Belike to hear
Auld voices fa'in saft an' slee
   On fancy's ear.

Thus, on the day o' solemn things,
The bell that in the steeple swings
To fauld a scaittered faim'ly rings
   Its walcome screed;
An' just a wee thing nearer brings
   The quick an' deid.

But noo the bell is ringin' in;
To tak their places, folk begin;
The minister himsel' will shune
   Be up the gate,
Filled fu' wi' clavers about sin
   An' man's estate.

The tünes are up—*French*, to be shüre,
The faithfü' *French*, an' twa-three mair;
The auld prezentor, hoastin' sair,
   Wales out the portions,
An' yirks the tüne into the air
   Wi' queer contortions.

Follows the prayer, the readin' next,
An' than the fisslin' for the text—
The twa-three last to find it, vext
   But kind o' proud;
An' than the peppermints are raxed,
   An' southernwood.

For noo's the time whan pews are seen
Nid-noddin' like a mandareen;
When tenty mithers stap a preen
   In sleepin' weans;
An' nearly half the parochine
   Forget their pains.

There's just a waukrif' twa or three:
Thrawn commentautors sweer to 'gree,
Weans glowrin' at the bumlin' bee
   On windie-glasses,
Or lads that tak a keek a-glee
   At sonsie lasses.

Himsel', meanwhile, frae whaur he cocks
An' bobs belaw the soundin'-box,
The treesures of his words unlocks
   Wi' prodigality,
An' deals some unco dingin' knocks
   To infidality.

Wi' sappy unction, hoo he burkes
The hopes o' men that trust in works,
Expounds the fau'ts o' ither kirks,
   An' shaws the best o' them
No muckle better than mere Turks,
   When a's confessed o' them.

Bethankit! what a bonny creed!
What mair would ony Christian need?-
The braw words rumm'le ower his heid,
   Nor steer the sleeper;
And in their restin' graves, the deid
   Sleep aye the deeper.

NOTE.—It may be guessed by some that I had a certain parish in my eye, and this makes it proper I should add a word of disclamation. In my time there have been two ministers in that parish. Of the first I have a special reason to speak well, even had there been any to think ill. The second I have often met in private and long (in the due phrase) "sat under" in his church, and neither here nor there have I heard an unkind or ugly word upon his lips. The preacher of the text had thus no original in that particular parish; but when I was a boy, he might have been observed in many others; he was then (like the schoolmaster) abroad; and by recent advices, it would seem he has not yet entirely disappeared. [R.L.S.]

VI—THE SPAEWIFE

O, I wad like to ken—to the beggar-wife says I—
Why chops are guid to brander and nane sae guid to fry.
An' siller, that's sae braw to keep, is brawer still to gi'e.
—*It's gey an' easy speirin'*, says the beggar-wife to me.

O, I wad like to ken—to the beggar-wife says I—
Hoo a' things come to be whaur we find them when we try,
The lasses in their claes an' the fishes in the sea.
—*It's gey an' easy speirin'*, says the beggar-wife to me.

O, I wad like to ken—to the beggar-wife says I—
Why lads are a' to sell an' lasses a' to buy;
An' naebody for dacency but barely twa or three
—*It's gey an' easy speirin'*, says the beggar-wife to me.

O, I wad like to ken—to the beggar-wife says I—
Gin death's as shure to men as killin' is to kye,
Why God has filled the yearth sae fu' o' tasty things to pree.
—*It's gey an' easy speirin'*, says the beggar-wife to me.

O, I wad like to ken—to the beggar wife says I—
The reason o' the cause an' the wherefore o' the why,
Wi' mony anither riddle brings the tear into my e'e.
—*It's gey an' easy speirin'*, says the beggar-wife to me.

VII—THE BLAST—1875

It's rainin'. Weet's the gairden sod,
Weet the lang roads whaur gangrels plod—
A maist unceevil thing o' God
   In mid July—
If ye'll just curse the sneckdraw, dod!
   An' sae wull I!

He's a braw place in Heev'n, ye ken,
An' lea's us puir, forjaskit men
Clamjamfried in the but and ben
   He ca's the earth—
A wee bit inconvenient den
   No muckle worth;

An' whiles, at orra times, keeks out,
Sees what puir mankind are about;
An' if He can, I've little doubt,
   Upsets their plans;
He hates a' mankind, brainch and root,
   An' a' that's man's.

An' whiles, whan they tak heart again,
An' life i' the sun looks braw an' plain,
Doun comes a jaw o' droukin' rain
   Upon their honours—
God sends a spate outower the plain,
   Or mebbe thun'ers.

Lord safe us, life's an unco thing!
Simmer an' Winter, Yule an' Spring,
The damned, dour-heartit seasons bring
   A feck o' trouble.
I wadnae try't to be a king—
   No, nor for double.

But since we're in it, willy-nilly,
We maun be watchfu', wise an' skilly,
An' no mind ony ither billy,
   Lassie nor God.
But drink—that's my best counsel till 'e:
   Sae tak the nod.

VIII—THE COUNTERBLAST—1886

My bonny man, the warld, it's true,
Was made for neither me nor you;
It's just a place to warstle through,
   As job confessed o't;
And aye the best that we'll can do
   Is mak the best o't.

There's rowth o' wrang, I'm free to say:
The simmer brunt, the winter blae,
The face of earth a' fyled wi' clay
   An' dour wi' chuckies,
An' life a rough an' land'art play
   For country buckies.

An' food's anither name for clart;
An' beasts an' brambles bite an' scart;
An' what would WE be like, my heart!
   If bared o' claethin'?
—Aweel, I cannae mend your cart:
   It's that or naethin'.

A feek o' folk frae first to last
Have through this queer experience passed;
Twa-three, I ken, just damn an' blast
   The hale transaction;
But twa-three ithers, east an' wast,
    Fand satisfaction,

Whaur braid the briery muirs expand,
A waefü'an' a weary land,
The bumblebees, a gowden band,
   Are blithely hingin';
An' there the canty wanderer fand
   The laverock singin'.

Trout in the burn grow great as herr'n,
The simple sheep can find their fair'n';
The wind blaws clean about the cairn
   Wi' caller air;
The muircock an' the barefit bairn
   Are happy there.

Sic-like the howes o' life to some:
Green loans whaur they ne'er fash their thumb.
But mark the muckle winds that come
   Soopin' an' cool,
Or hear the powrin' burnie drum
   In the shilfa's pool.

The evil wi' the guid they tak;
They ca' a gray thing gray, no black;
To a steigh brae, a stubborn back
   Addressin' daily;
An' up the rude, unbieldy track
   O' life, gang gaily.

What you would like's a palace ha',
Or Sinday parlour dink an' braw
Wi' a' things ordered in a raw
   By denty leddies.
Weel, than, ye cannae hae't: that's a'
   That to be said is.

An' since at life ye've taen the grue,
An' winnae blithely hirsle through,
Ye've fund the very thing to do—
   That's to drink speerit;
An' shüne we'll hear the last o' you—
   An' blithe to hear it!

The shoon ye coft, the life ye lead,
Ithers will heir when aince ye're deid;
They'll heir your tasteless bite o' breid,
   An' find it sappy;
They'll to your dulefü' house succeed,
   An' there be happy.

As whan a glum an' fractious wean
Has sat an' sullened by his lane
Till, wi' a rowstin' skelp, he's taen
   An' shoo'd to bed—
The ither bairns a' fa' to play'n',
   As gleg's a gled.

IX—THE COUNTERBLAST IRONICAL

It's strange that God should fash to frame
   The yearth and lift sae hie,
An' clean forget to explain the same
   To a gentleman like me.

They gutsy, donnered ither folk,
   Their weird they weel may dree;
But why present a pig in a poke
   To a gentleman like me?

They ither folk their parritch eat
   An' sup their sugared tea;
But the mind is no to be wyled wi' meat
   Wi' a gentleman like me.

They ither folk, they court their joes
   At gloamin' on the lea;
But they're made of a commoner clay, I suppose,
   Than a gentleman like me.

They ither folk, for richt or wrang,
   They suffer, bleed, or dee;
But a' thir things are an emp'y sang
   To a gentleman like me.

It's a different thing that I demand,
   Tho' humble as can be—
A statement fair in my Maker's hand
   To a gentleman like me:

A clear account writ fair an' broad,
   An' a plain apologie;
Or the deevil a ceevil word to God
   From a gentleman like me.

X—THEIR LAUREATE TO AN ACADEMY CLASS DINNER CLUB

Dear Thamson class, whaure'er I gang
It aye comes ower me wi' a spang:
"Lordsake! Thae Thamson lads—(deil hang
   Or else Lord mend them!)—
An' that wanchancy annual sang
   I ne'er can send them!"

Straucht, at the name, a trusty tyke,
My conscience girrs ahint the dyke;
Straucht on my hinderlands I fyke
   To find a rhyme t' ye;
Pleased—although mebbe no pleased-like—
   To gie my time t'ye.

"*Weel*," an' says you, wi' heavin' breist,
"*Sae far, sae guid, but what's the neist?*
Yearly we gaither to the feast,
   A' hopefu' men—
Yearly we skelloch 'Hang the beast—
   Nae sange again!'"

My lads, an' what am I to say?
Ye shurely ken the Muse's way:
Yestreen, as gleg's a tyke—the day,
   Thrawn like a cuddy:
Her conduc', that to her's a play,
   Deith to a body.

Aft whan I sat an' made my mane,
Aft whan I laboured burd-alane
Fishin' for rhymes an' findin' nane,
   Or nane were fit for ye—
Ye judged me cauld's a chucky stane—
   No car'n' a bit for ye!

But saw ye ne'er some pingein' bairn
As weak as a pitaty-par'n'—
Less used wi' guidin' horse-shoe airn
   Than steerin' crowdie—
Packed aff his lane, by moss an' cairn,
   To ca' the howdie.

Wae's me, for the puir callant than!
He wambles like a poke o' bran,
An' the lowse rein, as hard's he can,
   Pu's, trem'lin' handit;
Till, blaff! upon his hinderlan'
   Behauld him landit.

Sic-like—I awn the weary fac'—
Whan on my muse the gate I tak,
An' see her gleed e'e raxin' back
   To keek ahint her;—
To me, the brig o' Heev'n gangs black
   As blackest winter.

"Lordsake! We're aff," thinks I, "but whaur?
On what abhorred an' whinny scaur,
Or whammled in what sea o' glaur,
   Will she desert me?
An' will she just disgrace? Or waur—
   Will she no' hurt me?"

Kittle the quære! But at least
The day I've backed the fashious beast,
While she, wi' mony a spang an' reist,
   Flang heels ower bonnet;
An' a' triumphant—for your feast,
   Hae! there's your sonnet!

XI—EMBRO HIE KIRK

The Lord Himsel' in former days
Waled out the proper tunes for praise
An' named the proper kind o' claes
   For folk to preach in:
Preceese and in the chief o' ways
   Important teachin'.

He ordered a' things late and air';
He ordered folk to stand at prayer,
(Although I cannae just mind where
   He gave the warnin',)
An' pit pomatum on their hair
   On Sabbath mornin'.

The hale o' life by His commands
Was ordered to a body's hands;
But see! this *corpus juris* stands
   By a' forgotten;
An' God's religion in a' lands
   Is deid an' rotten.

While thus the lave o' mankind's lost,
O' Scotland still God maks His boast—
Puir Scotland, on whase barren coast
   A score or twa
Auld wives wi' mutches an' a hoast
   Still keep His law.

In Scotland, a wheen canty, plain,
Douce, kintry-leevin' folk retain
The Truth—or did so aince—alane
   Of a' men leevin';
An' noo just twa o' them remain—
   Just Begg an' Niven.

For noo, unfaithfu', to the Lord
Auld Scotland joins the rebel horde;
Her human hymn-books on the board
   She noo displays:
An' Embro Hie Kirk's been restored
   In popish ways.

O punctum temporis for action
To a' o' the reformin' faction,
If yet, by ony act or paction,
   Thocht, word, or sermon,
This dark an' damnable transaction
   Micht yet determine!

For see—as Doctor Begg explains—
Hoo easy 't's dune! a pickle weans,
Wha in the Hie Street gaither stanes
   By his instruction,
The uncovenantit, pentit panes
   Ding to destruction.

Up, Niven, or ower late—an' dash
Laigh in the glaur that carnal hash;
Let spires and pews wi' gran' stramash
   Thegether fa';
The rumlin' kist o' whustles smash
   In pieces sma'.

Noo choose ye out a walie hammer;
About the knottit buttress clam'er;
Alang the steep roof stoyt an' stammer,
   A gate mis-chancy;
On the aul' spire, the bells' hie cha'mer,
   Dance your bit dancie.

Ding, devel, dunt, destroy, an' ruin,
Wi' carnal stanes the square bestrewin',
Till your loud chaps frae Kyle to Fruin,
   Frae Hell to Heeven,
Tell the guid wark that baith are doin'—
   Baith Begg an' Niven.

XII—THE SCOTSMAN'S RETURN FROM ABROAD

(IN A LETTER FROM MR. THOMSON TO MR. JOHNSTONE)

In mony a foreign pairt I've been,
An' mony an unco ferlie seen,
Since, Mr. Johnstone, you and I
Last walkit upon Cocklerye.
Wi' gleg, observant een, I pass't
By sea an' land, through East an' Wast,
And still in ilka age an' station
Saw naething but abomination.
In thir uncovenantit lands
The gangrel Scot uplifts his hands
At lack of a' sectarian füsh'n,
An' cauld religious destitütion.
He rins, puir man, frae place to place,
Tries a' their graceless means o' grace,
Preacher on preacher, kirk on kirk—

This yin a stot an' thon a stirk [6]—
A bletherin' clan, no warth a preen,
As bad as Smith of Aiberdeen! [7]

[6] "Stot" and "stirk," *lit.* cattle, used to express stupidity.
[7] The late Professor Robertson Smith of Cambridge, formerly of Aberdeen, a leader of the school of advanced Biblical criticism.

At last, across the weary faem,
Frae far, outlandish pairts I came.
On ilka side o' me I fand
Fresh tokens o' my native land.
Wi' whatna joy I hailed them a'—
The hilltaps standin' raw by raw,
The public house, the Hielan' birks,
And a' the bonny U.P. kirks!
But maistly thee, the bluid o' Scots,
Frae Maidenkirk to John o' Grots,
The king o' drinks, as I conceive it,
Talisker, Isla, or Glenlivet!

For after years wi' a pockmantie
Frae Zanzibar to Alicante,
In mony a fash and sair affliction
I gie't as my sincere conviction—
Of a' their foreign tricks an' pliskies,
I maist abominate their whiskies.
Nae doot, themsel's, they ken it weel,
An' wi' a hash o' leemon peel,
And ice an' siccan filth, they ettle
The stawsome kind o' goo to settle;
Sic wersh apothecary's broos wi'
As Scotsmen scorn to fyle their moo's wi'.

An', man, I was a blithe hame-comer
Whan first I syndit out my rummer.
Ye should hae seen me then, wi' care
The less important pairts prepare;
Syne, weel contentit wi' it a',
Pour in the sperrits wi' a jaw!
I didnae drink, I didnae speak,—
I only snowkit up the reek.
I was sae pleased therein to paidle,
I sat an' plowtered wi' my ladle.

An' blithe was I, the morrow's morn,
To daunder through the stookit corn,
And after a' my strange mishanters,

Sit doun amang my ain dissenters.
An', man, it was a joy to me
The pu'pit an' the pews to see,
The pennies dirlin' in the plate,
The elders lookin' on in state;
An' 'mang the first, as it befell,
Wha should I see, sir, but yoursel'

I was, and I will no deny it,
At the first gliff a hantle tryit
To see yoursel' in sic a station—
It seemed a doubtfü' dispensation.
The feelin' was a mere digression;
For shüne I understood the session,
An' mindin' Aiken an' M'Neil,
I wondered they had dune sae weel.
I saw I had mysel' to blame;
For had I but remained at hame,
Aiblins—though no ava' deservin' 't—
They micht hae named your humble servant.

The kirk was filled, the door was steeked;
Up to the pu'pit ance I keeked;
I was mair pleased than I can tell—
It was the minister himsel'!
Proud, proud was I to see his face,
After sae lang awa' frae grace.
Pleased as I was, I'm no denyin'
Some maitters were not edifyin';
For first I fand—an' here was news!—
Mere hymn-books cockin' in the pews—
A humanised abomination,
Unfit for ony congregation.
Syne, while I still was on the tenter,
I scunnered at the new prezentor;
I thocht him gesterin' an' cauld—
A sair declension frae the auld.
Syne, as though a' the faith was wreckit,
The prayer was not what I'd exspeckit.
Himsel', as it appeared to me,
Was no the man he üsed to be.
But just as I was growin' vext
He waled a maist judeecious text,
An', launchin' into his prelections,
Swoopt, wi' a skirl, on a' defections.

O what a gale was on my speerit
To hear the p'ints o' doctrine clearit,
And a' the horrors o' damnation
Set furth wi' faithfü' ministration!
Nae shauchlin' testimony here—
We were a' damned, an' that was clear,
I owned, wi' gratitude an' wonder,
He was a pleisure to sit under.

XIII

Late in the nicht in bed I lay,
The winds were at their weary play,
An' tirlin' wa's an' skirlin' wae
   Through Heev'n they battered;—
On-ding o' hail, on-blaff o' spray,
   The tempest blattered.

The masoned house it dinled through;
It dung the ship, it cowped the coo'.
The rankit aiks it overthrew,
   Had braved a' weathers;
The strang sea-gleds it took an' blew
   Awa' like feathers.

The thrawes o' fear on a' were shed,
An' the hair rose, an' slumber fled,
An' lichts were lit an' prayers were said
   Through a' the kintry;
An' the cauld terror clum in bed
   Wi' a' an' sindry.

To hear in the pit-mirk on hie
The brangled collieshangie flie,
The warl', they thocht, wi' land an' sea,
   Itsel' wad cowpit;
An' for auld airn, the smashed debris
   By God be rowpit.

Meanwhile frae far Aldeboran,
To folks wi' talescopes in han',
O' ships that cowpit, winds that ran,
   Nae sign was seen,
But the wee warl' in sunshine span
   As bricht's a preen.

I, tae, by God's especial grace,
Dwall denty in a bieldy place,
Wi' hosened feet, wi' shaven face,
   Wi' dacent mainners:
A grand example to the race
   O' tautit sinners!

The wind may blaw, the heathen rage,
The deil may start on the rampage;—
The sick in bed, the thief in cage—
   What's a' to me?
Cosh in my house, a sober sage,
   I sit an' see.

An' whiles the bluid spangs to my bree,
To lie sae saft, to live sae free,
While better men maun do an' die
   In unco places.
"Whaur's God?" I cry, an' *"Whae is me*
   To hae sic graces?"

I mind the fecht the sailors keep,
But fire or can'le, rest or sleep,
In darkness an' the muckle deep;
   An' mind beside
The herd that on the hills o' sheep
   Has wandered wide.

I mind me on the hoastin' weans—
The penny joes on causey stanes—
The auld folk wi' the crazy banes,
   Baith auld an' puir,
That aye maun thole the winds an' rains
   An' labour sair.

An' whiles I'm kind o' pleased a blink,
An' kind o' fleyed forby, to think,
For a' my rowth o' meat an' drink
   An' waste o' crumb,
I'll mebbe have to thole wi' skink
   In Kingdom Come.

For God whan jowes the Judgment bell,
Wi' His ain Hand, His Leevin' Sel',
Sall ryve the guid (as Prophets tell)
   Frae them that had it;
And in the reamin' pat o' Hell,
   The rich be scaddit.

O Lord, if this indeed be sae,
Let daw that sair an' happy day!
Again' the warl', grawn auld an' gray,
   Up wi' your aixe!
An' let the puir enjoy their play—
   I'll thole my paiks.

XIV—MY CONSCIENCE!

Of a' the ills that flesh can fear,
The loss o' frien's, the lack o' gear,
A yowlin' tyke, a glandered mear,
   A lassie's nonsense—
There's just ae thing I cannae bear,
   An' that's my conscience.

Whan day (an' a' excuse) has gane,
An' wark is dune, and duty's plain,
An' to my charmer a' my lane
   I creep apairt,
My conscience! hoo the yammerin' pain
   Stends to my heart!

A' day wi' various ends in view
The hairsts o' time I had to pu',
An' made a hash wad staw a soo,
   Let be a man!—
My conscience! whan my han's were fu',
   Whaur were ye than?

An' there were a' the lures o' life,
There pleesure skirlin' on the fife,
There anger, wi' the hotchin' knife
   Ground shairp in Hell—
My conscience!—you that's like a wife!—
   Whaur was yoursel'?

I ken it fine: just waitin' here,
To gar the evil waur appear,
To clart the guid, confuse the clear,
   Misca' the great,
My conscience! an' to raise a steer
   When a's ower late.

Sic-like, some tyke grawn auld and blind,
Whan thieves brok' through the gear to p'ind,
Has lain his dozened length an' grinned
   At the disaster;
An' the morn's mornin', wud's the wind,
   Yokes on his master.

XV—TO DOCTOR JOHN BROWN

Whan the dear doctor, dear to a',
Was still amang us here belaw,
I set my pipes his praise to blaw
   Wi' a' my speerit;
But noo, Dear Doctor! he's awa',
   An' ne'er can hear it.

By Lyne and Tyne, by Thames and Tees,
By a' the various river-Dee's,
In Mars and Manors 'yont the seas
   Or here at hame,
Whaure'er there's kindly folk to please,
   They ken your name.

They ken your name, they ken your tyke,
They ken the honey from your byke;
But mebbe after a' your fyke,
   (The trüth to tell)
It's just your honest Rab they like,
   An' no yoursel'.

As at the gowff, some canny play'r
Should tee a common ba' wi' care—
Should flourish and deleever fair
   His souple shintie—
An' the ba' rise into the air,
   A leevin' lintie:

Sae in the game we writers play,
There comes to some a bonny day,
When a dear ferlie shall repay
   Their years o' strife,
An' like your Rab, their things o' clay,
   Spreid wings o' life.

Ye scarce deserved it, I'm afraid—
You that had never learned the trade,
But just some idle mornin' strayed
   Into the schüle,
An' picked the fiddle up an' played
   Like Neil [8] himsel'.

[8] Neil Gow, the great Highland fiddler.

Your e'e was gleg, your fingers dink;
Ye didnae fash yoursel' to think,
But wove, as fast as puss can link,
   Your denty wab:-
Ye stapped your pen into the ink,
   An' there was Rab!

Sinsyne, whaure'er your fortune lay
By dowie den, by canty brae,
Simmer an' winter, nicht an' day,
   Rab was aye wi' ye;
An' a' the folk on a' the way
   Were blithe to see ye.

O sir, the gods are kind indeed,
An' hauld ye for an honoured heid,
That for a wee bit clarkit screed
   Sae weel reward ye,
An' lend—puir Rabbie bein' deid—
   His ghaist to guard ye.

For though, whaure'er yoursel' may be,
We've just to turn an' glisk a wee,
An' Rab at heel we're shure to see
   Wi' gladsome caper:—
The bogle of a bogle, he—
   A ghaist o' paper!

And as the auld-farrand hero sees
In Hell a bogle Hercules,
Pit there the lesser deid to please,
   While he himsel'
Dwalls wi' the muckle gods at ease
   Far raised frae hell:

Sae the true Rabbie far has gane
On kindlier business o' his ain
Wi' aulder frien's; an' his breist-bane
   An' stumpie tailie,
He birstles at a new hearth stane
   By James and Ailie.

XVI

It's an owercome sooth for age an' youth
   And it brooks wi' nae denial,
That the dearest friends are the auldest friends
   And the young are just on trial.

There's a rival bauld wi' young an' auld
   And it's him that has bereft me;
For the sürest friends are the auldest friends
   And the maist o' mines hae left me.

There are kind hearts still, for friends to fill
   And fools to take and break them;
But the nearest friends are the auldest friends
   And the grave's the place to seek them.

III. SONGS OF TRAVEL AND OTHER VERSES

I—THE VAGABOND
(To an air of Schubert)

Give to me the life I love,
   Let the lave go by me,
Give the jolly heaven above
   And the byway nigh me.
Bed in the bush with stars to see,
   Bread I dip in the river—
There's the life for a man like me,
   There's the life for ever.

Let the blow fall soon or late,
   Let what will be o'er me;
Give the face of earth around
   And the road before me.
Wealth I seek not, hope nor love,
   Nor a friend to know me;
All I seek, the heaven above
   And the road below me.

Or let autumn fall on me
   Where afield I linger,
Silencing the bird on tree,
   Biting the blue finger.
White as meal the frosty field—
   Warm the fireside haven—
Not to autumn will I yield,
   Not to winter even!

Let the blow fall soon or late,
   Let what will be o'er me;
Give the face of earth around,
   And the road before me.
Wealth I ask not, hope nor love,
   Nor a friend to know me;
All I ask, the heaven above
   And the road below me.

II—YOUTH AND LOVE—I

Once only by the garden gate
   Our lips we joined and parted.
I must fulfil an empty fate
   And travel the uncharted.

Hail and farewell! I must arise,
   Leave here the fatted cattle,
And paint on foreign lands and skies
   My Odyssey of battle.

The untented Kosmos my abode,
   I pass, a wilful stranger:
My mistress still the open road
   And the bright eyes of danger.

Come ill or well, the cross, the crown,
   The rainbow or the thunder,
I fling my soul and body down
   For God to plough them under.

III—YOUTH AND LOVE—II

To the heart of youth the world is a highwayside.
   Passing for ever, he fares; and on either hand,
Deep in the gardens golden pavilions hide,
   Nestle in orchard bloom, and far on the level land
Call him with lighted lamp in the eventide.

Thick as the stars at night when the moon is down,
   Pleasures assail him. He to his nobler fate
Fares; and but waves a hand as he passes on,
   Cries but a wayside word to her at the garden gate,
Sings but a boyish stave and his face is gone.

IV—THE UNFORGOTTEN—I

I

In dreams, unhappy, I behold you stand
     As heretofore:
The unremembered tokens in your hand
     Avail no more.

No more the morning glow, no more the grace,
     Enshrines, endears.
Cold beats the light of time upon your face
     And shows your tears.

He came and went. Perchance you wept a while
     And then forgot.
Ah me! but he that left you with a smile
     Forgets you not.

V—THE UNFORGOTTEN—II

V

She rested by the Broken Brook,
    She drank of Weary Well,
She moved beyond my lingering look,
    Ah, whither none can tell!

She came, she went. In other lands,
    Perchance in fairer skies,
Her hands shall cling with other hands,
    Her eyes to other eyes.

She vanished. In the sounding town,
    Will she remember too?
Will she recall the eyes of brown
    As I recall the blue?

VI

The infinite shining heavens
    Rose and I saw in the night
Uncountable angel stars
    Showering sorrow and light.

I saw them distant as heaven,
    Dumb and shining and dead,
And the idle stars of the night
    Were dearer to me than bread.

Night after night in my sorrow
    The stars stood over the sea,
Till lo! I looked in the dusk
    And a star had come down to me.

VII

Plain as the glistering planets shine
    When winds have cleaned the skies,
Her love appeared, appealed for mine,
    And wantoned in her eyes.

Clear as the shining tapers burned
    On Cytherea's shrine,
Those brimming, lustrous beauties turned,
    And called and conquered mine.

The beacon-lamp that Hero lit
   No fairer shone on sea,
No plainlier summoned will and wit,
   Than hers encouraged me.

I thrilled to feel her influence near,
   I struck my flag at sight.
Her starry silence smote my ear
   Like sudden drums at night.

I ran as, at the cannon's roar,
   The troops the ramparts man—
As in the holy house of yore
   The willing Eli ran.

Here, lady, lo! that servant stands
   You picked from passing men,
And should you need nor heart nor hands
   He bows and goes again.

VIII

To you, let snow and roses
   And golden locks belong.
These are the world's enslavers,
   Let these delight the throng.
For her of duskier lustre
   Whose favour still I wear,
The snow be in her kirtle,
   The rose be in her hair!

The hue of highland rivers
   Careering, full and cool,
From sable on to golden,
   From rapid on to pool—
The hue of heather-honey,
   The hue of honey-bees,
Shall tinge her golden shoulder,
   Shall gild her tawny knees.

IX

Let Beauty awake in the morn from beautiful dreams,
    Beauty awake from rest!
    Let Beauty awake
    For Beauty's sake
In the hour when the birds awake in the brake
    And the stars are bright in the west!

Let Beauty awake in the eve from the slumber of day,
    Awake in the crimson eve!
    In the day's dusk end
    When the shades ascend,
Let her wake to the kiss of a tender friend
    To render again and receive!

X

I know not how it is with you—
    I love the first and last,
The whole field of the present view,
    The whole flow of the past.

One tittle of the things that are,
    Nor you should change nor I—
One pebble in our path—one star
    In all our heaven of sky.

Our lives, and every day and hour,
    One symphony appear:
One road, one garden—every flower
    And every bramble dear.

XI

I will make you brooches and toys for your delight
Of bird-song at morning and star-shine at night.
I will make a palace fit for you and me
Of green days in forests and blue days at sea.

I will make my kitchen, and you shall keep your room,
Where white flows the river and bright blows the broom,
And you shall wash your linen and keep your body white
In rainfall at morning and dewfall at night.

And this shall be for music when no one else is near,
The fine song for singing, the rare song to hear!
That only I remember, that only you admire,
Of the broad road that stretches and the roadside fire.

XII—WE HAVE LOVED OF YORE

(TO AN AIR OF DIABELLI)

Berried brake and reedy island,
    Heaven below, and only heaven above,
Through the sky's inverted azure
   Softly swam the boat that bore our love.
      Bright were your eyes as the day;
      Bright ran the stream,
      Bright hung the sky above.
Days of April, airs of Eden,
   How the glory died through golden hours,
And the shining moon arising,
   How the boat drew homeward filled with flowers!
      Bright were your eyes in the night:
      We have lived, my love—
      O, we have loved, my love.

Frost has bound our flowing river,
   Snow has whitened all our island brake,
And beside the winter fagot
   Joan and Darby doze and dream and wake.
      Still, in the river of dreams
      Swims the boat of love—
      Hark! chimes the falling oar!
And again in winter evens
   When on firelight dreaming fancy feeds,
In those ears of agèd lovers
   Love's own river warbles in the reeds.
Love still the past, O my love!
     We have lived of yore,
     O, we have loved of yore.

XIII—DITTY

(TO AN AIR FROM BACH)

The cock shall crow
    In the morning grey,
The bugles blow
    At the break of day:
The cock shall sing and the merry bugles ring,
And all the little brown birds sing upon the spray.

The thorn shall blow
    In the month of May,
And my love shall go
    In her holiday array:
But I shall lie in the kirkyard nigh
While all the little brown birds sing upon the spray.

XIV—MATER TRIUMPHANS

Son of my woman's body, you go, to the drum and fife,
To taste the colour of love and the other side of life—
From out of the dainty the rude, the strong from out of the frail,
Eternally through the ages from the female comes the male.

The ten fingers and toes, and the shell-like nail on each,
The eyes blind as gems and the tongue attempting speech;
Impotent hands in my bosom, and yet they shall wield the sword!
Drugged with slumber and milk, you wait the day of the Lord.

Infant bridegroom, uncrowned king, unanointed priest,
Soldier, lover, explorer, I see you nuzzle the breast.
You that grope in my bosom shall load the ladies with rings,
You, that came forth through the doors, shall burst the doors of kings.

XV

Bright is the ring of words
    When the right man rings them,
Fair the fall of songs
    When the singer sings them.
Still they are carolled and said—
    On wings they are carried—
After the singer is dead
    And the maker buried.

Low as the singer lies
   In the field of heather,
Songs of his fashion bring
   The swains together.
And when the west is red
   With the sunset embers,
The lover lingers and sings
   And the maid remembers.

XVI

In the highlands, in the country places,
Where the old plain men have rosy faces,
And the young fair maidens
Quiet eyes;
Where essential silence cheers and blesses,
And for ever in the hill-recesses
Her more lovely music
Broods and dies.

O to mount again where erst I haunted;
Where the old red hills are bird-enchanted,
And the low green meadows
Bright with sward;
And when even dies, the million-tinted,
And the night has come, and planets glinted,
Lo, the valley hollow
Lamp-bestarred!

O to dream, O to awake and wander
There, and with delight to take and render,
Through the trance of silence,
Quiet breath;
Lo! for there, among the flowers and grasses,
Only the mightier movement sounds and passes;
Only winds and rivers,
Life and death.

XVII

(TO THE TUNE OF WANDERING WILLIE)

Home no more home to me, whither must I wander?
   Hunger my driver, I go where I must.
Cold blows the winter wind over hill and heather;
   Thick drives the rain, and my roof is in the dust.
Loved of wise men was the shade of my roof-tree.
   The true word of welcome was spoken in the door—
Dear days of old, with the faces in the firelight,
   Kind folks of old, you come again no more.

Home was home then, my dear, full of kindly faces,
   Home was home then, my dear, happy for the child.
Fire and the windows bright glittered on the moorland;
   Song, tuneful song, built a palace in the wild.
Now, when day dawns on the brow of the moorland,
   Lone stands the house, and the chimney-stone is cold.
Lone let it stand, now the friends are all departed,
   The kind hearts, the true hearts, that loved the place of old.

Spring shall come, come again, calling up the moorfowl,
   Spring shall bring the sun and rain, bring the bees and flowers;
Red shall the heather bloom over hill and valley,
   Soft flow the stream through the even-flowing hours;
Fair the day shine as it shone on my childhood—
   Fair shine the day on the house with open door;
Birds come and cry there and twitter in the chimney—
   But I go for ever and come again no more.

XVII—TO DR. HAKE
(On receiving a Copy of Verses)

In the belovèd hour that ushers day,
In the pure dew, under the breaking grey,
One bird, ere yet the woodland quires awake,
With brief réveillé summons all the brake:
Chirp, chirp, it goes; nor waits an answer long;
And that small signal fills the grove with song.

Thus on my pipe I breathed a strain or two;
It scarce was music, but 'twas all I knew.
It was not music, for I lacked the art,
Yet what but frozen music filled my heart?
Chirp, chirp, I went, nor hoped a nobler strain;
But Heaven decreed I should not pipe in vain,
For, lo! not far from there, in secret dale,
All silent, sat an ancient nightingale.
My sparrow notes he heard; thereat awoke;
And with a tide of song his silence broke.

XIX—TO ——

I knew thee strong and quiet like the hills;
I knew thee apt to pity, brave to endure,
In peace or war a Roman full equipt;
And just I knew thee, like the fabled kings
Who by the loud sea-shore gave judgment forth,
From dawn to eve, bearded and few of words.
What, what, was I to honour thee? A child;
A youth in ardour but a child in strength,
Who after virtue's golden chariot-wheels
Runs ever panting, nor attains the goal.
So thought I, and was sorrowful at heart.

Since then my steps have visited that flood
Along whose shore the numerous footfalls cease,
The voices and the tears of life expire.
Thither the prints go down, the hero's way
Trod large upon the sand, the trembling maid's:
Nimrod that wound his trumpet in the wood,
And the poor, dreaming child, hunter of flowers,
That here his hunting closes with the great:
So one and all go down, nor aught returns.

For thee, for us, the sacred river waits,
For me, the unworthy, thee, the perfect friend;
There Blame desists, there his unfaltering dogs
He from the chase recalls, and homeward rides;
Yet Praise and Love pass over and go in.
So when, beside that margin, I discard
My more than mortal weakness, and with thee
Through that still land unfearing I advance:
If then at all we keep the touch of joy
Thou shalt rejoice to find me altered—I,
O Felix, to behold thee still unchanged.

XX

The morning drum-call on my eager ear
Thrills unforgotten yet; the morning dew
Lies yet undried along my field of noon.
But now I pause at whiles in what I do,
And count the bell, and tremble lest I hear
(My work untrimmed) the sunset gun too soon.

XXI

I have trod the upward and the downward slope;
I have endured and done in days before;
I have longed for all, and bid farewell to hope;
And I have lived and loved, and closed the door.

XXII

He hears with gladdened heart the thunder
   Peal, and loves the falling dew;
He knows the earth above and under—
   Sits and is content to view.

He sits beside the dying ember,
   God for hope and man for friend,
Content to see, glad to remember,
   Expectant of the certain end.

XXIII—THE LOST OCCAISON

Farewell, fair day and fading light!
The clay-born here, with westward sight,
Marks the huge sun now downward soar.
Farewell. We twain shall meet no more.

Farewell. I watch with bursting sigh
My late contemned occasion die.
I linger useless in my tent:
Farewell, fair day, so foully spent!

Farewell, fair day. If any God
At all consider this poor clod,
He who the fair occasion sent
Prepared and placed the impediment.

Let him diviner vengeance take—
Give me to sleep, give me to wake
Girded and shod, and bid me play
The hero in the coming day!

XXIV—IF THIS WERE FAITH

God, if this were enough,
That I see things bare to the buff
And up to the buttocks in mire;
That I ask nor hope nor hire,
Nut in the husk,
Nor dawn beyond the dusk,
Nor life beyond death:
God, if this were faith?

Having felt thy wind in my face
Spit sorrow and disgrace,
Having seen thine evil doom
In Golgotha and Khartoum,
And the brutes, the work of thine hands,
Fill with injustice lands
And stain with blood the sea:
If still in my veins the glee
Of the black night and the sun
And the lost battle, run:
If, an adept,
The iniquitous lists I still accept
With joy, and joy to endure and be withstood,
And still to battle and perish for a dream of good:
God, if that were enough?

If to feel, in the ink of the slough,
And the sink of the mire,
Veins of glory and fire
Run through and transpierce and transpire,
And a secret purpose of glory in every part,
And the answering glory of battle fill my heart;
To thrill with the joy of girded men
To go on for ever and fail and go on again,
And be mauled to the earth and arise,
And contend for the shade of a word and a thing not seen with the eyes:
With the half of a broken hope for a pillow at night
That somehow the right is the right
And the smooth shall bloom from the rough:
Lord, if that were enough?

XXV—MY WIFE

Trusty, dusky, vivid, true,
With eyes of gold and bramble-dew,
Steel-true and blade-straight,
The great artificer
Made my mate.

Honour, anger, valour, fire;
A love that life could never tire,
Death quench or evil stir,
The mighty master
Gave to her.

Teacher, tender, comrade, wife,
A fellow-farer true through life,
Heart-whole and soul-free
The august father
Gave to me.

XXVI—WINTER

In rigorous hours, when down the iron lane
The redbreast looks in vain
For hips and haws,
Lo, shining flowers upon my window-pane
   The silver pencil of the winter draws.

When all the snowy hill
And the bare woods are still;
When snipes are silent in the frozen bogs,
   And all the garden garth is whelmed in mire,
Lo, by the hearth, the laughter of the logs—
   More fair than roses, lo, the flowers of fire!

SARANAC LAKE.

XXVII

The stormy evening closes now in vain,
   Loud wails the wind and beats the driving rain,
      While here in sheltered house
         With fire-ypainted walls,
      I hear the wind abroad,
         I hark the calling squalls—
'Blow, blow,' I cry, 'you burst your cheeks in vain!
Blow, blow,' I cry, 'my love is home again!'

Yon ship you chase perchance but yesternight
Bore still the precious freight of my delight,
  That here in sheltered house
   With fire-ypainted walls,
  Now hears the wind abroad,
   Now harks the calling squalls.
'Blow, blow,' I cry, 'in vain you rouse the sea,
My rescued sailor shares the fire with me!'

XXVIII—TO AN ISLAND PRINCESS

Since long ago, a child at home,
I read and longed to rise and roam,
Where'er I went, whate'er I willed,
One promised land my fancy filled.
Hence the long roads my home I made;
Tossed much in ships; have often laid
Below the uncurtained sky my head,
Rain-deluged and wind-buffeted:
And many a thousand hills I crossed
And corners turned—Love's labour lost,
Till, Lady, to your isle of sun
I came, not hoping; and, like one
Snatched out of blindness, rubbed my eyes,
And hailed my promised land with cries.

Yes, Lady, here I was at last;
Here found I all I had forecast:
The long roll of the sapphire sea
That keeps the land's virginity;
The stalwart giants of the wood
Laden with toys and flowers and food;
The precious forest pouring out
To compass the whole town about;
The town itself with streets of lawn,
Loved of the moon, blessed by the dawn,
Where the brown children all the day
Keep up a ceaseless noise of play,
Play in the sun, play in the rain,
Nor ever quarrel or complain;—
And late at night, in the woods of fruit,
Hark! do you hear the passing flute?

I threw one look to either hand,
And knew I was in Fairyland.
And yet one point of being so
I lacked. For, Lady (as you know),
Whoever by his might of hand,
Won entrance into Fairyland,
Found always with admiring eyes
A Fairy princess kind and wise.

It was not long I waited; soon
Upon my threshold, in broad noon,
Gracious and helpful, wise and good,
The Fairy Princess Moë stood.

TANTIRA, TAHITI, NOV. 5, 1888.

XXIX—TO KALAKAUA

(WITH A PRESENT OF A PEARL)

The Silver Ship, my King—that was her name
In the bright islands whence your fathers came—
The Silver Ship, at rest from winds and tides,
Below your palace in your harbour rides:
And the seafarers, sitting safe on shore,
Like eager merchants count their treasures o'er.
One gift they find, one strange and lovely thing,
Now doubly precious since it pleased a king.

The right, my liege, is ancient as the lyre
For bards to give to kings what kings admire.
'Tis mine to offer for Apollo's sake;
And since the gift is fitting, yours to take.
To golden hands the golden pearl I bring:
The ocean jewel to the island king.

HONOLULU, FEB. 3, 1889.

XXX—TO PRINCESS KAIULANI

Forth from her land to mine she goes,
The island maid, the island rose,
Light of heart and bright of face:
The daughter of a double race.
Her islands here, in Southern sun,
Shall mourn their Kaiulani gone,
And I, in her dear banyan shade,
Look vainly for my little maid.
But our Scots islands far away
Shall glitter with unwonted day,
And cast for once their tempests by
To smile in Kaiulani's eye.

HONOLULU.

[Written in April to Kaiulani in the April of her age; and at Waikiki, within easy walk of Kaiulani's banyan! When she comes to my land and her father's, and the rain beats upon the window (as I fear it will), let her look at this page; it will be like a weed gathered and pressed at home; and she will remember her own islands, and the shadow of the mighty tree; and she will hear the peacocks screaming in the dusk and the wind blowing in the palms; and she will think of her father sitting there alone.—R. L. S.]

XXXI—TO MOTHER MARYANNE

To see the infinite pity of this place,
The mangled limb, the devastated face,
The innocent sufferer smiling at the rod—
A fool were tempted to deny his God.
He sees, he shrinks. But if he gaze again,
Lo, beauty springing from the breast of pain!
He marks the sisters on the mournful shores;
And even a fool is silent and adores.

GUEST HOUSE, KALAWAO, MOLOKAI.

XXXII—IN MEMORIAM E. H.

I knew a silver head was bright beyond compare,
I knew a queen of toil with a crown of silver hair.
Garland of valour and sorrow, of beauty and renown,
Life, that honours the brave, crowned her himself with the crown.

The beauties of youth are frail, but this was a jewel of age.
Life, that delights in the brave, gave it himself for a gage.
Fair was the crown to behold, and beauty its poorest part—
At once the scar of the wound and the order pinned on the heart.

The beauties of man are frail, and the silver lies in the dust,
And the queen that we call to mind sleeps with the brave and the just;
Sleeps with the weary at length; but, honoured and ever fair,
Shines in the eye of the mind the crown of the silver hair.

HONOLULU.

XXXIII—TO MY WIFE

(A FRAGMENT)

Long must elapse ere you behold again
Green forest frame the entry of the lane—
The wild lane with the bramble and the brier,
The year-old cart-tracks perfect in the mire,
The wayside smoke, perchance, the dwarfish huts,
And ramblers' donkey drinking from the ruts:—
Long ere you trace how deviously it leads,
Back from man's chimneys and the bleating meads
To the woodland shadow, to the sylvan hush,
When but the brooklet chuckles in the brush—
Back from the sun and bustle of the vale
To where the great voice of the nightingale
Fills all the forest like a single room,
And all the banks smell of the golden broom;
So wander on until the eve descends.
And back returning to your firelit friends,
You see the rosy sun, despoiled of light,
Hung, caught in thickets, like a schoolboy's kite.

Here from the sea the unfruitful sun shall rise,
Bathe the bare deck and blind the unshielded eyes;
The allotted hours aloft shall wheel in vain
And in the unpregnant ocean plunge again.
Assault of squalls that mock the watchful guard,
And pluck the bursting canvas from the yard,
And senseless clamour of the calm, at night
Must mar your slumbers. By the plunging light,
In beetle-haunted, most unwomanly bower
Of the wild-swerving cabin, hour by hour . . .

SCHOONER 'EQUATOR.'

XXXIV—TO THE MUSE

Resign the rhapsody, the dream,
   To men of larger reach;
Be ours the quest of a plain theme,
   The piety of speech.

As monkish scribes from morning break
   Toiled till the close of light,
Nor thought a day too long to make
   One line or letter bright:

We also with an ardent mind,
   Time, wealth, and fame forgot,
Our glory in our patience find
   And skim, and skim the pot:

Till last, when round the house we hear
   The evensong of birds,
One corner of blue heaven appear
   In our clear well of words.

Leave, leave it then, muse of my heart!
   Sans finish and sans frame,
Leave unadorned by needless art
   The picture as it came.

APEMAMA.

XXXV—TO MY OLD FAMILIARS

Do you remember—can we e'er forget?—
How, in the coiled-perplexities of youth,
In our wild climate, in our scowling town,
We gloomed and shivered, sorrowed, sobbed and feared?
The belching winter wind, the missile rain,
The rare and welcome silence of the snows,
The laggard morn, the haggard day, the night,
The grimy spell of the nocturnal town,
Do you remember?—Ah, could one forget!

As when the fevered sick that all night long
Listed the wind intone, and hear at last
The ever-welcome voice of chanticleer
Sing in the bitter hour before the dawn,—
With sudden ardour, these desire the day:
So sang in the gloom of youth the bird of hope;
So we, exulting, hearkened and desired.
For lo! as in the palace porch of life
We huddled with chimeras, from within—
How sweet to hear!—the music swelled and fell,
And through the breach of the revolving doors
What dreams of splendour blinded us and fled!

I have since then contended and rejoiced;
Amid the glories of the house of life
Profoundly entered, and the shrine beheld:
Yet when the lamp from my expiring eyes
Shall dwindle and recede, the voice of love
Fall insignificant on my closing ears,
What sound shall come but the old cry of the wind
In our inclement city? what return
But the image of the emptiness of youth,
Filled with the sound of footsteps and that voice
Of discontent and rapture and despair?
So, as in darkness, from the magic lamp,
The momentary pictures gleam and fade
And perish, and the night resurges—these
Shall I remember, and then all forget.

APEMAMA.

XXXVI

The tropics vanish, and meseems that I,
From Halkerside, from topmost Allermuir,
Or steep Caerketton, dreaming gaze again.
Far set in fields and woods, the town I see
Spring gallant from the shallows of her smoke,
Cragged, spired, and turreted, her virgin fort
Beflagged. About, on seaward-drooping hills,
New folds of city glitter. Last, the Forth
Wheels ample waters set with sacred isles,
And populous Fife smokes with a score of towns.
There, on the sunny frontage of a hill,
Hard by the house of kings, repose the dead,
My dead, the ready and the strong of word.
Their works, the salt-encrusted, still survive;

The sea bombards their founded towers; the night
Thrills pierced with their strong lamps. The artificers,
One after one, here in this grated cell,
Where the rain erases, and the rust consumes,
Fell upon lasting silence. Continents
And continental oceans intervene;
A sea uncharted, on a lampless isle,
Environs and confines their wandering child
In vain. The voice of generations dead
Summons me, sitting distant, to arise,
My numerous footsteps nimbly to retrace,
And, all mutation over, stretch me down
In that denoted city of the dead.

APEMAMA.

XXXVII—TO S. C. [9]

[9] Sidney Colvin.

I heard the pulse of the besieging sea
Throb far away all night. I heard the wind
Fly crying and convulse tumultuous palms.
I rose and strolled. The isle was all bright sand,
And flailing fans and shadows of the palm;
The heaven all moon and wind and the blind vault;
The keenest planet slain, for Venus slept.
   The king, my neighbour, with his host of wives,
Slept in the precinct of the palisade;
Where single, in the wind, under the moon,
Among the slumbering cabins, blazed a fire,
Sole street-lamp and the only sentinel.
   To other lands and nights my fancy turned—
To London first, and chiefly to your house,
The many-pillared and the well-beloved.
There yearning fancy lighted; there again
In the upper room I lay, and heard far off
The unsleeping city murmur like a shell;
The muffled tramp of the Museum guard
Once more went by me; I beheld again
Lamps vainly brighten the dispeopled street;
Again I longed for the returning morn,
The awaking traffic, the bestirring birds,
The consentaneous trill of tiny song
That weaves round monumental cornices
A passing charm of beauty. Most of all,
For your light foot I wearied, and your knock
That was the glad réveillé of my day.

Lo, now, when to your task in the great house
At morning through the portico you pass,
One moment glance, where by the pillared wall
Far-voyaging island gods, begrimed with smoke,
Sit now unworshipped, the rude monument
Of faiths forgot and races undivined:
Sit now disconsolate, remembering well
The priest, the victim, and the songful crowd,
The blaze of the blue noon, and that huge voice,
Incessant, of the breakers on the shore.
As far as these from their ancestral shrine,
So far, so foreign, your divided friends
Wander, estranged in body, not in mind.

APEMAMA.

XXXVIII—THE HOUSE OF TEMBINOKA

At my departure from the island of Apemama, for which you will look in vain in most atlases, the King and I agreed, since we both set up to be in the poetical way, that we should celebrate our separation in verse. Whether or not his Majesty has been true to his bargain, the laggard posts of the Pacific may perhaps inform me in six months, perhaps not before a year. The following lines represent my part of the contract, and it is hoped, by their pictures of strange manners, they may entertain a civilised audience. Nothing throughout has been invented or exaggerated; the lady herein referred to as the author's muse has confined herself to stringing into rhyme facts or legends that I saw or heard during two months' residence upon the island.—R. L. S.

ENVOI

Let us, who part like brothers, part like bards;
And you in your tongue and measure, I in mine,
Our now division duly solemnise.
Unlike the strains, and yet the theme is one:
The strains unlike, and how unlike their fate!
You to the blinding palace-yard shall call
The prefect of the singers, and to him,
Listening devout, your valedictory verse
Deliver; he, his attribute fulfilled,
To the island chorus hand your measures on,
Wed now with harmony: so them, at last,
Night after night, in the open hall of dance,
Shall thirty matted men, to the clapped hand,
Intone and bray and bark. Unfortunate!
Paper and print alone shall honour mine.

THE SONG

Let now the King his ear arouse
And toss the bosky ringlets from his brows,
The while, our bond to implement,
My muse relates and praises his descent.

I

Bride of the shark, her valour first I sing
Who on the lone seas quickened of a King.
She, from the shore and puny homes of men,
Beyond the climber's sea-discerning ken,
Swam, led by omens; and devoid of fear,
Beheld her monstrous paramour draw near.
She gazed; all round her to the heavenly pale,
The simple sea was void of isle or sail—
Sole overhead the unsparing sun was reared—
When the deep bubbled and the brute appeared.
But she, secure in the decrees of fate,
Made strong her bosom and received the mate,
And, men declare, from that marine embrace
Conceived the virtues of a stronger race.

II

Her stern descendant next I praise,
Survivor of a thousand frays:—
In the hall of tongues who ruled the throng;
Led and was trusted by the strong;
And when spears were in the wood,
Like a tower of vantage stood:—
Whom, not till seventy years had sped,
Unscarred of breast, erect of head,
Still light of step, still bright of look,
The hunter, Death, had overtook.

III

His sons, the brothers twain, I sing,
Of whom the elder reigned a King.
No Childeric he, yet much declined
From his rude sire's imperious mind,
Until his day came when he died,
He lived, he reigned, he versified.
But chiefly him I celebrate
That was the pillar of the state,

Ruled, wise of word and bold of mien,
The peaceful and the warlike scene;
And played alike the leader's part
In lawful and unlawful art.
His soldiers with emboldened ears
Heard him laugh among the spears.
He could deduce from age to age
The web of island parentage;
Best lay the rhyme, best lead the dance,
For any festal circumstance:
And fitly fashion oar and boat,
A palace or an armour coat.
None more availed than he to raise
The strong, suffumigating blaze,
Or knot the wizard leaf: none more,
Upon the untrodden windward shore
Of the isle, beside the beating main,
To cure the sickly and constrain,
With muttered words and waving rods,
The gibbering and the whistling gods.
But he, though thus with hand and head
He ruled, commanded, charmed, and led,
And thus in virtue and in might
Towered to contemporary sight—
Still in fraternal faith and love,
Remained below to reach above,
Gave and obeyed the apt command,
Pilot and vassal of the land.

IV

My Tembinok' from men like these
Inherited his palaces,
His right to rule, his powers of mind,
His cocoa-islands sea-enshrined.
Stern bearer of the sword and whip,
A master passed in mastership,
He learned, without the spur of need,
To write, to cipher, and to read;
From all that touch on his prone shore
Augments his treasury of lore,
Eager in age as erst in youth
To catch an art, to learn a truth,
To paint on the internal page
A clearer picture of the age.
His age, you say? But ah, not so!
In his lone isle of long ago,
A royal Lady of Shalott,

Sea-sundered, he beholds it not;
He only hears it far away.
The stress of equatorial day
He suffers; he records the while
The vapid annals of the isle;
Slaves bring him praise of his renown,
Or cackle of the palm-tree town;
The rarer ship and the rare boat
He marks; and only hears remote,
Where thrones and fortunes rise and reel,
The thunder of the turning wheel.

V

For the unexpected tears he shed
At my departing, may his lion head
Not whiten, his revolving years
No fresh occasion minister of tears;
At book or cards, at work or sport,
Him may the breeze across the palace court
For ever fan; and swelling near
For ever the loud song divert his ear.

SCHOONER 'EQUATOR,' AT SEA.

XXXVIII—THE WOODMAN

In all the grove, nor stream nor bird
Nor aught beside my blows was heard,
And the woods wore their noonday dress—
The glory of their silentness.
From the island summit to the seas,
Trees mounted, and trees drooped, and trees
Groped upward in the gaps. The green
Inarboured talus and ravine
By fathoms. By the multitude
The rugged columns of the wood
And bunches of the branches stood;
Thick as a mob, deep as a sea,
And silent as eternity.

With lowered axe, with backward head,
Late from this scene my labourer fled,
And with a ravelled tale to tell,
Returned. Some denizen of hell,
Dead man or disinvested god,
Had close behind him peered and trod,
And triumphed when he turned to flee.

How different fell the lines with me!
Whose eye explored the dim arcade
Impatient of the uncoming shade—
Shy elf, or dryad pale and cold,
Or mystic lingerer from of old:
Vainly. The fair and stately things,
Impassive as departed kings,
All still in the wood's stillness stood,
And dumb. The rooted multitude
Nodded and brooded, bloomed and dreamed,
Unmeaning, undivined. It seemed
No other art, no hope, they knew,
Than clutch the earth and seek the blue.

'Mid vegetable king and priest
And stripling, I (the only beast)
Was at the beast's work, killing; hewed
The stubborn roots across, bestrewed
The glebe with the dislustred leaves,
And bade the saplings fall in sheaves;
Bursting across the tangled math
A ruin that I called a path,
A Golgotha that, later on,
When rains had watered, and suns shone,
And seeds enriched the place, should bear
And be called garden. Here and there,
I spied and plucked by the green hair
A foe more resolute to live,
The toothed and killing sensitive.
He, semi-conscious, fled the attack;
He shrank and tucked his branches back;
And straining by his anchor-strand,
Captured and scratched the rooting hand.
I saw him crouch, I felt him bite;
And straight my eyes were touched with sight.
I saw the wood for what it was:
The lost and the victorious cause,
The deadly battle pitched in line,
Saw silent weapons cross and shine:
Silent defeat, silent assault,
A battle and a burial vault.

Thick round me in the teeming mud
Brier and fern strove to the blood:
The hooked liana in his gin
Noosed his reluctant neighbours in:
There the green murderer throve and spread,
Upon his smothering victims fed,

And wantoned on his climbing coil.
Contending roots fought for the soil
Like frightened demons: with despair
Competing branches pushed for air.
Green conquerors from overhead
Bestrode the bodies of their dead:
The Caesars of the sylvan field,
Unused to fail, foredoomed to yield:
For in the groins of branches, lo!
The cancers of the orchid grow.

Silent as in the listed ring
Two chartered wrestlers strain and cling;
Dumb as by yellow Hooghly's side
The suffocating captives died;
So hushed the woodland warfare goes
Unceasing; and the silent foes
Grapple and smother, strain and clasp
Without a cry, without a gasp.
Here also sound thy fans, O God,
Here too thy banners move abroad:
Forest and city, sea and shore,
And the whole earth, thy threshing-floor!
The drums of war, the drums of peace,
Roll through our cities without cease,
And all the iron halls of life
Ring with the unremitting strife.

The common lot we scarce perceive.
Crowds perish, we nor mark nor grieve:
The bugle calls—we mourn a few!
What corporal's guard at Waterloo?
What scanty hundreds more or less
In the man-devouring Wilderness?
What handful bled on Delhi ridge?
—See, rather, London, on thy bridge
The pale battalions trample by,
Resolved to slay, resigned to die.
Count, rather, all the maimed and dead
In the unbrotherly war of bread.
See, rather, under sultrier skies
What vegetable Londons rise,
And teem, and suffer without sound:
Or in your tranquil garden ground,
Contented, in the falling gloom,
Saunter and see the roses bloom.
That these might live, what thousands died!
All day the cruel hoe was plied;

The ambulance barrow rolled all day;
Your wife, the tender, kind, and gay,
Donned her long gauntlets, caught the spud,
And bathed in vegetable blood;
And the long massacre now at end,
See! where the lazy coils ascend,
See, where the bonfire sputters red
At even, for the innocent dead.

Why prate of peace? when, warriors all,
We clank in harness into hall,
And ever bare upon the board
Lies the necessary sword.
In the green field or quiet street,
Besieged we sleep, beleaguered eat;
Labour by day and wake o' nights,
In war with rival appetites.
The rose on roses feeds; the lark
On larks. The sedentary clerk
All morning with a diligent pen
Murders the babes of other men;
And like the beasts of wood and park,
Protects his whelps, defends his den.

Unshamed the narrow aim I hold;
I feed my sheep, patrol my fold;
Breathe war on wolves and rival flocks,
A pious outlaw on the rocks
Of God and morning; and when time
Shall bow, or rivals break me, climb
Where no undubbed civilian dares,
In my war harness, the loud stairs
Of honour; and my conqueror
Hail me a warrior fallen in war.

VAILIMA.

XL—TROPIC RAIN

As the single pang of the blow, when the metal is mingled well,
Rings and lives and resounds in all the bounds of the bell,
So the thunder above spoke with a single tongue,
So in the heart of the mountain the sound of it rumbled and clung.

Sudden the thunder was drowned—quenched was the levin light—
And the angel-spirit of rain laughed out loud in the night.
Loud as the maddened river raves in the cloven glen,
Angel of rain! you laughed and leaped on the roofs of men;

And the sleepers sprang in their beds, and joyed and feared as you fell.
You struck, and my cabin quailed; the roof of it roared like a bell.
You spoke, and at once the mountain shouted and shook with brooks.
You ceased, and the day returned, rosy, with virgin looks.

And methought that beauty and terror are only one, not two;
And the world has room for love, and death, and thunder, and dew;
And all the sinews of hell slumber in summer air;
And the face of God is a rock, but the face of the rock is fair.
Beneficent streams of tears flow at the finger of pain;
And out of the cloud that smites, beneficent rivers of rain.

VAILIMA.

XLI—AN END OF TRAVEL

Let now your soul in this substantial world
Some anchor strike. Be here the body moored;—
This spectacle immutably from now
The picture in your eye; and when time strikes,
And the green scene goes on the instant blind—
The ultimate helpers, where your horse to-day
Conveyed you dreaming, bear your body dead.

VAILIMA.

XLII

We uncommiserate pass into the night
From the loud banquet, and departing leave
A tremor in men's memories, faint and sweet
And frail as music. Features of our face,
The tones of the voice, the touch of the loved hand,
Perish and vanish, one by one, from earth:
Meanwhile, in the hall of song, the multitude
Applauds the new performer. One, perchance,
One ultimate survivor lingers on,
And smiles, and to his ancient heart recalls
The long forgotten. Ere the morrow die,
He too, returning, through the curtain comes,
And the new age forgets us and goes on.

XLIII—THE LAST SIGHT

Once more I saw him. In the lofty room,
Where oft with lights and company his tongue
Was trump to honest laughter, state attired.
A something in his likeness.—"Look!" said one,
Unkindly kind, "look up, it is your boy!"
And the dread changeling gazed on me in vain.

XLIV

Sing me a song of a lad that is gone,
   Say, could that lad be I?
Merry of soul he sailed on a day
   Over the sea to Skye.

Mull was astern, Rum on the port,
   Egg on the starboard bow;
Glory of youth glowed in his soul:
   Where is that glory now?

Sing me a song of a lad that is gone,
   Say, could that lad be I?
Merry of soul he sailed on a day
   Over the sea to Skye.

Give me again all that was there,
   Give me the sun that shone!
Give me the eyes, give me the soul,
   Give me the lad that's gone!

Sing me a song of a lad that is gone,
   Say, could that lad be I?
Merry of soul he sailed on a day
   Over the sea to Skye.

Billow and breeze, islands and seas,
   Mountains of rain and sun,
All that was good, all that was fair,
   All that was me is gone.

XLV—TO S. R. CROCKETT

(ON RECEIVING A DEDICATION)

Blows the wind to-day, and the sun and the rain are flying,
    Blows the wind on the moors to-day and now,
Where about the graves of the martyrs the whaups are crying,
    My heart remembers how!

Grey recumbent tombs of the dead in desert places,
    Standing stones on the vacant wine-red moor,
Hills of sheep, and the homes of the silent vanished races,
    And winds, austere and pure:

Be it granted me to behold you again in dying,
    Hills of home! and to hear again the call;
Hear about the graves of the martyrs the peewees crying,
    And hear no more at all.

VAILIMA.

XLVI—EVENSONG

The embers of the day are red
Beyond the murky hill.
The kitchen smokes: the bed
In the darkling house is spread:
The great sky darkens overhead,
And the great woods are shrill.
So far have I been led,
Lord, by Thy will:
So far I have followed, Lord, and wondered still.

The breeze from the enbalmèd land
Blows sudden toward the shore,
And claps my cottage door.
I hear the signal, Lord—I understand.
The night at Thy command
Comes. I will eat and sleep and will not question more.

VAILIMA.

IV. BALLADS

THE SONG OF RAHÉRO

A LEGEND OF TAHITI

TO ORI A ORI

Ori, my brother in the island mode,
In every tongue and meaning much my friend,
This story of your country and your clan,
In your loved house, your too much honoured guest,
I made in English. Take it, being done;
And let me sign it with the name you gave.

TERIITERA.

INTRODUCTION.—This tale, which I have not consciously changed a single feature, I received from tradition. It is highly popular through all the country of the eight Tevas, the clan to which Rohéro belonged; and particularly in Taiárapu, the windward peninsula of Tahiti, where we lived. I have heard from end to end two versions; and as many as five different persons have helped me with details. There seems no reasons why the tale should not be true.

I. THE SLAYING OF TÁMATÉA

It fell in the days of old, as the men of Taiárapu tell,
A youth went forth to the fishing, and fortune favoured him well.
Támatéa his name: gullible, simple, and kind,
Comely of countenance, nimble of body, empty of mind,
His mother ruled him and loved him beyond the wont of a wife,
Serving the lad for eyes and living herself in his life.
Alone from the sea and the fishing came Támatéa the fair,
Urging his boat to the beach, and the mother awaited him there,
—"Long may you live!" said she. "Your fishing has sped to a wish.
And now let us choose for the king the fairest of all your fish.
For fear inhabits the palace and grudging grows in the land,
Marked is the sluggardly foot and marked the niggardly hand,
The hours and the miles are counted, the tributes numbered and weighed,
And woe to him that comes short, and woe to him that delayed!"

So spake on the beach the mother, and counselled the wiser thing.
For Rahéro stirred in the country and secretly mined the king.
Nor were the signals wanting of how the leaven wrought,
In the cords of obedience loosed and the tributes grudgingly brought.
And when last to the temple of Oro the boat with the victim sped,
And the priest uncovered the basket and looked on the face of the dead,
Trembling fell upon all at sight of an ominous thing,
For there was the aito [10] dead, and he of the house of the king.

[10] "*The aito,*" *quasi* champion, or brave. One skilled in the use of some weapon, who wandered the country challenging distinguished rivals and taking part in local quarrels. It was in the natural course of his advancement to be at last employed by a chief, or king; and it would then be a part of his duties to purvey the victim for sacrifice. One of the doomed families was indicated; the aito took his weapon and went forth alone; a little behind him bearers followed with the sacrificial basket. Sometimes the victim showed fight, sometimes prevailed; more often, without doubt, he fell. But whatever body was found, the bearers indifferently took up.

So spake on the beach the mother, matter worthy of note,
And wattled a basket well, and chose a fish from the boat;
And Támatéa the pliable shouldered the basket and went,
And travelled, and sang as he travelled, a lad that was well content.
Still the way of his going was round by the roaring coast,
Where the ring of the reef is broke and the trades run riot the most.
On his left, with smoke as of battle, the billows battered the land;
Unscalable, turreted mountains rose on the inner hand.
And cape, and village, and river, and vale, and mountain above,
Each had a name in the land for men to remember and love;
And never the name of a place, but lo! a song in its praise:
Ancient and unforgotten, songs of the earlier days,
That the elders taught to the young, and at night, in the full of the moon,
Garlanded boys and maidens sang together in tune.
Támatéa the placable went with a lingering foot;
He sang as loud as a bird, he whistled hoarse as a flute;
He broiled in the sun, he breathed in the grateful shadow of trees,
In the icy stream of the rivers he waded over the knees;
And still in his empty mind crowded, a thousand-fold,
The deeds of the strong and the songs of the cunning heroes of old.

And now was he come to a place Taiárapu honoured the most,
Where a silent valley of woods debouched on the noisy coast,
Spewing a level river. There was a haunt of Pai. [11]
There, in his potent youth, when his parents drove him to die,
Honoura lived like a beast, lacking the lamp and the fire,
Washed by the rains of the trade and clotting his hair in the mire;
And there, so mighty his hands, he bent the tree to his foot—
So keen the spur of his hunger, he plucked it naked of fruit.

There, as she pondered the clouds for the shadow of coming ills,
Ahupu, the woman of song, walked on high on the hills.
Of these was Rahéro sprung, a man of a godly race;
And inherited cunning of spirit and beauty of body and face.
Of yore in his youth, as an aito, Rahéro wandered the land,
Delighting maids with his tongue, smiting men with his hand.
Famous he was in his youth; but before the midst of his life
Paused, and fashioned a song of farewell to glory and strife.

[11] "*Pai*," "*Honoura*," and "*Ahupu*." Legendary persons of Tahiti, all natives of Taiárapu. Of the two first, I have collected singular, although imperfect, legends, which I hope soon to lay before the public in another place. Of Ahupu, except in snatches of song, little memory appears to linger. She dwelt at least about Tepari,—"the sea-cliffs,"—the eastern fastness of the isle; walked by paths known only to herself upon the mountains; was courted by dangerous suitors who came swimming from adjacent islands, and defended and rescued (as I gather) by the loyalty of native fish. My anxiety to learn more of "Ahupu Vehine" became (during my stay in Taiárapu) a cause of some diversion to that mirthful people, the inhabitants.

House of mine (it went), *house upon the sea,*
Belov'd of all my fathers, more belov'd by me!
Vale of the strong Honoura, deep ravine of Pai,
Again in your woody summits I hear the trade-wind cry.

House of mine, in your walls, strong sounds the sea,
Of all sounds on earth, dearest sound to me.
I have heard the applause of men, I have heard it arise and die:
Sweeter now in my house I hear the trade-wind cry.

These were the words of his singing, other the thought of his heart;
For secret desire of glory vexed him, dwelling apart.
Lazy and crafty he was, and loved to lie in the sun,
And loved the cackle of talk and the true word uttered in fun;
Lazy he was, his roof was ragged, his table was lean,
And the fish swam safe in his sea, and he gathered the near and the green.
He sat in his house and laughed, but he loathed the king of the land,
And he uttered the grudging word under the covering hand.
Treason spread from his door; and he looked for a day to come,
A day of the crowding people, a day of the summoning drum,
When the vote should be taken, the king be driven forth in disgrace,
And Rahéro, the laughing and lazy, sit and rule in his place,

           Here Támatéa came, and beheld the house on the brook;
           And Rahéro was there by the way and covered an oven to cook. [12]
           Naked he was to the loins, but the tattoo covered the lack,
           And the sun and the shadow of palms dappled his muscular back.
           Swiftly he lifted his head at the fall of the coming feet,
           And the water sprang in his mouth with a sudden desire of meat;
           For he marked the basket carried, covered from flies and the sun; [13]
           And Rahéro buried his fire, but the meat in his house was done.

[12] "*Covered an oven.*" The cooking fire is made in a hole in the ground, and is then buried.
[13] "*Flies.*" This is perhaps an anachronism. Even speaking of to-day in Tahiti, the phrase would have to be understood as referring mainly to mosquitoes, and these only in watered valleys with close woods, such as I suppose to form the surroundings of Rahéro's homestead. A quarter of a mile away, where the air moves freely, you shall look in vain for one.

           Forth he stepped; and took, and delayed the boy, by the hand;
           And vaunted the joys of meat and the ancient ways of the land:
           —"Our sires of old in Taiárapu, they that created the race,
           Ate ever with eager hand, nor regarded season or place,
           Ate in the boat at the oar, on the way afoot; and at night
           Arose in the midst of dreams to rummage the house for a bite.
           It is good for the youth in his turn to follow the way of the sire;
           And behold how fitting the time! for here do I cover my fire."
           —"I see the fire for the cooking but never the meat to cook,"
           Said Támatéa.—"Tut!" said Rahéro. "Here in the brook
           And there in the tumbling sea, the fishes are thick as flies,
           Hungry like healthy men, and like pigs for savour and size:
           Crayfish crowding the river, sea-fish thronging the sea."
           —"Well it may be," says the other, "and yet be nothing to me.
           Fain would I eat, but alas! I have needful matter in hand,
           Since I carry my tribute of fish to the jealous king of the land."

           Now at the word a light sprang in Rahéro's eyes.
           "I will gain me a dinner," thought he, "and lend the king a surprise."
           And he took the lad by the arm, as they stood by the side of the track,
           And smiled, and rallied, and flattered, and pushed him forward and back.
           It was "You that sing like a bird, I never have heard you sing,"
           And "The lads when I was a lad were none so feared of a king.
           And of what account is an hour, when the heart is empty of guile?
           But come, and sit in the house and laugh with the women awhile;
           And I will but drop my hook, [14] and behold! the dinner made."

[14] "*Hook*" of mother-of-pearl. Bright-hook fishing, and that with the spear, appear to be the favourite native methods.

So Támatéa the pliable hung up his fish in the shade
On a tree by the side of the way; and Rahéro carried him in,
Smiling as smiles the fowler when flutters the bird to the gin,
And chose him a shining hook, and viewed it with sedulous eye,
And breathed and burnished it well on the brawn of his naked thigh,
And set a mat for the gull, and bade him be merry and bide,
Like a man concerned for his guest, and the fishing, and nothing beside.

Now when Rahéro was forth, he paused and hearkened, and heard
The gull jest in the house and the women laugh at his word;
And stealthily crossed to the side of the way, to the shady place
Where the basket hung on a mango; and craft transfigured his face.
Deftly he opened the basket, and took of the fat of the fish,
The cut of kings and chieftains, enough for a goodly dish.
This he wrapped in a leaf, set on the fire to cook
And buried; and next the marred remains of the tribute he took,
And doubled and packed them well, and covered the basket close
—"There is a buffet, my king," quoth he, "and a nauseous dose!"—
And hung the basket again in the shade, in a cloud of flies
—"And there is a sauce to your dinner, king of the crafty eyes!"

Soon as the oven was open, the fish smelt excellent good.
In the shade, by the house of Rahéro, down they sat to their food,
And cleared the leaves [15] in silence, or uttered a jest and laughed,
And raising the cocoanut bowls, buried their faces and quaffed.
But chiefly in silence they ate; and soon as the meal was done,
Rahéro feigned to remember and measured the hour by the sun,
And "Támatéa," quoth he, "it is time to be jogging, my lad."

[15] "*Leaves*," the plates of Tahiti.

So Támatéa arose, doing ever the thing he was bade,
And carelessly shouldered the basket, and kindly saluted his host;
And again the way of his going was round by the roaring coast.
Long he went; and at length was aware of a pleasant green,
And the stems and shadows of palms, and roofs of lodges between
There sate, in the door of his palace, the king on a kingly seat,
And aitos stood armed around, and the yottowas [16] sat at his feet.
But fear was a worm in his heart: fear darted his eyes;
And he probed men's faces for treasons and pondered their speech for lies.
To him came Támatéa, the basket slung in his hand,
And paid him the due obeisance standing as vassals stand.
In silence hearkened the king, and closed the eyes in his face,
Harbouring odious thoughts and the baseless fears of the base;
In silence accepted the gift and sent the giver away.
So Támatéa departed, turning his back on the day.
And lo! as the king sat brooding, a rumour rose in the crowd;

The yottowas nudged and whispered, the commons murmured aloud;
Tittering fell upon all at sight of the impudent thing,
At the sight of a gift unroyal flung in the face of a king.
And the face of the king turned white and red with anger and shame
In their midst; and the heart in his body was water and then was flame;
Till of a sudden, turning, he gripped an aito hard,
A youth that stood with his ómare, [17] one of the daily guard,
And spat in his ear a command, and pointed and uttered a name,
And hid in the shade of the house his impotent anger and shame.

[16] "*Yottowas*," so spelt for convenience of pronunciation, *quasi* Tacksmen in the Scottish Hoghlands. The organization of eight sub-districts and eight yottowas to a division, which was in use (until yesterday) among the Tevas, I have attributed without authority to the next clan: see verses 341-2.

[17] "*Ómare*," pronounced as a dactyl. A loaded quarter-staff, one of the two favourite weapons of the Tahitian brave: the javelin, or casting spear, was the other.

Now Támatéa the fool was far on the homeward way,
The rising night in his face, behind him the dying day.
Rahéro saw him go by, and the heart of Rahéro was glad,
Devising shame to the king and nowise harm to the lad;
And all that dwelt by the way saw and saluted him well,
For he had the face of a friend and the news of the town to tell;
And pleased with the notice of folk, and pleased that his journey was done,
Támatéa drew homeward, turning his back to the sun.

And now was the hour of the bath in Taiárapu: far and near
The lovely laughter of bathers rose and delighted his ear.
Night massed in the valleys; the sun on the mountain coast
Struck, end-long; and above the clouds embattled their host,
And glowed and gloomed on the heights; and the heads of the palms were gems,
And far to the rising eve extended the shade of their stems;
And the shadow of Támatéa hovered already at home.

And sudden the sound of one coming and running light as the foam
Struck on his ear; and he turned, and lo! a man on his track,
Girded and armed with an ómare, following hard at his back.
At a bound the man was upon him;—and, or ever a word was said,
The loaded end of the ómare fell and laid him dead.

II. THE VENGING OF TÁMATÉA

Thus was Rahéro's treason; thus and no further it sped
The king sat safe in his place and a kindly fool was dead.

But the mother of Támatéa arose with death in her eyes.
All night long, and the next, Taiárapu rang with her cries.
As when a babe in the wood turns with a chill of doubt
And perceives nor home, nor friends, for the trees have closed her about,
The mountain rings and her breast is torn with the voice of despair:
So the lion-like woman idly wearied the air
For awhile, and pierced men's hearing in vain, and wounded their hearts.
But as when the weather changes at sea, in dangerous parts,
And sudden the hurricane wrack unrolls up the front of the sky,
At once the ship lies idle, the sails hang silent on high,
The breath of the wind that blew is blown out like the flame of a lamp,
And the silent armies of death draw near with inaudible tramp:
So sudden, the voice of her weeping ceased; in silence she rose
And passed from the house of her sorrow, a woman clothed with repose,
Carrying death in her breast and sharpening death with her hand.

Hither she went and thither in all the coasts of the land.
They tell that she feared not to slumber alone, in the dead of night,
In accursed places; beheld, unblenched, the ribbon of light [18]
Spin from temple to temple; guided the perilous skiff,
Abhorred not the paths of the mountain and trod the verge of the cliff;
From end to end of the island, thought not the distance long,
But forth from king to king carried the tale of her wrong.
To king after king, as they sat in the palace door, she came,
Claiming kinship, declaiming verses, naming her name
And the names of all of her fathers; and still, with a heart on the rack,
Jested to capture a hearing and laughed when they jested back:
So would deceive them awhile, and change and return in a breath,
And on all the men of Vaiau imprecate instant death;
And tempt her kings—for Vaiau was a rich and prosperous land,
And flatter—for who would attempt it but warriors mighty of hand?
And change in a breath again and rise in a strain of song,
Invoking the beaten drums, beholding the fall of the strong,
Calling the fowls of the air to come and feast on the dead.
And they held the chin in silence, and heard her, and shook the head;
For they knew the men of Taiárapu famous in battle and feast,
Marvellous eaters and smiters: the men of Vaiau not least.

[18] "*The ribbon of light.*" Still to be seen (and heard) spinning from one marae to another on Tahiti; or so I have it upon evidence that would rejoice the Physical Society.

To the land of the Námunu-úra, [19] to Paea, at length she came,
To men who were foes to the Tevas and hated their race and name.
There was she well received, and spoke with Hiopa the king. [20]
And Hiopa listened, and weighed, and wisely considered the thing.
"Here in the back of the isle we dwell in a sheltered place,"
Quoth he to the woman, "in quiet, a weak and peaceable race.
But far in the teeth of the wind lofty Taiárapu lies;
Strong blows the wind of the trade on its seaward face, and cries
Aloud in the top of arduous mountains, and utters its song
In green continuous forests. Strong is the wind, and strong
And fruitful and hardy the race, famous in battle and feast,
Marvellous eaters and smiters: the men of Vaiau not least.
Now hearken to me, my daughter, and hear a word of the wise:
How a strength goes linked with a weakness, two by two, like the eyes.
They can wield the ómare well and cast the javelin far;
Yet are they greedy and weak as the swine and the children are.
Plant we, then, here at Paea, a garden of excellent fruits;
Plant we bananas and kava and taro, the king of roots;
Let the pigs in Paea be tapu [21] and no man fish for a year;
And of all the meat in Tahiti gather we threefold here.
So shall the fame of our plenty fill the island, and so,
At last, on the tongue of rumour, go where we wish it to go.
Then shall the pigs of Taiárapu raise their snouts in the air;
But we sit quiet and wait, as the fowler sits by the snare,
And tranquilly fold our hands, till the pigs come nosing the food:
But meanwhile build us a house of Trotéa, the stubborn wood,
Bind it with incombustible thongs, set a roof to the room,
Too strong for the hands of a man to dissever or fire to consume;
And there, when the pigs come trotting, there shall the feast be spread,
There shall the eye of the morn enlighten the feasters dead.
So be it done; for I have a heart that pities your state,
And Nateva and Námunu-úra are fire and water for hate."

[19] "*Námunu-úra.*" The complete name is Námunu-úra te aropa. Why it should be pronounced Námunu, dactylically, I cannot see, but so I have always heard it. This was the clan immediately beyond the Tevas on the south coast of the island. At the date of the tale the clan organization must have been very weak. There is no particular mention of Támatéa mother going to Pápara, to the head chief of her own clan, which would appear her natural recourse. On the other hand, she seems to have visited various lesser chiefs among the Tevas, and these to have excused themselves solely on the danger of the enterprise. The broad distinction here drawn between Nateva and Námunu-úra is therefore not impossibly anachronistic.

[20] "*Hiopa the King.*" Hiopa was really the name of the king (chief) of Vaiau; but I could never learn that of the king of Paea—pronounce to rhyme with the Indian *ayah*—and I gave the name where it was most needed. This note must appear otiose indeed to readers who have never heard of either of these two gentleman; and perhaps there is only one person in the world capable at once of reading my verses

and spying the inaccuracy. For him, for Mr. Tati Salmon, hereditary high chief of the Tevas, the note is solely written: a small attention from a clansman to his chief.

[21] "*Let the pigs be tapu.*" It is impossible to explain *tapu* in a note; we have it as an English word, taboo. Suffice it, that a thing which was *tapu* must not be touched, nor a place that was *tapu* visited.

>All was done as he said, and the gardens prospered; and now
>The fame of their plenty went out, and word of it came to Vaiau.
>For the men of Námunu-úra sailed, to the windward far,
>Lay in the offing by south where the towns of the Tevas are,
>And cast overboard of their plenty; and lo! at the Tevas feet
>The surf on all of the beaches tumbled treasures of meat.
>In the salt of the sea, a harvest tossed with the refluent foam;
>And the children gleaned it in playing, and ate and carried it home;
>And the elders stared and debated, and wondered and passed the jest,
>But whenever a guest came by eagerly questioned the guest;
>And little by little, from one to another, the word went round:
>"In all the borders of Paea the victual rots on the ground,
>And swine are plenty as rats. And now, when they fare to the sea,
>The men of the Námunu-úra glean from under the tree
>And load the canoe to the gunwale with all that is toothsome to eat;
>And all day long on the sea the jaws are crushing the meat,
>The steersman eats at the helm, the rowers munch at the oar,
>And at length, when their bellies are full, overboard with the store!"
>Now was the word made true, and soon as the bait was bare,
>All the pigs of Taiárapu raised their snouts in the air.
>Songs were recited, and kinship was counted, and tales were told
>How war had severed of late but peace had cemented of old
>The clans of the island. "To war," said they, "now set we an end,
>And hie to the Námunu-úra even as a friend to a friend."
>
>So judged, and a day was named; and soon as the morning broke,
>Canoes were thrust in the sea and the houses emptied of folk.
>Strong blew the wind of the south, the wind that gathers the clan;
>Along all the line of the reef the clamorous surges ran;
>And the clouds were piled on the top of the island mountain-high,
>A mountain throned on a mountain. The fleet of canoes swept by
>In the midst, on the green lagoon, with a crew released from care,
>Sailing an even water, breathing a summer air,
>Cheered by a cloudless sun; and ever to left and right,
>Bursting surge on the reef, drenching storms on the height.
>So the folk of Vaiau sailed and were glad all day,
>Coasting the palm-tree cape and crossing the populous bay
>By all the towns of the Tevas; and still as they bowled along,
>Boat would answer to boat with jest and laughter and song,
>And the people of all the towns trooped to the sides of the sea
>And gazed from under the hand or sprang aloft on the tree,
>Hailing and cheering. Time failed them for more to do;

The holiday village careened to the wind, and was gone from view
Swift as a passing bird; and ever as onward it bore,
Like the cry of the passing bird, bequeathed its song to the shore—
Desirable laughter of maids and the cry of delight of the child.
And the gazer, left behind, stared at the wake and smiled.
By all the towns of the Tevas they went, and Pápara last,
The home of the chief, the place of muster in war; and passed
The march of the lands of the clan, to the lands of an alien folk.
And there, from the dusk of the shoreside palms, a column of smoke
Mounted and wavered and died in the gold of the setting sun,
"Paea!" they cried. "It is Paea." And so was the voyage done.
In the early fall of the night, Hiopa came to the shore,
And beheld and counted the comers, and lo, they were forty score:
The pelting feet of the babes that ran already and played,
The clean-lipped smile of the boy, the slender breasts of the maid,
And mighty limbs of women, stalwart mothers of men.
The sires stood forth unabashed; but a little back from his ken
Clustered the scarcely nubile, the lads and maids, in a ring,
Fain of each other, afraid of themselves, aware of the king
And aping behaviour, but clinging together with hands and eyes,
With looks that were kind like kisses, and laughter tender as sighs.
There, too, the grandsire stood, raising his silver crest,
And the impotent hands of a suckling groped in his barren breast.
The childhood of love, the pair well married, the innocent brood,
The tale of the generations repeated and ever renewed—
Hiopa beheld them together, all the ages of man,
And a moment shook in his purpose.

    But these were the foes of his clan,
And he trod upon pity, and came, and civilly greeted the king,
And gravely entreated Rahéro; and for all that could fight or sing,
And claimed a name in the land, had fitting phrases of praise;
But with all who were well-descended he spoke of the ancient days.
And "'Tis true," said he, "that in Paea the victual rots on the ground;
But, friends, your number is many; and pigs must be hunted and found,
And the lads troop to the mountains to bring the féis down,
And around the bowls of the kava cluster the maids of the town.
So, for to-night, sleep here; but king, common, and priest
To-morrow, in order due, shall sit with me in the feast."
Sleepless the live-long night, Hiopa's followers toiled.
The pigs screamed and were slaughtered; the spars of the guest-house oiled,
The leaves spread on the floor. In many a mountain glen
The moon drew shadows of trees on the naked bodies of men
Plucking and bearing fruits; and in all the bounds of the town
Red glowed the cocoanut fires, and were buried and trodden down.
Thus did seven of the yottowas toil with their tale of the clan,
But the eighth wrought with his lads, hid from the sight of man.
In the deeps of the woods they laboured, piling the fuel high

In fagots, the load of a man, fuel seasoned and dry,
Thirsty to seize upon fire and apt to blurt into flame.

And now was the day of the feast. The forests, as morning came,
Tossed in the wind, and the peaks quaked in the blaze of the day
And the cocoanuts showered on the ground, rebounding and rolling away:
A glorious morn for a feast, a famous wind for a fire.
To the hall of feasting Hiopa led them, mother and sire
And maid and babe in a tale, the whole of the holiday throng.
Smiling they came, garlanded green, not dreaming of wrong;
And for every three, a pig, tenderly cooked in the ground,
Waited, and féi, the staff of life, heaped in a mound
For each where he sat;—for each, bananas roasted and raw
Piled with a bountiful hand, as for horses hay and straw
Are stacked in a stable; and fish, the food of desire, [22]
And plentiful vessels of sauce, and breadfruit gilt in the fire;—
And kava was common as water. Feasts have there been ere now,
And many, but never a feast like that of the folk of Vaiau.

[22] "*Fish, the food of desire.*" There is a special word in the Tahitian language to signify *hungering after fish.* I may remark that here is one of my chief difficulties about the whole story. How did king, commons, women, and all come to eat together at the feast? But it troubled none of my numerous authorities; so there must certainly be some natural explanation.

All day long they ate with the resolute greed of brutes,
And turned from the pigs to the fish, and again from the fish to the fruits,
And emptied the vessels of sauce, and drank of the kava deep;
Till the young lay stupid as stones, and the strongest nodded to sleep.
Sleep that was mighty as death and blind as a moonless night
Tethered them hand and foot; and their souls were drowned, and the light
Was cloaked from their eyes. Senseless together, the old and the young,
The fighter deadly to smite and the prater cunning of tongue,
The woman wedded and fruitful, inured to the pangs of birth,
And the maid that knew not of kisses, blindly sprawled on the earth.

From the hall Hiopa the king and his chiefs came stealthily forth.
Already the sun hung low and enlightened the peaks of the north;
But the wind was stubborn to die and blew as it blows at morn,
Showering the nuts in the dusk, and e'en as a banner is torn,
High on the peaks of the island, shattered the mountain cloud.
And now at once, at a signal, a silent, emulous crowd
Set hands to the work of death, hurrying to and fro,
Like ants, to furnish the fagots, building them broad and low,
And piling them high and higher around the walls of the hall.
Silence persisted within, for sleep lay heavy on all;
But the mother of Támatéa stood at Hiopa's side,
And shook for terror and joy like a girl that is a bride.

Night fell on the toilers, and first Hiopa the wise
Made the round of the house, visiting all with his eyes;
And all was piled to the eaves, and fuel blockaded the door;
And within, in the house beleaguered, slumbered the forty score.
Then was an aito dispatched and came with fire in his hand,
And Hiopa took it.—"Within," said he, "is the life of a land;
And behold! I breathe on the coal, I breathe on the dales of the east,
And silence falls on forest and shore; the voice of the feast
Is quenched, and the smoke of cooking; the rooftree decays and falls
On the empty lodge, and the winds subvert deserted walls."

Therewithal, to the fuel, he laid the glowing coal;
And the redness ran in the mass and burrowed within like a mole,
And copious smoke was conceived. But, as when a dam is to burst,
The water lips it and crosses in silver trickles at first,
And then, of a sudden, whelms and bears it away forthright:
So now, in a moment, the flame sprang and towered in the night,
And wrestled and roared in the wind, and high over house and tree,
Stood, like a streaming torch, enlightening land and sea.

But the mother of Támatéa threw her arms abroad,
"Pyre of my son," she shouted, 'debited vengeance of God,
Late, late, I behold you, yet I behold you at last,
And glory, beholding! For now are the days of my agony past,
The lust that famished my soul now eats and drinks its desire,
And they that encompassed my son shrivel alive in the fire.
Tenfold precious the vengeance that comes after lingering years!
Ye quenched the voice of my singer?—hark, in your dying ears,
The song of the conflagration! Ye left me a widow alone?
—Behold, the whole of your race consumes, sinew and bone
And torturing flesh together: man, mother, and maid
Heaped in a common shambles; and already, borne by the trade,
The smoke of your dissolution darkens the stars of night."

Thus she spoke, and her stature grew in the people's sight.

III. RAHÉRO

Rahéro was there in the hall asleep: beside him his wife,
Comely, a mirthful woman, one that delighted in life;
And a girl that was ripe for marriage, shy and sly as a mouse;
And a boy, a climber of trees: all the hopes of his house.
Unwary, with open hands, he slept in the midst of his folk,
And dreamed that he heard a voice crying without, and awoke,
Leaping blindly afoot like one from a dream that he fears.
A hellish glow and clouds were about him;—it roared in his ears
Like the sound of the cataract fall that plunges sudden and steep;
And Rahéro swayed as he stood, and his reason was still asleep.

Now the flame struck hard on the house, wind-wielded, a fracturing blow,
And the end of the roof was burst and fell on the sleepers below;
And the lofty hall, and the feast, and the prostrate bodies of folk,
Shone red in his eyes a moment, and then were swallowed of smoke.
In the mind of Rahéro clearness came; and he opened his throat;
And as when a squall comes sudden, the straining sail of a boat
Thunders aloud and bursts, so thundered the voice of the man.
—"The wind and the rain!" he shouted, the mustering word of the clan, [23]
And "up!" and "to arms men of Vaiau!" But silence replied,
Or only the voice of the gusts of the fire, and nothing beside.

[23] *"The mustering word of the clan."*

>*Teva te ua,*
>*Teva te matai!*
>
>Teva the wind,
>Teva the rain!

Rahéro stooped and groped. He handled his womankind,
But the fumes of the fire and the kava had quenched the life of their mind,
And they lay like pillars prone; and his hand encountered the boy,
And there sprang in the gloom of his soul a sudden lightning of joy.
"Him can I save!" he thought, "if I were speedy enough."
And he loosened the cloth from his loins, and swaddled the child in the stuff;
And about the strength of his neck he knotted the burden well.

There where the roof had fallen, it roared like the mouth of hell.
Thither Rahéro went, stumbling on senseless folk,
And grappled a post of the house, and began to climb in the smoke:
The last alive of Vaiau; and the son borne by the sire.
The post glowed in the grain with ulcers of eating fire,
And the fire bit to the blood and mangled his hands and thighs;
And the fumes sang in his head like wine and stung in his eyes;
And still he climbed, and came to the top, the place of proof,
And thrust a hand through the flame, and clambered alive on the roof.
But even as he did so, the wind, in a garment of flames and pain,
Wrapped him from head to heel; and the waistcloth parted in twain;
And the living fruit of his loins dropped in the fire below.

About the blazing feast-house clustered the eyes of the foe,
Watching, hand upon weapon, lest ever a soul should flee,
Shading the brow from the glare, straining the neck to see
Only, to leeward, the flames in the wind swept far and wide,
And the forest sputtered on fire; and there might no man abide.
Thither Rahéro crept, and dropped from the burning eaves,
And crouching low to the ground, in a treble covert of leaves
And fire and volleying smoke, ran for the life of his soul

Unseen; and behind him under a furnace of ardent coal,
Cairned with a wonder of flame, and blotting the night with smoke,
Blazed and were smelted together the bones of all his folk.

He fled unguided at first; but hearing the breakers roar,
Thitherward shaped his way, and came at length to the shore.
Sound-limbed he was: dry-eyed; but smarted in every part;
And the mighty cage of his ribs heaved on his straining heart
With sorrow and rage. And "Fools!" he cried, "fools of Vaiau,
Heads of swine—gluttons—Alas! and where are they now?
Those that I played with, those that nursed me, those that I nursed?
God, and I outliving them! I, the least and the worst—
I, that thought myself crafty, snared by this herd of swine,
In the tortures of hell and desolate, stripped of all that was mine:
All!—my friends and my fathers—the silver heads of yore
That trooped to the council, the children that ran to the open door
Crying with innocent voices and clasping a father's knees!
And mine, my wife—my daughter—my sturdy climber of trees
Ah, never to climb again!"

    Thus in the dusk of the night,
(For clouds rolled in the sky and the moon was swallowed from sight,)
Pacing and gnawing his fists, Rahéro raged by the shore.
Vengeance: that must be his. But much was to do before;
And first a single life to be snatched from a deadly place,
A life, the root of revenge, surviving plant of the race:
And next the race to be raised anew, and the lands of the clan
Repeopled. So Rahéro designed, a prudent man
Even in wrath, and turned for the means of revenge and escape:
A boat to be seized by stealth, a wife to be taken by rape.

Still was the dark lagoon; beyond on the coral wall,
He saw the breakers shine, he heard them bellow and fall.
Alone, on the top of the reef, a man with a flaming brand
Walked, gazing and pausing, a fish-spear poised in his hand.
The foam boiled to his calf when the mightier breakers came,
And the torch shed in the wind scattering tufts of flame.
Afar on the dark lagoon a canoe lay idly at wait:
A figure dimly guiding it: surely the fisherman's mate.
Rahéro saw and he smiled. He straightened his mighty thews:
Naked, with never a weapon, and covered with scorch and bruise,
He straightened his arms, he filled the void of his body with breath,
And, strong as the wind in his manhood, doomed the fisher to death.

Silent he entered the water, and silently swam, and came
There where the fisher walked, holding on high the flame.
Loud on the pier of the reef volleyed the breach of the sea;
And hard at the back of the man, Rahéro crept to his knee
On the coral, and suddenly sprang and seized him, the elder hand
Clutching the joint of his throat, the other snatching the brand
Ere it had time to fall, and holding it steady and high.
Strong was the fisher, brave, and swift of mind and of eye—
Strongly he threw in the clutch; but Rahéro resisted the strain,
And jerked, and the spine of life snapped with a crack in twain,
And the man came slack in his hands and tumbled a lump at his feet.

One moment: and there, on the reef, where the breakers whitened and beat,
Rahéro was standing alone, glowing and scorched and bare,
A victor unknown of any, raising the torch in the air.
But once he drank of his breath, and instantly set him to fish
Like a man intent upon supper at home and a savoury dish.
For what should the woman have seen? A man with a torch—and then
A moment's blur of the eyes—and a man with a torch again.
And the torch had scarcely been shaken. "Ah, surely," Rahéro said,
"She will deem it a trick of the eyes, a fancy born in the head;
But time must be given the fool to nourish a fool's belief."
So for a while, a sedulous fisher, he walked the reef,
Pausing at times and gazing, striking at times with the spear:
—Lastly, uttered the call; and even as the boat drew near,
Like a man that was done with its use, tossed the torch in the sea.

Lightly he leaped on the boat beside the woman; and she
Lightly addressed him, and yielded the paddle and place to sit;
For now the torch was extinguished the night was black as the pit
Rahéro set him to row, never a word he spoke,
And the boat sang in the water urged by his vigorous stroke.
—"What ails you?" the woman asked, "and why did you drop the brand?
We have only to kindle another as soon as we come to land."
Never a word Rahéro replied, but urged the canoe.
And a chill fell on the woman.—"Atta! speak! is it you?
Speak! Why are you silent? Why do you bend aside?
Wherefore steer to the seaward?" thus she panted and cried.
Never a word from the oarsman, toiling there in the dark;
But right for a gate of the reef he silently headed the bark,
And wielding the single paddle with passionate sweep on sweep,
Drove her, the little fitted, forth on the open deep.
And fear, there where she sat, froze the woman to stone:
Not fear of the crazy boat and the weltering deep alone;
But a keener fear of the night, the dark, and the ghostly hour,
And the thing that drove the canoe with more than a mortal's power
And more than a mortal's boldness. For much she knew of the dead

That haunt and fish upon reefs, toiling, like men, for bread,
And traffic with human fishers, or slay them and take their ware,
Till the hour when the star of the dead [24] goes down, and the morning air
Blows, and the cocks are singing on shore. And surely she knew
The speechless thing at her side belonged to the grave. [25]

[24 & 25] "*The star of the dead.*" Venus as a morning star. I have collected much curious evidence as to this belief. The dead retain their taste for a fish diet, enter into copartnery with living fishers, and haunt the reef and the lagoon. The conclusion attributed to the nameless lady of the legend would be reached to-day, under the like circumstances, by ninety per cent. of Polynesians; and here I probably understate by one-tenth.

                It blew
All night from the south; all night, Rahéro contended and kept
The prow to the cresting sea; and, silent as though she slept,
The woman huddled and quaked. And now was the peep of day.
High and long on their left the mountainous island lay;
And over the peaks of Taiárapu arrows of sunlight struck.
On shore the birds were beginning to sing: the ghostly ruck
Of the buried had long ago returned to the covered grave;
And here on the sea, the woman, waxing suddenly brave,
Turned her swiftly about and looked in the face of the man.
And sure he was none that she knew, none of her country or clan:
A stranger, mother-naked, and marred with the marks of fire,
But comely and great of stature, a man to obey and admire.

And Rahéro regarded her also, fixed, with a frowning face,
Judging the woman's fitness to mother a warlike race.
Broad of shoulder, ample of girdle, long in the thigh,
Deep of bosom she was, and bravely supported his eye.

"Woman," said he, "last night the men of your folk—
Man, woman, and maid, smothered my race in smoke.
It was done like cowards; and I, a mighty man of my hands,
Escaped, a single life; and now to the empty lands
And smokeless hearths of my people, sail, with yourself, alone.
Before your mother was born, the die of to-day was thrown
And you selected:—your husband, vainly striving, to fall
Broken between these hands:—yourself to be severed from all,
The places, the people, you love—home, kindred, and clan—
And to dwell in a desert and bear the babes of a kinless man."

THE FEAST OF FAMINE

MARQUESAN MANNERS

In this ballad I have strung together some of the more striking particularities of the Marquesas. It rests upon no authority; it is in no sense, like "Rahéro," a native story; but a patchwork of details of manners and the impressions of a traveller. It may seem strange, when the scene is laid upon these profligate islands, to make the story hinge on love. But love is not less known in the Marquesas than elsewhere; nor is there any cause of suicide more common in the islands.

I. THE PRIEST'S VIGIL

In all the land of the tribe was neither fish nor fruit,
And the deepest pit of popoi stood empty to the foot. [26]
The clans upon the left and the clans upon the right
Now oiled their carven maces and scoured their daggers bright;
They gat them to the thicket, to the deepest of the shade,
And lay with sleepless eyes in the deadly ambuscade.
And oft in the starry even the song of morning rose,
What time the oven smoked in the country of their foes;
For oft to loving hearts, and waiting ears and sight,
The lads that went to forage returned not with the night.
Now first the children sickened, and then the women paled,
And the great arms of the warrior no more for war availed.
Hushed was the deep drum, discarded was the dance;
And those that met the priest now glanced at him askance.
The priest was a man of years, his eyes were ruby-red, [27]
He neither feared the dark nor the terrors of the dead,
He knew the songs of races, the names of ancient date;
And the beard upon his bosom would have bought the chief's estate.
He dwelt in a high-built lodge, hard by the roaring shore,
Raised on a noble terrace and with tikis [28] at the door.
Within it was full of riches, for he served his nation well,
And full of the sound of breakers, like the hollow of a shell.
For weeks he let them perish, gave never a helping sign,
But sat on his oiled platform to commune with the divine,
But sat on his high terrace, with the tikis by his side,
And stared on the blue ocean, like a parrot, ruby-eyed.

[26] "*Pit of popoi.*' Where the bread-fruit was stored for preservation.
[27] "*Ruby-red.*" The priest's eyes were probably red from the abuse of kava. His beard (verse 18) is said to be worth an estate; for the beards of old men are the favourite head-adornment of the Marquesans, as the hair of women formed their most costly girdle. The former, among this generally beardless and short-lived people, fetch to-day considerable sums.
[28] "*Tikis.*" The tiki is an ugly image hewn out of wood or stone.

Dawn as yellow as sulphur leaped on the mountain height:
Out on the round of the sea the gems of the morning light,
Up from the round of the sea the streamers of the sun;—
But down in the depths of the valley the day was not begun.
In the blue of the woody twilight burned red the cocoa-husk,
And the women and men of the clan went forth to bathe in the dusk,
A word that began to go round, a word, a whisper, a start:
Hope that leaped in the bosom, fear that knocked on the heart:
"See, the priest is not risen—look, for his door is fast!
He is going to name the victims; he is going to help us at last."

Thrice rose the sun to noon; and ever, like one of the dead,
The priest lay still in his house with the roar of the sea in his head;
There was never a foot on the floor, there was never a whisper of speech;
Only the leering tikis stared on the blinding beach.
Again were the mountains fired, again the morning broke;
And all the houses lay still, but the house of the priest awoke.
Close in their covering roofs lay and trembled the clan,
But the agèd, red-eyed priest ran forth like a lunatic man;
And the village panted to see him in the jewels of death again,
In the silver beards of the old and the hair of women slain.
Frenzy shook in his limbs, frenzy shone in his eyes,
And still and again as he ran, the valley rang with his cries.
All day long in the land, by cliff and thicket and den,
He ran his lunatic rounds, and howled for the flesh of men;
All day long he ate not, nor ever drank of the brook;
And all day long in their houses the people listened and shook—
All day long in their houses they listened with bated breath,
And never a soul went forth, for the sight of the priest was death.

Three were the days of his running, as the gods appointed of yore,
Two the nights of his sleeping alone in the place of gore:
The drunken slumber of frenzy twice he drank to the lees,
On the sacred stones of the High-place under the sacred trees;
With a lamp at his ashen head he lay in the place of the feast,
And the sacred leaves of the banyan rustled around the priest.
Last, when the stated even fell upon terrace and tree,
And the shade of the lofty island lay leagues away to sea,
And all the valleys of verdure were heavy with manna and musk,
The wreck of the red-eyed priest came gasping home in the dusk.
He reeled across the village, he staggered along the shore,
And between the leering tikis crept groping through his door.

There went a stir through the lodges, the voice of speech awoke;
Once more from the builded platforms arose the evening smoke.
And those who were mighty in war, and those renowned for an art
Sat in their stated seats and talked of the morrow apart.

II. THE LOVERS

Hark! away in the woods—for the ears of love are sharp—
Stealthily, quietly touched, the note of the one-stringed harp. [29]
In the lighted house of her father, why should Taheia start?
Taheia heavy of hair, Taheia tender of heart,
Taheia the well-descended, a bountiful dealer in love,
Nimble of foot like the deer, and kind of eye like the dove?
Sly and shy as a cat, with never a change of face,
Taheia slips to the door, like one that would breathe a space;
Saunters and pauses, and looks at the stars, and lists to the seas;
Then sudden and swift as a cat, she plunges under the trees.
Swift as a cat she runs, with her garment gathered high,
Leaping, nimble of foot, running, certain of eye;
And ever to guide her way over the smooth and the sharp,
Ever nearer and nearer the note of the one-stringed harp;
Till at length, in a glade of the wood, with a naked mountain above,
The sound of the harp thrown down, and she in the arms of her love.
"Rua,"—"Taheia," they cry—"my heart, my soul, and my eyes,"
And clasp and sunder and kiss, with lovely laughter and sighs,
"Rua!"—"Taheia, my love,"—"Rua, star of my night,
Clasp me, hold me, and love me, single spring of delight."

[29] *"The one-stringed harp."* Usually employed for serenades.

And Rua folded her close, he folded her near and long,
The living knit to the living, and sang the lover's song:

> *Night, night it is, night upon the palms.*
> *Night, night it is, the land wind has blown.*
> *Starry, starry night, over deep and height;*
> *Love, love in the valley, love all alone.*

"Taheia, heavy of hair, a foolish thing have we done,
To bind what gods have sundered unkindly into one.
Why should a lowly lover have touched Taheia's skirt,
Taheia the well-descended, and Rua child of the dirt?"

>   —On high with the haka-ikis my father sits in state,
>   Ten times fifty kinsmen salute him in the gate;
>   Round all his martial body, and in bands across his face,
>   The marks of the tattooer proclaim his lofty place.
>   I too, in the hands of the cunning, in the sacred cabin of palm, [30]
>   Have shrunk like the mimosa, and bleated like the lamb;
>   Round half my tender body, that none shall clasp but you,
>   For a crest and a fair adornment go dainty lines of blue.
>   Love, love, beloved Rua, love levels all degrees,
>   And the well-tattooed Taheia clings panting to your knees."

[30] *"The sacred cabin of palm."* Which, however, no woman could approach. I do not know where women were tattooed; probably in the common house, or in the bush, for a woman was a creature of small account. I must guard the reader against supposing Taheia was at all disfigured; the art of the Marquesan tattooer is extreme; and she would appear to be clothed in a web of lace, inimitably delicate, exquisite in pattern, and of a bluish hue that at once contrasts and harmonises with the warm pigment of the native skin. It would be hard to find a woman more becomingly adorned than "a well tattooed" Marquesan.

>   —Taheia, song of the morning, how long is the longest love?
>   A cry, a clasp of the hands, a star that falls from above!
>   Ever at morn in the blue, and at night when all is black,
>   Ever it skulks and trembles with the hunter, Death, on its track.
>   Hear me, Taheia, death! For to-morrow the priest shall awake,
>   And the names be named of the victims to bleed for the nation's sake;
>   And first of the numbered many that shall be slain ere noon,
>   Rua the child of the dirt, Rua the kinless loon.
>   For him shall the drum be beat, for him be raised the song,
>   For him to the sacred High-place the chaunting people throng,
>   For him the oven smoke as for a speechless beast,
>   And the sire of my Taheia come greedy to the feast."
>   "Rua, be silent, spare me. Taheia closes her ears.
>   Pity my yearning heart, pity my girlish years!
>   Flee from the cruel hands, flee from the knife and coal,
>   Lie hid in the deeps of the woods, Rua, sire of my soul!"
>
>   "Whither to flee, Taheia, whither in all of the land?
>   The fires of the bloody kitchen are kindled on every hand;
>   On every hand in the isle a hungry whetting of teeth,
>   Eyes in the trees above, arms in the brush beneath.
>   Patience to lie in wait, cunning to follow the sleuth,
>   Abroad the foes I have fought, and at home the friends of my youth."

"Love, love, beloved Rua, love has a clearer eye,
Hence from the arms of love you go not forth to die.
There, where the broken mountain drops sheer into the glen,
There shall you find a hold from the boldest hunter of men;
There, in the deep recess, where the sun falls only at noon,
And only once in the night enters the light of the moon,
Nor ever a sound but of birds, or the rain when it falls with a shout;
For death and the fear of death beleaguer the valley about.
Tapu it is, but the gods will surely pardon despair;
Tapu, but what of that? If Rua can only dare.
Tapu and tapu and tapu, I know they are every one right;
But the god of every tapu is not always quick to smite.
Lie secret there, my Rua, in the arms of awful gods,
Sleep in the shade of the trees on the couch of the kindly sods,
Sleep and dream of Taheia, Taheia will wake for you;
And whenever the land wind blows and the woods are heavy with dew,
Alone through the horror of night, [31] with food for the soul of her love,
Taheia the undissuaded will hurry true as the dove."

[31] "*The horror of night.*" The Polynesian fear of ghosts and of the dark has been already referred to. Their life is beleaguered by the dead.

"Taheia, the pit of the night crawls with treacherous things,
Spirits of ultimate air and the evil souls of things;
The souls of the dead, the stranglers, that perch in the trees of the wood,
Waiters for all things human, haters of evil and good."

"Rua, behold me, kiss me, look in my eyes and read;
Are these the eyes of a maid that would leave her lover in need?
Brave in the eye of day, my father ruled in the fight;
The child of his loins, Taheia, will play the man in the night."

So it was spoken, and so agreed, and Taheia arose
And smiled in the stars and was gone, swift as the swallow goes;
And Rua stood on the hill, and sighed, and followed her flight,
And there were the lodges below, each with its door alight;
From folk that sat on the terrace and drew out the even long
Sudden crowings of laughter, monotonous drone of song;
The quiet passage of souls over his head in the trees; [32]
And from all around the haven the crumbling thunder of seas.
"Farewell, my home," said Rua. "Farewell, O quiet seat!
To-morrow in all your valleys the drum of death shall beat."

[32] "*The quiet passage of souls.*" So, I am told, the natives explain the sound of a little wind passing overhead unfelt.

III. THE FEAST

Dawn as yellow as sulphur leaped on the naked peak,
And all the village was stirring, for now was the priest to speak.
Forth on his terrace he came, and sat with the chief in talk;
His lips were blackened with fever, his cheeks were whiter than chalk;
Fever clutched at his hands, fever nodded his head,
But, quiet and steady and cruel, his eyes shone ruby-red.
In the earliest rays of the sun the chief rose up content;
Braves were summoned, and drummers; messengers came and went;
Braves ran to their lodges, weapons were snatched from the wall;
The commons herded together, and fear was over them all.
Festival dresses they wore, but the tongue was dry in their mouth,
And the blinking eyes in their faces skirted from north to south.

Now to the sacred enclosure gathered the greatest and least,
And from under the shade of the banyan arose the voice of the feast,
The frenzied roll of the drum, and a swift, monotonous song.
Higher the sun swam up; the trade wind level and strong
Awoke in the tops of the palms and rattled the fans aloud,
And over the garlanded heads and shining robes of the crowd
Tossed the spiders of shadow, scattered the jewels of sun.
Forty the tale of the drums, and the forty throbbed like one;
A thousand hearts in the crowd, and the even chorus of song,
Swift as the feet of a runner, trampled a thousand strong.
And the old men leered at the ovens and licked their lips for the food;
And the women stared at the lads, and laughed and looked to the wood.
As when the sweltering baker, at night, when the city is dead,
Alone in the trough of labour treads and fashions the bread;
So in the heat, and the reek, and the touch of woman and man,
The naked spirit of evil kneaded the hearts of the clan.

Now cold was at many a heart, and shaking in many a seat;
For there were the empty baskets, but who was to furnish the meat?
For here was the nation assembled, and there were the ovens anigh,
And out of a thousand singers nine were numbered to die.
Till, of a sudden, a shock, a mace in the air, a yell,
And, struck in the edge of the crowd, the first of the victims fell. [33]
Terror and horrible glee divided the shrinking clan,
Terror of what was to follow, glee for a diet of man.
Frenzy hurried the chaunt, frenzy rattled the drums;
The nobles, high on the terrace, greedily mouthed their thumbs;
And once and again and again, in the ignorant crowd below,
Once and again and again descended the murderous blow.
Now smoked the oven, and now, with the cutting lip of a shell,
A butcher of ninety winters jointed the bodies well.
Unto the carven lodge, silent, in order due,

The grandees of the nation one after one withdrew;
And a line of laden bearers brought to the terrace foot,
On poles across their shoulders, the last reserve of fruit.
The victims bled for the nobles in the old appointed way;
The fruit was spread for the commons, for all should eat to-day.

[33] "*The first of the victims fell.*" Without doubt, this whole scene is untrue to fact. The victims were disposed of privately and some time before. And indeed I am far from claiming the credit of any high degree of accuracy for this ballad. Even in a time of famine, it is probable that Marquesan life went far more gaily than is here represented. But the melancholy of to-day lies in the writer's mind.

And now was the kava brewed, and now the cocoa ran,
Now was the hour of the dance for child and woman and man;
And mirth was in every heart, and a garland on every head,
And all was well with the living and well with the eight who were dead.
Only the chiefs and the priest talked and consulted awhile:
"To-morrow," they said, and "To-morrow," and nodded and seemed to smile:
"Rua the child of dirt, the creature of common clay,
Rua must die to-morrow, since Rua is gone to-day."

Out of the groves of the valley, where clear the blackbirds sang.
Sheer from the trees of the valley the face of the mountain sprang;
Sheer and bare it rose, unscalable barricade,
Beaten and blown against by the generous draught of the trade.
Dawn on its fluted brow painted rainbow light,
Close on its pinnacled crown trembled the stars at night.
Here and there in a cleft clustered contorted trees,
Or the silver beard of a stream hung and swung in the breeze.
High overhead, with a cry, the torrents leaped for the main,
And silently sprinkled below in thin perennial rain.
Dark in the staring noon, dark was Rua's ravine,
Damp and cold was the air, and the face of the cliffs was green.
Here, in the rocky pit, accursed already of old,
On a stone in the midst of a river, Rua sat and was cold.

"Valley of mid-day shadows, valley of silent falls,
Rua sang, and his voice went hollow about the walls,
"Valley of shadow and rock, a doleful prison to me,
What is the life you can give to a child of the sun and the sea?"

And Rua arose and came to the open mouth of the glen,
Whence he beheld the woods, and the sea, and houses of men.
Wide blew the riotous trade, and smelt in his nostrils good;
It bowed the boats on the bay, and tore and divided the wood;
It smote and sundered the groves as Moses smote with the rod,
And the streamers of all the trees blew like banners abroad;
And ever and on, in a lull, the trade wind brought him along
A far-off patter of drums and a far-off whisper of song.

Swift as the swallow's wings, the diligent hands on the drum
Fluttered and hurried and throbbed. "Ah, woe that I hear you come,"
Rua cried in his grief, "a sorrowful sound to me,
Mounting far and faint from the resonant shore of the sea!
Woe in the song! for the grave breathes in the singers' breath,
And I hear in the tramp of the drums the beat of the heart of death.
Home of my youth! no more, through all the length of the years,
No more to the place of the echoes of early laughter and tears,
No more shall Rua return; no more as the evening ends,
To crowded eyes of welcome, to the reaching hands of friends."

All day long from the High-place the drums and the singing came,
And the even fell, and the sun went down, a wheel of flame;
And night came gleaning the shadows and hushing the sounds of the wood;
And silence slept on all, where Rua sorrowed and stood.
But still from the shore of the bay the sound of the festival rang,
And still the crowd in the High-place danced and shouted and sang.

Now over all the isle terror was breathed abroad
Of shadowy hands from the trees and shadowy snares in the sod;
And before the nostrils of night, the shuddering hunter of men
Hurried, with beard on shoulder, back to his lighted den.
"Taheia, here to my side!"—"Rua, my Rua, you!"
And cold from the clutch of terror, cold with the damp of the dew,
Taheia, heavy of hair, leaped through the dark to his arms;
Taheia leaped to his clasp, and was folded in from alarms.

"Rua, beloved, here, see what your love has brought;
Coming—alas! returning—swift as the shuttle of thought;
Returning, alas! for to-night, with the beaten drum and the voice,
In the shine of many torches must the sleepless clan rejoice;
And Taheia the well-descended, the daughter of chief and priest,
Taheia must sit in her place in the crowded bench of the feast."
So it was spoken; and she, girding her garment high,
Fled and was swallowed of woods, swift as the sight of an eye.

Night over isle and sea rolled her curtain of stars,
Then a trouble awoke in the air, the east was banded with bars;
Dawn as yellow as sulphur leaped on the mountain height;
Dawn, in the deepest glen, fell a wonder of light;
High and clear stood the palms in the eye of the brightening east,
And lo! from the sides of the sea the broken sound of the feast!
As, when in days of summer, through open windows, the fly
Swift as a breeze and loud as a trump goes by,
But when frosts in the field have pinched the wintering mouse,
Blindly noses and buzzes and hums in the firelit house:
So the sound of the feast gallantly trampled at night,
So it staggered and drooped, and droned in the morning light.

IV. THE RAID

It chanced that as Rua sat in the valley of silent falls,
He heard a calling of doves from high on the cliffy walls.
Fire had fashioned of yore, and time had broken, the rocks;
There were rooting crannies for trees and nesting-places for flocks;
And he saw on the top of the cliffs, looking up from the pit of the shade,
A flicker of wings and sunshine, and trees that swung in the trade.
"The trees swing in the trade," quoth Rua, doubtful of words,
"And the sun stares from the sky, but what should trouble the birds?"
Up from the shade he gazed, where high the parapet shone,
And he was aware of a ledge and of things that moved thereon.
"What manner of things are these? Are they spirits abroad by day?
Or the foes of my clan that are come, bringing death by a perilous way?"

The valley was gouged like a vessel, and round like the vessel's lip,
With a cape of the side of the hill thrust forth like the bows of a ship.
On the top of the face of the cape a volley of sun struck fair,
And the cape overhung like a chin a gulph of sunless air.
"Silence, heart! What is that?—that, that flickered and shone,
Into the sun for an instant, and in an instant gone?
Was it a warrior's plume, a warrior's girdle of hair?
Swung in the loop of a rope, is he making a bridge of the air?"

Once and again Rua saw, in the trenchant edge of the sky,
The giddy conjuring done. And then, in the blink of an eye,
A scream caught in with the breath, a whirling packet of limbs,
A lump that dived in the gulph, more swift than a dolphin swims;
And there was the lump at his feet, and eyes were alive in the lump.
Sick was the soul of Rua, ambushed close in a clump;
Sick of soul he drew near, making his courage stout;
And he looked in the face of the thing, and the life of the thing went out.
And he gazed on the tattooed limbs, and, behold, he knew the man:
Hoka, a chief of the Vais, the truculent foe of his clan:
Hoka a moment since that stepped in the loop of the rope,
Filled with the lust of war, and alive with courage and hope.

Again to the giddy cornice Rua lifted his eyes,
And again beheld men passing in the armpit of the skies.
"Foes of my race!" cried Rua, "the mouth of Rua is true:
Never a shark in the deep is nobler of soul than you.
There was never a nobler foray, never a bolder plan;
Never a dizzier path was trod by the children of man;
And Rua, your evil-dealer through all the days of his years,
"Counts it honour to hate you, honour to fall by your spears."
And Rua straightened his back. "O Vais, a scheme for a scheme!"
Cried Rua and turned and descended the turbulent stair of the stream,
Leaping from rock to rock as the water-wagtail at home
Flits through resonant valleys and skims by boulder and foam.
And Rua burst from the glen and leaped on the shore of the brook,
And straight for the roofs of the clan his vigorous way he took.
Swift were the heels of his flight, and loud behind as he went
Rattled the leaping stones on the line of his long descent.
And ever he thought as he ran, and caught at his gasping breath,
"O the fool of a Rua, Rua that runs to his death!
But the right is the right," thought Rua, and ran like the wind on the foam,
"The right is the right for ever, and home for ever home.
For what though the oven smoke? And what though I die ere morn?
There was I nourished and tended, and there was Taheia born."
Noon was high on the High-place, the second noon of the feast;
And heat and shameful slumber weighed on people and priest;
And the heart drudged slow in bodies heavy with monstrous meals;
And the senseless limbs were scattered abroad like spokes of wheels;
And crapulous women sat and stared at the stones anigh
With a bestial droop of the lip and a swinish rheum in the eye.
As about the dome of the bees in the time for the drones to fall,
The dead and the maimed are scattered, and lie, and stagger, and crawl;
So on the grades of the terrace, in the ardent eye of the day,
The half-awake and the sleepers clustered and crawled and lay;
And loud as the dome of the bees, in the time of a swarming horde,
A horror of many insects hung in the air and roared.

Rua looked and wondered; he said to himself in his heart:
"Poor are the pleasures of life, and death is the better part."
But lo! on the higher benches a cluster of tranquil folk
Sat by themselves, nor raised their serious eyes, nor spoke:
Women with robes unruffled and garlands duly arranged,
Gazing far from the feast with faces of people estranged;
And quiet amongst the quiet, and fairer than all the fair,
Taheia, the well-descended, Taheia, heavy of hair.
And the soul of Rua awoke, courage enlightened his eyes,
And he uttered a summoning shout and called on the clan to rise.
Over against him at once, in the spotted shade of the trees,
Owlish and blinking creatures scrambled to hands and knees;
On the grades of the sacred terrace, the driveller woke to fear,
And the hand of the ham-drooped warrior brandished a wavering spear.
And Rua folded his arms, and scorn discovered his teeth;
Above the war-crowd gibbered, and Rua stood smiling beneath.
Thick, like leaves in the autumn, faint, like April sleet,
Missiles from tremulous hands quivered around his feet;
And Taheia leaped from her place; and the priest, the ruby-eyed,
Ran to the front of the terrace, and brandished his arms, and cried:
"Hold, O fools, he brings tidings!" and "Hold, 'tis the love of my heart!"
Till lo! in front of the terrace, Rua pierced with a dart.

Taheia cherished his head, and the aged priest stood by,
And gazed with eyes of ruby at Rua's darkening eye.
"Taheia, here is the end, I die a death for a man.
I have given the life of my soul to save an unsavable clan.
See them, the drooping of hams! behold me the blinking crew:
Fifty spears they cast, and one of fifty true!
And you, O priest, the foreteller, foretell for yourself if you can,
Foretell the hour of the day when the Vais shall burst on your clan!
By the head of the tapu cleft, with death and fire in their hand,
Thick and silent like ants, the warriors swarm in the land."

And they tell that when next the sun had climbed to the noonday skies,
It shone on the smoke of feasting in the country of the Vais.

TICONDEROGA

A LEGEND OF THE WEST HIGHLANDS

TICONDEROGA

INTRODUCTION.—I first heard this legend of my own country from that friend of men of letters, Mr. Alfred Nutt, "there in roaring London's central stream"; and since the ballad first saw the light of day in *Scribner's Magazine*, Mr. Nutt and Lord Archibald Campbell have been in public controversy on the facts. Two clans, the Camerons and the Campbells, lay claim to this branching story; and they do well: the man who preferred his plighted troth to the commands and menaces of the dead is an ancestor worth disputing. But the Campbells must rest content: they have the broad lands and the broad page of history; this appanage must be denied them; for between the name of *Cameron* and that of *Campbell*, the muse will never hesitate.

    This is the tale of the man
        Who heard a word in the night
    In the land of the heathery hills,
        In the days of the feud and the fight.
    By the sides of the rainy sea,
        Where never a stranger came,
    On the awful lips of the dead,
        He heard the outlandish name.
    It sang in his sleeping ears,
        It hummed in his waking head:
    The name—Ticonderoga,
        The utterance of the dead.

I. THE SAYING OF THE NAME

On the loch-sides of Appin,
    When the mist blew from the sea,
A Stewart stood with a Cameron:
    An angry man was he.
The blood beat in his ears,
    The blood ran hot to his head,
The mist blew from the sea,
    And there was the Cameron dead.

"O, what have I done to my friend,
    O, what have I done to mysel',
That he should be cold and dead,

And I in the danger of all?
Nothing but danger about me,
   Danger behind and before,
Death at wait in the heather
   In Appin and Mamore,
Hate at all of the ferries
   And death at each of the fords,
Camerons priming gunlocks
And Camerons sharpening swords."

But this was a man of counsel,
   This was a man of a score,
There dwelt no pawkier Stewart
   In Appin or Mamore.
He looked on the blowing mist,
   He looked on the awful dead,
And there came a smile on his face
   And there slipped a thought in his head.

Out over cairn and moss,
   Out over scrog and scaur,
He ran as runs the clansman
   That bears the cross of war.
His heart beat in his body,
   His hair clove to his face,
When he came at last in the gloaming
   To the dead man's brother's place.
The east was white with the moon,
   The west with the sun was red,
And there, in the house-doorway,
   Stood the brother of the dead.

"I have slain a man to my danger,
   I have slain a man to my death.
I put my soul in your hands,"
   The panting Stewart saith.
"I lay it bare in your hands,
   For I know your hands are leal;
And be you my targe and bulwark
   From the bullet and the steel."

Then up and spoke the Cameron,
    And gave him his hand again:
"There shall never a man in Scotland
    Set faith in me in vain;
And whatever man you have slaughtered,
    Of whatever name or line,
By my sword and yonder mountain,
    I make your quarrel mine. [34]
I bid you in to my fireside,
    I share with you house and hall;
It stands upon my honour
    To see you safe from all."

[34] Mr. Nutt reminds me it was. "by my sword and Ben Cruachan" the Cameron swore.

It fell in the time of midnight,
    When the fox barked in the den
And the plaids were over the faces
    In all the houses of men,
That as the living Cameron
    Lay sleepless on his bed,
Out of the night and the other world,
    Came in to him the dead.

"My blood is on the heather,
    My bones are on the hill;
There is joy in the home of ravens
    That the young shall eat their fill.
My blood is poured in the dust,
    My soul is spilled in the air;
And the man that has undone me
    Sleeps in my brother's care."

"I'm wae for your death, my brother,
    But if all of my house were dead,
I couldna withdraw the plighted hand,
    Nor break the word once said."

"O, what shall I say to our father,
    In the place to which I fare?
O, what shall I say to our mother,
    Who greets to see me there?
And to all the kindly Camerons
    That have lived and died long-syne—
Is this the word you send them,
    Fause-hearted brother mine?"

"It's neither fear nor duty,
   It's neither quick nor dead
Shall gar me withdraw the plighted hand,
   Or break the word once said."

Thrice in the time of midnight,
   When the fox barked in the den,
And the plaids were over the faces
   In all the houses of men,
Thrice as the living Cameron
   Lay sleepless on his bed,
Out of the night and the other world
   Came in to him the dead,
And cried to him for vengeance
   On the man that laid him low;
And thrice the living Cameron
   Told the dead Cameron, no.

"Thrice have you seen me, brother,
   But now shall see me no more,
Till you meet your angry fathers
   Upon the farther shore.
Thrice have I spoken, and now,
   Before the cock be heard,
I take my leave for ever
   With the naming of a word.
It shall sing in your sleeping ears,
   It shall hum in your waking head,
The name—Ticonderoga,
   And the warning of the dead."

Now when the night was over
   And the time of people's fears,
The Cameron walked abroad,
   And the word was in his ears.

"Many a name I know,
   But never a name like this;
O, where shall I find a skilly man
   Shall tell me what it is?"
With many a man he counselled
   Of high and low degree,
With the herdsmen on the mountains
   And the fishers of the sea.
And he came and went unweary,
   And read the books of yore,
And the runes that were written of old
   On stones upon the moor.
And many a name he was told,
   But never the name of his fears—
Never, in east or west,
   The name that rang in his ears:
Names of men and of clans;
   Names for the grass and the tree,
For the smallest tarn in the mountains,
   The smallest reef in the sea:
Names for the high and low,
   The names of the craig and the flat;
But in all the land of Scotland,
   Never a name like that.

II. THE SEEKING OF THE NAME

And now there was speech in the south,
   And a man of the south that was wise,
A periwig'd lord of London, [35]
   Called on the clans to rise.
And the riders rode, and the summons
   Came to the western shore,
To the land of the sea and the heather,
   To Appin and Mamore.
It called on all to gather
   From every scrog and scaur,
That loved their fathers' tartan
   And the ancient game of war.
And down the watery valley
   And up the windy hill,
Once more, as in the olden,
   The pipes were sounding shrill;
Again in highland sunshine
   The naked steel was bright;
And the lads, once more in tartan
   Went forth again to fight.

[35] "*A periwig'd lord of London.*" The first Pitt.

>"O, why should I dwell here
>   With a weird upon my life,
>When the clansmen shout for battle
>   And the war-swords clash in strife?
>I canna joy at feast,
>   I canna sleep in bed,
>For the wonder of the word
>   And the warning of the dead.
>It sings in my sleeping ears,
>   It hums in my waking head,
>The name—Ticonderoga,
>   The utterance of the dead.
>Then up, and with the fighting men
>   To march away from here,
>Till the cry of the great war-pipe
>   Shall drown it in my ear!"
>
>Where flew King George's ensign
>   The plaided soldiers went:
>They drew the sword in Germany,
>   In Flanders pitched the tent.
>The bells of foreign cities
>   Rang far across the plain:
>They passed the happy Rhine,
>   They drank the rapid Main.
>Through Asiatic jungles
>   The Tartans filed their way,
>And the neighing of the war-pipes
>   Struck terror in Cathay. [36]

[36] "*Cathay.*" There must be some omission in General Stewart's charming *History of the Highland Regiments*, a book that might well be republished and continued; or it scarce appears how our friend could have got to China.

>"Many a name have I heard," he thought,
>   "In all the tongues of men,
>Full many a name both here and there.
>   Full many both now and then.
>When I was at home in my father's house
>   In the land of the naked knee,
>Between the eagles that fly in the lift
>   And the herrings that swim in the sea,
>And now that I am a captain-man
>   With a braw cockade in my hat—
>Many a name have I heard," he thought,
>   "But never a name like that."

III. THE PLACE OF THE NAME

There fell a war in a woody place,
   Lay far across the sea,
A war of the march in the mirk midnight
   And the shot from behind the tree,
The shaven head and the painted face,
   The silent foot in the wood,
In a land of a strange, outlandish tongue
   That was hard to be understood.

It fell about the gloaming
   The general stood with his staff,
He stood and he looked east and west
   With little mind to laugh.
"Far have I been and much have I seen,
   And kennt both gain and loss,
But here we have woods on every hand
   And a kittle water to cross.
Far have I been and much have I seen,
   But never the beat of this;
And there's one must go down to that waterside
   To see how deep it is."

It fell in the dusk of the night
   When unco things betide,
The skilly captain, the Cameron,
   Went down to that waterside.
Canny and soft the captain went;
   And a man of the woody land,
With the shaven head and the painted face,
   Went down at his right hand.
It fell in the quiet night,
   There was never a sound to ken;
But all of the woods to the right and the left
   Lay filled with the painted men.

"Far have I been and much have I seen,
   Both as a man and boy,
But never have I set forth a foot
   On so perilous an employ."
It fell in the dusk of the night
   When unco things betide,
That he was aware of a captain-man
   Drew near to the waterside.
He was aware of his coming
   Down in the gloaming alone;
And he looked in the face of the man
   And lo! the face was his own.

"This is my weird," he said,
   "And now I ken the worst;
For many shall fall the morn,
   But I shall fall with the first.
O, you of the outland tongue,
   You of the painted face,
This is the place of my death;
   Can you tell me the name of the place?"

"Since the Frenchmen have been here
   They have called it Sault-Marie;
But that is a name for priests,
   And not for you and me.
It went by another word,"
   Quoth he of the shaven head:
"It was called Ticonderoga
   In the days of the great dead."

And it fell on the morrow's morning,
   In the fiercest of the fight,
That the Cameron bit the dust
   As he foretold at night;
And far from the hills of heather
   Far from the isles of the sea,
He sleeps in the place of the name
   As it was doomed to be.

HEATHER ALE

A GALLOWAY LEGEND

Among the curiosities of human nature, this legend claims a high place. It is needless to remind the reader that the Picts were never exterminated, and form to this day a large proportion of the folk in Scotland: occupying the eastern and the central parts, from the Firth of Forth, or perhaps the Lammermoors, upon the south, to the Ord of Caithness on the north. That the blundering guess of a dull chronicler should have inspired men with imaginary loathing for their own ancestors is already strange: that it should have begotten this wild legend seems incredible. It is possible the chronicler's error was merely nominal? That what he told, and what the people proved themselves so ready to receive, about the Picts, was true or partly true of some anterior and perhaps Lappish savages, small of stature, black of hue, dwelling underground—possibly also the distillers of some forgotten spirit? See Mr. Campbell's *Tales of the West Highlands*.

>From the bonny bells of heather
   They brewed a drink long-syne,
Was sweeter far than honey,
   Was stronger far than wine.
They brewed it and they drank it,
   And lay in a blessed swound
For days and days together
In their dwellings underground.

There rose a king in Scotland,
   A fell man to his foes,
He smote the Picts in battle,
   He hunted them like roes.
Over miles of the red mountain
   He hunted as they fled,
And strewed the dwarfish bodies
   Of the dying and the dead.

Summer came in the country,
   Red was the heather bell;
But the manner of the brewing
   Was none alive to tell.
In graves that were like children's
   On many a mountain head,
The Brewsters of the Heather
   Lay numbered with the dead.

The king in the red moorland
   Rode on a summer's day;
And the bees hummed, and the curlews
   Cried beside the way.
The king rode, and was angry,
   Black was his brow and pale,
To rule in a land of heather
   And lack the Heather Ale.

It fortuned that his vassals,
   Riding free on the heath,
Came on a stone that was fallen
   And vermin hid beneath.
Rudely plucked from their hiding,
   Never a word they spoke:
A son and his aged father—
   Last of the dwarfish folk.

The king sat high on his charger,
   He looked on the little men;
And the dwarfish and swarthy couple
   Looked at the king again.
Down by the shore he had them;
   And there on the giddy brink—
"I will give you life, ye vermin,
   For the secret of the drink."

There stood the son and father
   And they looked high and low;
The heather was red around them,
   The sea rumbled below.
And up and spoke the father,
   Shrill was his voice to hear:
"I have a word in private,
   A word for the royal ear.

"Life is dear to the aged,
   And honour a little thing;
I would gladly sell the secret,"
   Quoth the Pict to the King.
His voice was small as a sparrow's,
   And shrill and wonderful clear:
"I would gladly sell my secret,
   Only my son I fear.

"For life is a little matter,
   And death is nought to the young;
And I dare not sell my honour
   Under the eye of my son.
Take *him*, O king, and bind him,
   And cast him far in the deep;
And it's I will tell the secret
   That I have sworn to keep."

They took the son and bound him,
   Neck and heels in a thong,
And a lad took him and swung him,
   And flung him far and strong,
And the sea swallowed his body,
   Like that of a child of ten;—
And there on the cliff stood the father,
   Last of the dwarfish men.

"True was the word I told you:
   Only my son I feared;
For I doubt the sapling courage
   That goes without the beard.
But now in vain is the torture,
   Fire shall never avail:
Here dies in my bosom
   The secret of Heather Ale."

CHRISTMAS AT SEA

The sheets were frozen hard, and they cut the naked hand;
The decks were like a slide, where a seaman scarce could stand;
The wind was a nor'wester, blowing squally off the sea;
And cliffs and spouting breakers were the only things a-lee.

They heard the surf a-roaring before the break of day;
But 'twas only with the peep of light we saw how ill we lay.
We tumbled every hand on deck instanter, with a shout,
And we gave her the maintops'l, and stood by to go about.

All day we tacked and tacked between the South Head and the North;
All day we hauled the frozen sheets, and got no further forth;
All day as cold as charity, in bitter pain and dread,
For very life and nature we tacked from head to head.

We gave the South a wider berth, for there the tide-race roared;
But every tack we made we brought the North Head close aboard:
So's we saw the cliffs and houses, and the breakers running high,
And the coastguard in his garden, with his glass against his eye.

The frost was on the village roofs as white as ocean foam;
The good red fires were burning bright in every 'longshore home;
The windows sparkled clear, and the chimneys volleyed out;
And I vow we sniffed the victuals as the vessel went about.

The bells upon the church were rung with a mighty jovial cheer;
For it's just that I should tell you how (of all days in the year)
This day of our adversity was blessèd Christmas morn,
And the house above the coastguard's was the house where I was born.

O well I saw the pleasant room, the pleasant faces there,
My mother's silver spectacles, my father's silver hair;
And well I saw the firelight, like a flight of homely elves,
Go dancing round the china-plates that stand upon the shelves.

And well I knew the talk they had, the talk that was of me,
Of the shadow on the household and the son that went to sea;
And O the wicked fool I seemed, in every kind of way,
To be here and hauling frozen ropes on blessèd Christmas Day.

They lit the high sea-light, and the dark began to fall.
"All hands to loose topgallant sails," I heard the captain call.
"By the Lord, she'll never stand it," our first mate, Jackson, cried.
. . . "It's the one way or the other, Mr. Jackson," he replied.

She staggered to her bearings, but the sails were new and good,
And the ship smelt up to windward just as though she understood.
As the winter's day was ending, in the entry of the night,
We cleared the weary headland, and passed below the light.

And they heaved a mighty breath, every soul on board but me,
As they saw her nose again pointing handsome out to sea;
But all that I could think of, in the darkness and the cold,
Was just that I was leaving home and my folks were growing old.

V. NEW POEMS

I

SUMMER NIGHT

About us lies the summer night;
   The darkling earth is dusk below;
But high above, the sky is bright
   Between the eve and morning glow.

Clear white of dawn, and apple green,
   Sole lingering of the evening's hue,
Behind the clustered trees are seen,
   Across dark meadows drencht in dew.

So glow above the dusk of sin,
   Remembrance of Redemption vast,
And future hope of joy therein
   That shall be shed on us at last.

Each haloed in its husk of light,
   Atoms and worlds about us lie;
Though here we grope a while in night,
   'Tis always daylight up on high.

II

I sit up here at midnight,
   The wind is in the street,
The rain besieges the windows
   Like the sound of many feet.

I see the street lamps flicker,
   I see them wink and fail;
The streets are wet and empty,
   It blows an easterly gale.

Some think of the fisher skipper
   Beyond the Inchcape stone;
But I of the fisher woman
   That lies at home alone.

She raises herself on her elbow
   And watches the firelit floor;
Her eyes are bright with terror,
   Her heart beats fast and sore.

Between the roar of the flurries,
   When the tempest holds its breath,
She holds her breathing also—
   It is all as still as death.

She can hear the cinders dropping,
   The cat that purrs in its sleep—
The foolish fisher woman!
 Her heart is on the deep.

III

Lo! in thine honest eyes I read
The auspicious beacon that shall lead,
After long sailing in deep seas,
To quiet havens in June ease.

Thy voice sings like an inland bird
First by the seaworn sailor heard;
And like road sheltered from life's sea
Thine honest heart is unto me.

IV

Though deep indifference should drowse
The sluggish life beneath my brows,
And all the external things I see
Grow snow-showers in the street to me,
Yet inmost in my stormy sense
Thy looks shall be an influence.

Though other loves may come and go
And long years sever us below,
Shall the thin ice that grows above
Freeze the deep centre-well of love?
No, still below light amours, thou
Shalt rule me as thou rul'st me now.

Year following year shall only set
Fresh gems upon thy coronet;
And Time, grown lover, shall delight
To beautify thee in my sight;
And thou shalt ever rule in me
Crowned with the light of memory.

V

My heart, when first the blackbird sings,
    My heart drinks in the song:
Cool pleasure fills my bosom through
    And spreads each nerve along.

My bosom eddies quietly,
    My heart is stirred and cool
As when a wind-moved briar sweeps
    A stone into a pool

But unto thee, when thee I meet,
    My pulses thicken fast,
As when the maddened lake grows black
    And ruffles in the blast.

VI

1

I dreamed of forest alleys fair
    And fields of gray-flowered grass,
Where by the yellow summer moon
    My Jenny seemed to pass.

I dreamed the yellow summer moon,
    Behind a cedar wood,
Lay white on fields of rippling grass
    Where I and Jenny stood.

I dreamed—but fallen through my dream,
    In a rainy land I lie
Where wan wet morning crowns the hills
    Of grim reality.

2

I am as one that keeps awake
    All night in the month of June,
That lies awake in bed to watch
    The trees and great white moon.

For memories of love are more
    Than the white moon there above,
And dearer than quiet moonshine
    Are the thoughts of her I love.

3

Last night I lingered long without
   My last of loves to see.
Alas! the moon-white window-panes
   Stared blindly back on me.

To-day I hold her very hand,
   Her very waist embrace—
Like clouds across a pool, I read
   Her thoughts upon her face.

And yet, as now, through her clear eyes
   I seek the inner shrine—
I stoop to read her virgin heart
   In doubt if it be mine—

O looking long and fondly thus,
   What vision should I see?
No vision, but my own white face
   That grins and mimics me.

4

Once more upon the same old seat
In the same sunshiny weather,
The elm-trees' shadows at their feet
And foliage move together.

The shadows shift upon the grass,
The dial point creeps on;
The clear sun shines, the loiterers pass,
As then they passed and shone.

But now deep sleep is on my heart,
Deep sleep and perfect rest.
Hope's flutterings now disturb no more
The quiet of my breast.

VII

VERSES WRITTEN IN 1872

1

Though he that ever kind and true,
   Kept stoutly step by step with you
Your whole long gusty lifetime through
   Be gone a while before,
Be now a moment gone before,
   Yet, doubt not, soon the seasons shall restore
Your friend to you.

2

He has but turned a corner—still
He pushes on with right good will,
Thro' mire and marsh, by heuch and hill
      That self-same arduous way,—
That self-same upland hopeful way,
That you and he through many a doubtful day
      Attempted still.

3

He is not dead, this friend—not dead,
But, in the path we mortals tread,
Got some few, trifling steps ahead,
      And nearer to the end,
So that you, too, once past the bend,
Shall meet again, as face to face, this friend
      You fancy dead.

4

Push gayly on, strong heart! The while
You travel forward mile by mile,
He loiters with a backward smile
      Till you can overtake,
And strains his eyes, to search his wake,
Or whistling, as he sees you through the brake,
      Waits on a stile.

VIII

TO H. C. BUNNER

You know the way to Arcady
Where I was born;
You have been there, and fain
Would there return.
Some that go thither bring with them
Red rose or jewelled diadem
As secrets of the secret king:
I, only what a child would bring.
Yet I do think my song is true;
For this is how the children do;
This is the tune to which they go
In sunny pastures high and low;
The treble pipes not otherwise
Sing daily under sunny skies
In Arcady the dear;
And you who have been there before,
And love that country evermore,
May not disdain to hear.

IX

FROM WISHING-LAND

Dear Lady, tapping at your door,
   Some little verses stand,
And beg on this auspicious day
   To come and kiss your hand.

Their syllables all counted right
   Their rhymes each in its place,
Like birthday children, at the door
   They wait to see your face.

Rise, lady, rise and let them in;
   Fresh from the fairy shore,
They bring you things you wish to have,
   Each in its pinafore.

For they have been to Wishing-land
   This morning in the dew,
And all your dearest wishes bring—
   All granted—home to you.

What these may be, they would not tell,
    And could not if they would;
They take the packets sealed to you
    As trusty servants should.

But there was one that looked like love,
    And one that smelt like health,
And one that had a jingling sound—
    I fancy it might be wealth.

Ah, well, they are but wishes still;
    But, lady dear, for you
I know that all you wish is kind,
    I pray it all come true.

X

THE WELL-HEAD

The withered rushes made a flame
    Across the marsh of rusty red;
The dreary plover ever came
    And sang above the old well-head.

About it crouch the junipers,
    Green-black and dewed with berries white,
And in the grass the water stirs,
    Aloud all day, aloud all night.

The spring has scarcely come, 'tis said;
    Yet sweet and pleasant art thou still,
'Mong withered rushes, old well-head,
    Upon the sallow-shouldered hill.

The grass from which these waters came,
    These waters swelling from the sod,
Had been a bible unto some,
    A grave phylactery of God.

The Ayrshire peasant, years ago,
    Drank down religion in a cool
Deep draught of waters such as flow
    From out this pebbly little pool.

But different far is it with me,
   Here, where the piping curlews call;
The creatures will not let me see
   The great creator of them all.

And I should choose to go to sleep,
   With Merlin in Broceliande,
To hear the elm boughs hiss and sweep,
   In summer winds on either hand.

To cling to forest-trees and grass
   And this dear world of hill and plain,
For fear, whatever came to pass,
   God would not give as good again.

And some may use the gospel so,
   That is a pharos unto me,
And guide themselves to hell, although
   Their chart should lead them unto Thee.

Lord, shut our eyes or shut our mind,
   Or give us love, in case we fall;
'Tis better to go maim and blind
   Than not to reach the Lord at all.

XI

THE MILL-HOUSE

(A SICK-BED FANCY)

An alley ran across the pleasant wood,
On either side of whose broad opening stood
Wide-armed green elms of many a year, great bowers
Of perfect greenery in summer hours.
A small red pathway slow meandered there
Between two clumps of grapes, [both] lush and fair,
Well grown, that brushed a tall man past the knee.
No summer day grew therein over-hot,
For there was a pleasant freshness in the spot
Brought hither by a stream that men might see
Behind the rough-barked bole of every tree—
A little stream that ever murmured on
And here and there in sudden sunshine shone;
But for the most part, swept by shadowy boughs,
Among tall grass and fallen leaves did drowse,
With ever and anon, a leap, a gleam,

As some cross boulder lay athwart the stream.
Close following down this alley, one came near
The place where it descended sudden, sheer,
Into a dell betwixt two wooded hills,
Where ran a river made of many rills.
Near where to this the little alley stream
Lapsed in a turmoil, stood as in a dream
A lone, small mill-house in the vale aloof
With orange mosses on a grey slate roof
And all the walls and every lintel stone
With water mosses cunningly o'ergrown.
Its four-paned windows looked across a pool
By shadow of the house and trees kept cool;
Pent by the mossy weir that served the mill,
Its little waters lay unmoved and still,
Save for a circular, slow, eddy-wheeling
That on its bubble-spotted breast kept stealing,
And now and then the sudden, short wind-sway
Of some elm branch or beechen, that all day
Trailed in the shadowed pool; but far below
The enfranchised waters, in tumultuous flow,
Splashed round the boulders and leapt on in foam
Adown the sunshine way that led them home.
There was no noise at all about the mill
And the slope garden, like a dream, was still.
There came no sign at all into the glade,
Save when the white sack-laden waggons made
Wheel-creaking in the shadowy, slanting road,
And the great horses strained against the load;
Or when some trout would splash in the pool perhaps,
Or my old pointer from his pendulous chaps
Bayed at the very stillness. In the house
It was so strangely quiet that the mouse
Held carnival at mid-day on the floor.
The hearths were lined with Holland picture tiles
Of olden stories of enchanters' wiles;
And knights, stiff-seeming, upon stiffer steeds
Hastening to help fair ladies at their needs;
And bible tales, of prophets and of kings;
And faery ones, of midnight, meadow rings
Whereon, at mild star-rise, the wanton elves
Dance, having cleared the grass blades for themselves
As we men clear a forest; and besides
Of phantom castles and of woodland rides,
Of convent cloisters and religious veils
And all such like, were drawn a hundred tales;
And therein was the swinging censer showed,
And therein altar candles feebly glowed

And the bent priest upraised the sacred host.
And when the dusk drew on, in times of frost,
And new fires sparkled on the clean-swept hearth
And with pale tongues and laughing sound of mirth
Licked the dry wood and carven iron dogs
Whereon was piled the treasure of the logs,
In the red glow that rose and waned again
The picture figures writhed as if in pain,
Elijah shook his mantle, and the knight
His spear, and 'mong the elves of foot-fall light
One saw the dance grow faster, till the flame
Once more drew in, and all things were the same.

Nor were there wanting fleshlier joys than these;
For as the night grew closer and the trees
Hissed in the wind, before the ruddy fire
Was spread the napkin, white to a desire,
Laid out with silver vessels and brown bread
And some hot pasty smoking at the head
With odorous vapour, and the jug afloat
With bitter, amber ale that stings the throat,
Or figured glasses full of purple wine.
Or should one ask for pleasures more divine,
Then let him draw toward the pleasant blaze
And in the warm still chamber, let him raise
Blue wreaths of pungent vapour from the bowl,
That glows and dusks like an ignited coal
At every inhalation of sweet smoke.
So shall he clear a stage for that quaint folk,
The brood of dreams, that faëry puppet race
That will not dance but upon a vacant space;
And purge from every prejudice or creed
His easy spirit, that with greater speed,
He may outrun the boundaries of art
And grapple with grim questionings of heart.

XII

ST. MARTIN'S SUMMER

As swallows turning backward
   When half-way o'er the sea,
At one word's trumpet summons
   They came again to me—
The hopes I had forgotten
   Came back again to me.

I know not which to credit,
  O lady of my heart!
Your eyes that bade me linger,
  Your words that bade us part—
I know not which to credit,
  My reason or my heart.

But be my hopes rewarded,
  Or be they but in vain,
I have dreamed a golden vision,
  I have gathered in the grain—
I have dreamed a golden vision,
  I have not lived in vain.

XIII

All influences were in vain,
  The sun dripped gold among the trees,
The fresh breeze blew, the woody plain
  Ruffled and whispered in the breeze.

All day the sea was on one hand,
  The long beach shone with sun and wet—
We walked in trio on the sand,
  My shadow, I, and my regret!

Eve came. I clambered to my bed,
  Regret lay restless by my side,
The thought-wheels galloped in my head
  All night into the morning tide.

The thought-wheels span so madly quick,
  So many thousand times an hour,
Thought after thought took life, as thick
  As bats in some old belfry tower.

My mind was in *émeute*! each thought
  Usurped its individual right.
In vain, I temporised—I sought
  In vain to hold a plebiscite!

Thoughts jostled thoughts—By hill and glade
  They scattered far and wide like sheep,
I stretched my arms—I cried—I prayed—
  They heard not—I began to weep.

My head grew giddy-weak—I tried
   To drown my reason. All in vain.
I lay upon my face and cried
   Most bitterly to God again.

God put a thought into my hand,
   God gave me a resolve, an aim,
I blew it trumpet-wise—the band
   Of scattered fancies heard and came.

They heard the bugle tones I blew—
   The wandering thoughts came dropping in;
They took their ranks in silence due—
   One hour, and would the march begin?

The march began; and once begun
   The serious purpose, true design
Has held my being knit in one—
   My being kept the thoughts in line.

Since then, the waves are still. The tide
   Sets steadily and strongly out.
The sea shines tranquil, far and wide,
   My mind is past the surf of doubt.

The pole-star of my purpose keeps
   The constant line that I should steer.
At night my weary body sleeps,
   My brain works orderly and clear.

All things are altered since I set
   The steady goal before my face;
All things are changed; and my regret
   Is advertising for a place!

"Companion for an invalide—
The René-sort preferred—genteel
And orthodox." I wish it speed—
The creature kept so well to heel!

XIV

The old world moans and topes,
   Is restless and ill at ease;
And the old-world politicians
   Prescribe for the new disease.

I have stooped my head to listen
   (Its voice is far from strong)
For the burthen of its moanings
   As it topes all night long.

I have watched a patient vigil
   Beside its fever bed,
And I think that I can tell you
   The burthen of what it said:—

"As sick folk long for morning
   And long for night again,
So long for noble objects
   The hearts of noble men.

"They long and grope about them,
   With feverish hands they grope
For objects of endeavour,
   And exercise for hope.

"And they shall be our heroes
   And be our Avatar,
Who shall either reach the objects
   Or tell us what they are!"

XV

I am like one that has sat alone
   All day on a level plain,
With drooping head and trailing arms
   In a ceaseless pour of rain—

With drooping head and nerveless arms
   On the moorland flat and grey,
Till the clouds were severed suddenly
   About the end of day;

And the purple fringes of the rain
   Rose o'er the scarlet west,
And the birds sang in the soddened furze,
   And my heart sang in my breast.

XVI

The whole day thro', in contempt and pity,
   I pass your houses and beat my drum,
   In the roar of people that go and come,
In the sunlit streets of the city.

Hark! do you hear the ictus coming,
   Mid the roar and clatter of feet?
   Hark I in the ebb and flow of the street
Do you hear the sound of my drumming?

Sun and the fluttering ribbons blind me;
   But still I beat as I travel the town,
   And still the recruits come manfully down,
And the march grows long behind me.

In time to the drum the feet fall steady,
   The feet fall steady and firm to hear,
   And we cry, as we march, that the goal is near,
For all men are heroes already I

XVII

The old Chimaeras, old receipts
   For making "happy land,"
The old political beliefs
   Swam close before my hand.

The grand old communistic myths
   In a middle state of grace,
Quite dead, but not yet gone to Hell,
   And walking for a space,

Quite dead, and looking it, and yet
   All eagerness to show
The Social-Contract forgeries
   By Chatterton—Rousseau—

A hundred such as these I tried,
   And hundreds after that,
I fitted Social Theories
   As one would fit a hat!

Full many a marsh-fire lured me on,
   I reached at many a star,
I reached and grasped them and behold—
   The stump of a cigar!

All through the sultry, sweltering day
   The sweat ran down my brow,
The still plains heard my distant strokes
   That have been silenced now.

This way and that, now up, now down,
   I hailed full many a blow.
Alas! beneath my weary arm
   The thicket seemed to grow.

I take the lesson, wipe my brow
   And throw my axe aside,
And, sorely wearied, I go home
   In the tranquil eventide.

And soon the rising moon, that lights
   The eve of my defeat,
Shall see me sitting as of yore
   By my old master's feet.

XVIII

DEDICATION

My first gift and my last, to you
I dedicate this fascicle of songs—
The only wealth I have:
Just as they are, to you.

I speak the truth in soberness, and say
I had rather bring a light to your clear eyes,
Had rather hear you praise
This bosomful of songs

Than that the whole, hard world with one consent,
In one continuous chorus of applause
Poured forth for me and mine
The homage of ripe praise.

I write the finis here against my love,
This is my love's last epitaph and tomb.
Here the road forks, and I
Go my way, far from yours.

XIX

PRELUDE

By sunny market-place and street
Wherever I go my drum I beat,
And wherever I go in my coat of red
The ribbons flutter about my head.

I seek recruits for wars to come—
For slaughterless wars I beat the drum,
And the shilling I give to each new ally
Is hope to live and courage to die.

I know that new recruits shall come
Wherever I beat the sounding drum,
Till the roar of the march by country and town
Shall shake the tottering Dagons down.

For I was objectless as they
And loitering idly day by day;
But whenever I heard the recruiters come,
I left my all to follow the drum.

XX

THE VANQUISHED KNIGHT

I have left all upon the shameful field,
   Honour and Hope, my God, and all but life;
Spurless, with sword reversed and dinted shield,
   Degraded and disgraced, I leave the strife.

From him that hath not, shall there not be taken
   E'en that he hath, when he deserts the strife?
Life left by all life's benefits forsaken,
   O keep the promise, Lord, and take the life.

XXI

AULD REEKIE

When chitterin' cauld the day sall daw,
Loud may your bonny bugles blaw
   And loud your drums may beat.
Hie owre the land at evenfa'
Your lamps may glitter raw by raw,
   Along the gowsty street.

I gang nae mair where ance I gaed,
By Brunston, Fairmileheid, or Braid;
   But far frae Kirk or Tron.
O still ayont the muckle sea,
Still are ye dear, and dear to me,
   Auld Reekie, still and on!

XXII

ATHOLE BROSE

Willie an' I cam doun by Blair
   And in by Tullibardine,
The Rye were at the waterside,
   An' bee-skeps in the garden.
I saw the reek of a private still—
   Says I, 'Gud Lord, I thank ye!'
As Willie and I cam in by Blair
   And out by Killiekrankie.

Ye hinny bees, ye smuggler lads,
   Thou, Muse, the bard's protector,
I never kent what Rye were for
   Till I had drunk the nectar!
And shall I never drink it mair?
   Gud troth, I beg your pardon!
The neiest time I come doun by Blair
   And in by Tullibardine.

XXIII

OVER THE WATER WI'CHAIRLIE

(IN MEMORY OF A TRIP TO MALIE, MAY 27TH, 1892)

Come boat me o'er, come row me o'er!
   But fate constrained us sairly
And gied us our paiks and a hantle mair
   That ever we lippened to Charlie.
For naething o' this would hae happened to hiz
   If we had but stairted airly.
O we had won there and back again fair,
   If it hadnae been for Chairlie.

My Minnie sat cocked on a coggly canoe
   And, wow! But she lookit a ferlie!
Her fit asleep and the sea in her shoe,
   And a' on account o' Chairlie.
     O sair is my sorrow wi' seas and rocks!
       And the rain, says she, and Charlie,
     To sit cogglin' here on a biscuit box,
       My lee alane wi' Chairlie!

While Bell and mysel' and the strong chief wife,
   As stark as any kerlie,
We waded and paidled stachered for life,
   And banned the face o' Chairlie!
     I kilted my breeks and they their coats
       O! glam to the knee, and merrily,
     And we were a' in our Sinday's best,
       Black be the fa' o' Chairlie.

That we should be forced to kilt our duds,
   And show our shanks sae barely,
And stacher in a' kinds o' muds,
   And a' on account o' Chairlie.
     Oursel' we came there at the hinder end,
       And the dances were over fairly;
     O sure as death if we had but kenned,
       We would never have lippened to Chairlie!

But we had still to get home again,
   And the rain it rained full sairly,
I gie you my word as man to man,
   I think we were used unfairly!
      The rain it rained like never was,
         The wind it blew contrarily;
      But what constrained us mair than a'
         Was the pizon smiles o' Chairlie.
      He dipped his oar blade into the sea,
         He ladled it but sparsely,
      The gait the gude wife steers her tea
         Was the gait to row for Chairlie.

We threesome sat like dreepin' hens,
   And wow! we chittered sairly,
We dreeped and ran and clustered close,
   And flytit sair on Chairlie.
      O where is the rudder and where are the oars,
         And where is the boat plug, Chairlie?
      The sea it swells above our houghs,
         The boat is sinking fairly!
      O, if we put win hame again,
         And we expect it barely,
      The toot of judgement sure shall sound,
         Or we lippen again to Chairlie!

XXIV

TO THE COMMISSIONERS OF NORTHERN LIGHTS

I send to you, commissioners,
   A paper that may please ye, sirs,
(For troth they say it might be worse
   An' I believe't)
And on your business lay my curse
   Before I leav't.

I thocht I'd serve wi' you, sirs, yince,
But I've thocht better of it since,
The maitter I will nowise mince,
   But tell ye true:
I'll service wi' some ither prince,
   An' no' wi' you.

I've no' been very deep, ye'll think,
Cam' delicately to the brink
An' when the water gart me shrink
   Straucht took the rue,
An' didna stoop my fill to drink—
   I own it true.

I kennt on cape and isle, a light
Burnt fair an' clearly ilka night;
But at the service I took fright,
   As sune's I saw,
An' being still a neophite
   Gaed straucht awa'.

Anither course I now begin,
The weeg I'll cairry for my sin,
The court my voice shall echo in,
   An'—wha can tell?—
Some ither day I may be yin
   O you mysel'.

XXV

AFTER READING "ANTONY AND CLEOPATRA"

As when the hunt by holt and field
   Drives on with horn and strife,
Hunger of hopeless things pursues
   Our spirits throughout life.

The sea's roar fills us aching full
   Of objectless desire—
The sea's roar, and the white moon-shine,
   And the reddening of the fire.

Who talks to me of reason now?
   It would be more delight
To have died in Cleopatra's arms
   Than be alive to-night.

XXVI

The relic taken, what avails the shrine?
The locket, pictureless? O heart of mine,
Art thou not worse than that,
Still warm, a vacant nest where love once sat?

Her image nestled closer at my heart
Than cherished memories, healed every smart
And warmed it more than wine
Or the full summer sun in noon-day shine.

This was the little weather gleam that lit
The cloudy promontories—the real charm was it
That gilded hills and woods
And walked beside me thro' the solitudes.

That sun is set. My heart is widowed now
Of that companion-thought. Alone I plough
The seas of life, and trace
A separate furrow far from her and grace.

XXVII

About the sheltered garden ground
    The trees stand strangely still.
The vale ne'er seemed so deep before,
    Nor yet so high the hill.

An awful sense of quietness,
    A fulness of repose,
Breathes from the dewy garden-lawns,
    The silent garden rows.

As the hoof-beats of a troop of horse
    Heard far across a plain,
A nearer knowledge of great thoughts
    Thrills vaguely through my brain.

I lean my head upon my arm,
    My heart's too full to think;
Like the roar of seas, upon my heart
    Doth the morning stillness sink.

XXVIII

I know not how, but as I count
    The beads of former years,
Old laughter catches in my throat
    With the very feel of tears.

XXIX

Take not my hand as mine alone—
   You do not trust to me—
I hold the hand of greater men
   Too far before to see.

Follow not me, who only trace
   Stoop-head the prints of those
Our mighty predecessors, whom
   The darknesses enclose.

I cannot lead who follow—I
   Who learn, am dumb to teach;
I can but indicate the goals
   That greater men shall reach.

XXX

The angler rose, he took his rod,
He kneeled and made his prayers to God.
The living God sat overhead:
The angler tripped, the eels were fed.

XXXI

SPRING SONG

The air was full of sun and birds,
   The fresh air sparkled clearly.
Remembrance wakened in my heart
   And I knew I loved her dearly.

The fallows and the leafless trees
   And all my spirit tingled.
My earliest thought of love, and Spring's
   First puff of perfume mingled.

In my still heart the thoughts awoke,
   Came lone by lone together—
Say, birds and Sun and Spring, is Love
   A mere affair of weather?

XXXII

(A FRAGMENT)

Thou strainest through the mountain fern,
   A most exiguously thin
      Burn.
For all thy foam, for all thy din,
Thee shall the pallid lake inurn,
With well-a-day for Mr. Swin-
      Burn!
Take then this quarto in thy fin
And, O thou stoker huge and stern,
The whole affair, outside and in,
      Burn!
But save the true poetic kin,
The works of Mr. Robert Burn'
And William Wordsworth upon Tin-
      Tern!

XXXIII

The summer sun shone round me,
   The folded valley lay
In a stream of sun and odour,
   That sultry summer day.

The tall trees stood in the sunlight
   As still as still could be,
But the deep grass sighed and rustled
   And bowed and beckoned me.

The deep grass moved and whispered
   And lowed and brushed my face.
It whispered in the sunshine:
   "The winter comes apace."

XXXIV

You looked so tempting in the pew,
   You looked so sly and calm—
My trembling fingers played with yours
   As both looked out the Psalm.

Your heart beat hard against my arm,
   My foot to yours was set,
Your loosened ringlet burned my cheek
   Whenever they two met.

O little, little we hearkened, dear,
   And little, little cared,
Although the parson sermonised,
   The congregation stared.

XXXV

LOVE'S VICISSITUDES

As Love and Hope together
   Walk by me for a while,
Link-armed the ways they travel
   For many a pleasant mile—
Link-armed and dumb they travel,
   They sing not, but they smile.

Hope leaving, Love commences
   To practise on the lute;
And as he sings and travels
   With lingering, laggard foot,
Despair plays *obbligato*
   The sentimental flute.

Until in singing garments,
   Comes royally, at call—
Comes limber-hipped Indiff'rence
   Free stepping, straight and tall—
Comes singing and lamenting,
   The sweetest pipe of all.

XXVI

The moon is sinking—the tempestuous
   Grows worse, the squalls disputing our advance;
And as the feet fall well and true together
   In the last moonlight, see! the standards glance!

One hour, one moment, and that light for ever.
   Quite so.
     Jes' so.

XXXVII

DEATH

We are as maidens one and all,
   In some shut convent place,
Pleased with the flowers, the service bells,
   The cloister's shady grace,

That whiles, with fearful, fluttering hearts,
   Look outward thro' the grate
And down the long white road, up which,
   Some morning, soon or late,

Shall canter on his great grey horse
   That splendid acred Lord
Who comes to lead us forth—his wife,
   But half with our accord.

With fearful, fluttered hearts we wait—
   We meet him, bathed in tears;
We are so loath to leave behind
   Those tranquil convent years;

So loath to meet the pang, to take
   (On some poor chance of bliss)
Life's labour on the windy sea
   For a bower as still as this.

Weeping, we mount the crowded aisle,
   And weeping after us
The bridesmaids follow—Come to me!
   I will not meet you thus,

Pale rider to the convent gate.
   Come, O rough bridegroom, Death,
Where, bashful bride, I wait you, veiled,
   Flush-faced, with shaken breath;

I do not fear your kiss. I dream
   New days, secure from strife,
And, bride-like, in the future hope—
   A quiet household life.

XXXVIII

DUDDINGSTONE

With caws and chirrupings, the woods
   In this thin sun rejoice.
The Psalm seems but the little kirk
   That sings with its own voice.

The cloud-rifts share their amber light
   With the surface of the mere—
I think the very stones are glad
   To feel each other near.

Once more my whole heart leaps and swells
   And gushes o'er with glee;
The fingers of the sun and shade
   Touch music stops in me.

Now fancy paints that bygone day
   When you were here, my fair—
The whole lake rang with rapid skates
   In the windless winter air.

You leaned to me, I leaned to you,
   Our course was smooth as flight—
We steered—a heel-touch to the left,
   A heel-touch to the right.

We swung our way through flying men,
   Your hand lay fast in mine:
We saw the shifting crowd dispart,
   The level ice-reach shine.

I swear by yon swan-travelled lake,
   By yon calm hill above,
I swear had we been drowned that day
   We had been drowned in love.

XXXIX

Stout marches lead to certain ends,
We seek no Holy Grail, my friends—
That dawn should find us every day
Some fraction farther on our way.

The dumb lands sleep from east to west,
They stretch and turn and take their rest.
The cock has crown in the steading-yard,
But priest and people slumber hard.

We two are early forth, and hear
The nations snoring far and near.
So peacefully their rest they take,
It seems we are the first awake!

—Strong heart! this is no royal way,
A thousand cross-roads seek the day;
And, hid from us, to left and right,
A thousand seekers seek the light.

XL

Away with funeral music—set
   The pipe to powerful lips—
The cup of life's for him that drinks
   And not for him that sips.

XLI

TO SYDNEY [37]

[37] Stevenson's cousin, Robert Alan Stevenson

Not thine where marble-still and white
Old statues share the tempered light
And mock the uneven modern flight,
   But in the stream
Of daily sorrow and delight
   To seek a theme.

I too, O friend, have steeled my heart
Boldly to choose the better part,
To leave the beaten ways of art,
   And wholly free
To dare, beyond the scanty chart,
   The deeper sea.

All vain restrictions left behind,
Frail bark! I loose my anchored mind
And large, before the prosperous wind
   Desert the strand—
A new Columbus sworn to find
   The morning land.

Nor too ambitious, friend. To thee
I own my weakness. Not for me
To sing the enfranchised nations' glee,
   Or count the cost
Of warships foundered far at sea
   And battles lost.

High on the far-seen, sunny hills,
Morning-content my bosom fills;
Well-pleased, I trace the wandering rills
   And learn their birth.
Far off, the clash of sovereign wills
   May shake the earth.

The nimble circuit of the wheel,
The uncertain poise of merchant weal,
Heaven of famine, fire and steel
   When nations fall;
These, heedful, from afar I feel—
   I mark them all.

But not, my friend, not these I sing,
My voice shall fill a narrower ring.
Tired souls, that flag upon the wing,
   I seek to cheer:
Brave wines to strengthen hope I bring,
   Life's cantineer!

Some song that shall be suppling oil
To weary muscles strained with toil,
Shall hearten for the daily moil,
   Or widely read
Make sweet for him that tills the soil
   His daily bread—

Such songs in my flushed hours I dream
(High thought) instead of armour gleam
Or warrior cantos ream by ream
   To load the shelves—
Songs with a lilt of words, that seem
   To sing themselves.

XLII

Had I the power that have the will,
   The enfeebled will—a modern curse—
This book of mine should blossom still
   A perfect garden-ground of verse.

White placid marble gods should keep
   Good watch in every shadowy lawn;
And from clean, easy-breathing sleep
   The birds should waken me at dawn.

—A fairy garden;—none the less
   Throughout these gracious paths of mine
All day there should be free access
   For stricken hearts and lives that pine;

And by the folded lawns all day—
   No idle gods for such a land—
All active Love should take its way
   With active Labour hand in hand.

XLIII

O dull cold northern sky,
   O brawling sabbath bells,
   O feebly twittering Autumn bird that tells
The year is like to die!

O still, spoiled trees, O city ways,
O sun desired in vain,
O dread presentiment of coming rain
That cloys the sullen days!

Thee, heart of mine, I greet.
   In what hard mountain pass
   Striv'st thou? In what importunate morass
Sink now thy weary feet?

Thou run'st a hopeless race
   To win despair. No crown
   Awaits success, but leaden gods look down
On thee, with evil face.

And those that would befriend
   And cherish thy defeat,
   With angry welcome shall turn sour the sweet
Home-coming of the end.

Yea, those that offer praise
   To idleness, shall yet
   Insult thee, coming glorious in the sweat
Of honourable ways.

XLIV

APOLOGETIC POSTSCRIPT OF A YEAR LATER

If you see this song, my dear,
   And last year's toast,
I'm confoundedly in fear
You'll be serious and severe
   About the boast.

Blame not that I sought such aid
   To cure regret.
I was then so lowly laid
I used all the Gasconnade
   That I could get.

Being snubbed is somewhat smart,
   Believe, my sweet;
And I needed all my art
To restore my broken heart
   To its conceit.

Come and smile, dear, and forget
   I boasted so,
I apologise—regret—
It was all a jest;—and— yet—
   I do not know.

XLV

TO MARCUS [38]

[38] Charles Baxter.

You have been far, and I
    Been farther yet,
  Since last, in foul or fair
  An impecunious pair,
Below this northern sky
    Of ours, we met.

Now winter night shall see
    Again us two,
  While howls the tempest higher,
  Sit warmly by the fire
And dream and plan, as we
    Were wont to do.

And, hand in hand, at large
    Our thoughts shall walk
  While storm and gusty rain,
  Again and yet again,
Shall drive their noisy charge
    Across the talk.

The pleasant future still
    Shall smile to me,
  And hope with wooing hands
  Wave on to fairy lands
All over dale and hill
    And earth and sea.

And you who doubt the sky
    And fear the sun—
  You—*Christian* with the pack—
  You shall not wander back
For I am *Hopeful*—I
    Will cheer you on.

Come—where the great have trod,
    The great shall lead—
  Come, elbow through the press,
  Pluck Fortune by the dress—
By God, we must—by God,
    We shall succeed.

XLVI

TO OTTILIE

You remember, I suppose,
    How the August sun arose,
  And how his face
Woke to trill and carolette
All the cages that were set
    About the place.

In the tender morning light
All around lay strange and bright
    And still and sweet,
And the gray doves unafraid
Went their morning promenade
    Along the street.

XLVII

This gloomy northern day,
     Or this yet gloomier night,
    Has moved a something high
    In my cold heart; and I,
That do not often pray,
    Would pray to-night.

And first on Thee I call
    For bread, O God of might!
Enough of bread for all,—
     That through the famished town
     Cold hunger may lie down
    With none to-night.

I pray for hope no less,
    Strong-sinewed hope, O Lord,
     That to the struggling young
     May preach with brazen tongue
Stout Labour, high success,
    And bright reward.

And last, O Lord, I pray
    For hearts resigned and bold
To trudge the dusty way—
     Hearts stored with song and joke
     And warmer than a cloak
    Against the cold.

If nothing else he had,
  He who has this, has all.
    This comforts under pain;
    This, through the stinging rain,
Keeps ragamuffin glad
  Behind the wall.

This makes the sanded inn
  A palace for a Prince,
And this, when griefs begin
    And cruel fate annoys,
    Can bring to mind the joys
Of ages since.

XLVIII

TO A YOUTH [39]

[39] Doubtless Stevenson's cousin, "Bob," Robert Alan Stevenson.

See, with strong heart, O youth, the change
Of mood and season in thy breast.
The intrepid soul that dares the wider range
Shall find securer rest.

The variable moods they breed
Are but as April sun and shower,
That only seem to hinder—truly speed
Against the harvest hour.

Thy net in all rough waters cast,
In all fair pasturelands rejoice,
Thee shall such wealth of trials lead at last
To thy true home of choice.

So shalt thou grow, O youth, at length
Strong in endeavour, strong to bear
As having all things borne, thy lease of strength
Not perishable hair.

Not the frail tenement of health,
The uneasy mail of stoic pride
(A Nessus-shirt indeed!) the veer of wealth
In strong continual tide.

Not these, but in the constant heart,
That having all ways tried, at last
Holds, stout and patient, to the eternal chart,
Well tested in the past.

O, more than garlands for our heads,
Than drum and trumpet sounding loud,
As the long line of fluttering banners threads
The many-coloured crowd;

That sense of progress won with ease,
Of unconstrained advance in both,
Of the full circle finished—such as trees
Feel in their own free growth.

So shall thy life to plains below,
O not unworthy of the crown!
Equal and pure, by lives yet purer, flow
Companionably down.

XLIX

JOHN CAVALIER

These are your hills, John Cavalier.
Your father s kids you tended here,
And grew, among these mountains wild,
A humble and religious child.—
Fate turned the wheel; you grew and grew;
Bold Marshalls doffed the hat to you;
God whispered counsels in your ear
To guide your sallies, Cavalier.

You shook the earth with martial tread;
The ensigns fluttered by your head;
In Spain or France, Velay or Kent,
The music sounded as you went.—
Much would I give if I might spy
Your brave battalions marching by;
Or, on the wind, if I might hear
Your drums and bugles, Cavalier.

In vain. O'er all the windy hill,
The ways are void, the air is still,
Alone, below the echoing rock,
The shepherd calls upon his flock.—
The wars of Spain and of Cevennes,
The bugles and the marching men,
The horse you rode for many a year—
Where are they now, John Cavalier?

All armies march the selfsame way
Far from the cheerful eye of day;
And you and yours marched down below
About two hundred years ago.
Over the hills, into the shade,
Journeys each mortal cavalcade;
Out of the sound, out of the sun,
They go when their day s work is done;
And all shall doff the bandoleer
To sleep with dead John Cavalier.

L

PRAISE AND PRAYER

I have been well, I have been ill,
    I have been rich and poor;
I have set my back against the wall
    And fought it by the hour;

I have been false, I have been true;
    And thro' grief and mirth,
I have done all that man can do
    To be a man of worth;

And now, when from an unknown shore,
    I dare an unknown wave,
God, who has helped me heretofore,
    O help me wi' the lave!

LI

HOPES

Tho' day by day old hopes depart,
    Yet other hopes arise
If still we bear a hopeful heart
    And forward-looking eyes.

Of all that entered hand in hand
   With me the dusty plains—
   Look round!—not one remains,
Not one remains of all the jovial band.

Some fell behind, some hastened on;
   Some, scattered far and wide,
   Sought lands on every side;
One way or other, all the band are gone.

Yes, all are gone; and yet, at night,
New objects of desire
People the sunken fire
And new hopes whisper sweetly new delight;

And still, flush-faced, new goals I see,
   New finger-posts I find,
   And still thro' rain and wind
A troop of shouting hopes keep step with me.

Tho' day by day old hopes depart,
   Yet other hopes arise
If still we bear a hopeful heart
   And forward-looking eyes.

LII

I have a friend; I have a story;
   I have a life that's hard to live;
I love; my love is all my glory;
   I have been hurt and I forgive.

I have a friend; none could be better;
   I stake my heart upon my friend!
I love; I trust her to the letter;
   Will she deceive me in the end?

She is my love, my life, my jewel;
   My hope, my star, my dear delight.
God! but the ways of God are cruel,—
   That love should bow the knee to spite!

She loves, she hates,—a foul alliance!
   One King shall rule in one estate.
I only love; 'tis all my science;
   A while, and she will only hate.

LIII

Link your arm in mine, my lad—
 You and I together,
You and I and all the rest
 Shall face the winter weather.

Chorus

Some to good, and some to harm,
 Some to cheer the others,
All the world goes arm in arm,
 And all the men are brothers.

Fortune kicks us here and there,
 Small our role in life, lad.
Better paltry pace, howe'er,
 Than hero-laurelled strife, lad.

While there's liquor to be had,
 Deeply drain the bickers.
Ocean plays at marbles, lad,
 With men of war for knickers.

Who will ever hear of me?
 Who will hear of you, lad?
Devil take posterity
 And present people too, lad!

I have work enough to do,
 Strength enough to do it—
I have work and so have you,
 So put your shoulder to it!

Some do half that I can do,
 Some can do the double,
Some must rule for me and you,
 To save ourselves the trouble!

Who would envy yonder man
 Decorated thus, lad?
We are workingmen for him,
 And he's an earl for us, lad!

LIV

The wind is without there and howls in the trees,
    And the rain-flurries drum on the glass:
Alone by the fireside with elbows on knees
    I can number the hours as they pass.
Yet now, when to cheer me the crickets begin
    And my pipe is just happily lit,
Believe me, my friend, tho' the evening draws in,
    That not all uncontented I sit.

Alone, did I say? O no, nowise alone
    With the Past sitting warm on my knee,
To gossip of days that are over and gone,
    But still charming to her and to me.
With much to be glad of and much to deplore,
    Yet, as these days with those we compare,
Believe me, my friend, tho' the sorrows seem more
    They are somehow more easy to bear.

And thou, faded Future, uncertain and frail,
    As I cherish thy light in each draught,
His lamp is not more to the miner—their sail
    Is not more to the crew on the raft.
For Hope can make feeble ones earnest and brave,
    And, as forth thro' the years I look on,
Believe me, my friend, [40] between this and the grave,
    I see wonderful things to be done.

[40] This poem is addressed to Charles Baxter.

To do or to try; and, believe me, my friend,
    If the call should come early for me,
I can leave these foundations uprooted, and tend
    For some new city over the sea.
To do or to try; and if failure be mine,
    And if Fortune go cross to my plan,
Believe me, my friend, tho' I mourn the design
    I shall never lament for the man.

LV

A VALENTINE'S SONG

Motley I count the only wear
   That suits, in this mixed world, the truly wise,
Who boldly smile upon despair
   And shake their bells in Grandam Grundy's eyes.
Singers should sing with such a goodly cheer
   That the bare listening should make strong like wine,
At this unruly time of year,
   The Feast of Valentine.

We do not now parade our "oughts"
   And "shoulds" and motives and beliefs in God.
Their life lies all indoors; sad thoughts
   Must keep the house, while gay thoughts go abroad,
Within we hold the wake for hopes deceased;
   But in the public streets, in wind or sun,
Keep open, at the annual feast,
   The puppet-booth of fun.

Our powers, perhaps, are small to please,
   But even negro-songs and castanettes,
Old jokes and hackneyed repartees
   Are more than the parade of vain regrets.
Let Jacques stand Wert[h]ering by the wounded deer—
   We shall make merry, honest friends of mine,
At this unruly time of year,
   The Feast of Valentine.

I know how, day by weary day,
   Hope fades, love fades, a thousand pleasures fade.
I have not trudged in vain that way
   On which life's daylight darkens, shade by shade.
And still, with hopes decreasing, griefs increased,
   Still, with what wit I have shall I, for one,
Keep open, at the annual feast,
   The puppet-booth of fun.

I care not if the wit be poor,
   The old worn motley stained with rain and tears,
If but the courage still endure
   That filled and strengthened hope in earlier years;
If still, with friends averted, fate severe,
   A glad, untainted cheerfulness be mine
To greet the unruly time of year,
   The Feast of Valentine.

Priest, I am none of thine, and see
   In the perspective of still hopeful youth
That Truth shall triumph over thee—
   Truth to one's self—I know no other truth.
I see strange days for thee and thine, O priest,
   And how your doctrines, fallen one by one,
Shall furnish at the annual feast
   The puppet-booth of fun.

Stand on your putrid ruins—stand,
   White neck-clothed bigot, fixedly the same,
Cruel with all things but the hand,
   Inquisitor in all things but the name.
Back, minister of Christ and source of fear—
   We cherish freedom—back with thee and thine
From this unruly time of year,
   The Feast of Valentine.

Blood thou mayest spare; but what of tears?
   But what of riven households, broken faith—
Bywords that cling through all men's years
   And drag them surely down to shame and death?
Stand back, O cruel man, O foe of youth,
   And let such men as hearken not thy voice
Press freely up the road to truth,
   The King's highway of choice.

LVI

Hail! Childish slaves of social rules
   You had yourselves a hand in making!
How I could shake your faith, ye fools,
   If but I thought it worth the shaking.
I see, and pity you; and then
   Go, casting off the idle pity,
In search of better, braver men,
   My own way freely through the city.

My own way freely, and not yours;
   And, careless of a town's abusing,
Seek real friendship that endures
   Among the friends of my own choosing.
I'll choose my friends myself, do you hear?
   And won't let Mrs. Grundy do it,
Tho' all I honour and hold dear
   And all I hope should move me to it.

I take my old coat from the shelf—
   I am a man of little breeding.
And only dress to please myself—
   I own, a very strange proceeding.
I smoke a pipe abroad, because
   To all cigars I much prefer it,
And as I scorn your social laws
   My choice has nothing to deter it.

Gladly I trudge the footpath way,
   While you and yours roll by in coaches
In all the pride of fine array,
   Through all the city's thronged approaches.
O fine religious, decent folk,
   In Virtue's flaunting gold and scarlet,
I sneer between two puffs of smoke,—
   Give me the publican and harlot.

Ye dainty-spoken, stiff, severe
   Seed of the migrated Philistian,
One whispered question in your ear—
   Pray, what was Christ, if you be Christian?
If Christ were only here just now,
   Among the city's wynds and gables
Teaching the life he taught us, how
   Would he be welcome to your tables?

I go and leave your logic-straws,
   Your former-friends with face averted,
Your petty ways and narrow laws,
   Your Grundy and your God, deserted.
From your frail ark of lies, I flee
   I know not where, like Noah's raven.
Full to the broad, unsounded sea
   I swim from your dishonest haven.

Alone on that unsounded deep,
   Poor waif, it may be I shall perish,
Far from the course I thought to keep,
   Far from the friends I hoped to cherish.
It may be that I shall sink, and yet
   Hear, thro' all taunt and scornful laughter,
Through all defeat and all regret,
   The stronger swimmers coming after.

LVII

Swallows travel to and fro,
And the great winds come and go,
And the steady breezes blow,
   Bearing perfume, bearing love.
Breezes hasten, swallows fly,
Towered clouds forever ply,
And at noonday, you and I
   See the same sunshine above.

Dew and rain fall everywhere,
Harvests ripen, flowers are fair,
And the whole round earth is bare
   To the moonshine and the sun;
And the live air, fanned with wings,
Bright with breeze and sunshine, brings
Into contact distant things,
   And makes all the countries one.

Let us wander where we will,
Something kindred greets us still;
Something seen on vale or hill
   Falls familiar on the heart;
So, at scent or sound or sight,
Severed souls by day and night
Tremble with the same delight—
   Tremble, half the world apart.

LVIII

TO MESDAMES ZASSETSKY AND GARSCHINE [41]

[41] Two Russian princesses whom Stevenson met at Mentone.

The wind may blaw the lee-gang way
And aye the lift be mirk an' gray,
An deep the moss and steigh the brae
   Where a' maun gang—
There's still an hoor in ilka day
   For luve and sang.

And canty hearts are strangely steeled.
By some dikeside they'll find a bield,
Some couthy neuk by muir or field
   They're sure to hit,
Where, frae the blatherin' wind concealed,
   They'll rest a bit.

An' weel for them if kindly fate
Send ower the hills to them a mate;
They'll crack a while o' kirk an' State,
   O' yowes an' rain:
An' when it's time to take the gate,
   Tak' ilk his ain.

—Sic neuk beside the southern sea
I soucht—sic place o' quiet lee
Frae a' the winds o' life. To me,
   Fate, rarely fair,
Had set a freendly company
   To meet me there.

Kindly by them they gart me sit,
An' blythe was I to bide a bit.
Licht as o' some hame fireside lit
   My life for me.
—Ower early maun I rise an' quit
   This happy lee.

LIX

TO MADAME GARSCHINE

What is the face, the fairest face, till Care,
   Till Care the graver—Care with cunning hand,
Etches content thereon and makes it fair,
   Or constancy, and love, and makes it grand?

LX

MUSIC AT THE VILLA MARINA

Form some abiding central source of power,
   Strong-smitten steady chords, ye seem to flow
   And, flowing, carry virtue. Far below,
The vain tumultuous passions of the hour
Fleet fast and disappear; and as the sun
   Shines on the wake of tempests, there is cast
   O'er all the shattered ruins of my past
A strong contentment as of battles won.

And yet I cry in anguish, as I hear
   The long drawn pageant of your passage roll
   Magnificently forth into the night.
To yon fair land ye come from, to yon sphere
Of strength and love where now ye shape your flight,
O even wings of music, bear my soul!

Ye have the power, if but ye had the will,
   Strong-smitten steady chords in sequence grand,
   To bear me forth into that tranquil land
Where good is no more ravelled up with ill;
Where she and I, remote upon some hill
   Or by some quiet river's windless strand,
   May live, and love, and wander hand in hand,
And follow nature simply, and be still.

From this grim world, where, sadly, prisoned, we
   Sit bound with others' heart-strings as with chains,
   And, if one moves, all suffer,—to that Goal,
If such a land, if such a sphere, there be,
   Thither, from life and all life's joys and pains,
   O even wings of music, bear my soul!

LXI

Fear not, dear friend, but freely live your days
   Though lesser lives should suffer. Such am I,
   A lesser life, that what is his of sky
Gladly would give for you, and what of praise.
Step, without trouble, down the sunlit ways.
   We that have touched your raiment, are made whole
   From all the selfish cankers of man's soul,
And we would see you happy, dear, or die.
Therefore be brave, and therefore, dear, be free;
Try all things resolutely, till the best,
Out of all lesser betters, you shall find;
And we, who have learned greatness from you, we,
   Your lovers, with a still, contented mind,
   See you well anchored in some port of rest.

LXII

Let love go, if go she will.
Seek not, O fool, her wanton flight to stay.
Of all she gives and takes away
The best remains behind her still.

The best remains behind; in vain
Joy she may give and take again,
Joy she may take and leave us pain,
   If yet she leave behind
   The constant mind
To meet all fortunes nobly, to endure
All things with a good heart, and still be pure,
Still to be foremost in the foremost cause,
And still be worthy of the love that was.
Love coming is omnipotent indeed,
But not Love going. Let her go. The seed
Springs in the favouring Summer air, and grows,
And waxes strong; and when the Summer goes,
   Remains, a perfect tree.

Joy she may give and take again,
Joy she may take and leave us pain.
   O Love, and what care we?
For one thing thou hast given, O Love, one thing
Is ours that nothing can remove;
And as the King discrowned is still a King,
   The unhappy lover still preserves his love.

LXIII

I do not fear to own me kin
To the glad clods in which spring flowers begin;
Or to my brothers, the great trees,
That speak with pleasant voices in the breeze,
Loud talkers with the winds that pass;
Or to my sister, the deep grass.

Of such I am, of such my body is,
That thrills to reach its lips to kiss.
That gives and takes with wind and sun and rain
And feels keen pleasure to the point of pain.
Of such are these,
The brotherhood of stalwart trees,
The humble family of flowers,
That make a light of shadowy bowers
Or star the edges of the bent:
They give and take sweet colour and sweet scent;
They joy to shed themselves abroad;
And tree and flower and grass and sod
Thrill and leap and live and sing
With silent voices in the Spring.

Hence I not fear to yield my breath,
Since all is still unchanged by death;
Since in some pleasant valley I may be,
Clod beside clod, or tree by tree,
Long ages hence, with her I love this hour;
And feel a lively joy to share
With her the sun and rain and air,
To taste her quiet neighbourhood
As the dumb things of field and wood,
The clod, the tree, and starry flower,
Alone of all things have the power.

LXIV

I am like one that for long days had sate,
    With seaward eyes set keen against the gale,
On some lone foreland, watching sail by sail,
The portbound ships for one ship that was late;
And sail by sail, his heart burned up with joy,
    And cruelly was quenched, until at last
    One ship, the looked-for pennant at its mast,
Bore gaily, and dropt safely past the buoy;
And lo! the loved one was not there—was dead.
Then would he watch no more; no more the sea
    With myriad vessels, sail by sail, perplex
His eyes and mock his longing. Weary head,
Take now thy rest; eyes, close; for no more me
    Shall hopes untried elate, or ruined vex.

For thus on love I waited; thus for love
    Strained all my senses eagerly and long;
    Thus for her coming ever trimmed my song;
Till in the far skies coloured as a dove,
A bird gold-coloured flickered far and fled
    Over the pathless waterwaste for me;
    And with spread hands I watched the bright bird flee
And waited, till before me she dropped dead.
    O golden bird in these dove-coloured skies
    How long I sought, how long with wearied eyes
I sought, O bird, the promise of thy flight!
And now the morn has dawned, the morn has died,
The day has come and gone; and once more night
    About my lone life settles, wild and wide.

LXV

Sit doon by me, my canty freend,
    Sit doon, an' snuff the licht!
A boll o' bear's in ilka glass
    Ye'se drink wi' me the nicht!

    Chorus

Let preachers prate o' soberness
    An' brand us ripe for doom,
Yet still we'll lo'e the brimmin' glass,
    And still we'll hate the toom.

There's fire an' life in ilka glass,
   There's blythesomeness an' cheer,
There's thirst an' what'll slocken it,
   There's love and laughter here.

O mirk an' black the lee lang gate
   That we maun gang the nicht,
But aye we'll pass the brimmin' glass
   An' aye we'll snuff the licht.

We'll draw the closer roond the fire
   And aye the closer get.
Without, the ways may thaw or freeze,
   Within we're roar in' wet!

LXVI

Here he [42] comes, big with statistics,
   Troubled and sharp about fac's.
He has heap of the *Form* that is thinkable—
   The *stuff* that is feeling, he lacks.

Do you envy this whiskered absurdity,
   With *pince-nez* and clerical tie?
Poor fellow, he's blind of a sympathy!
   I'd rather be blind of an eye.

[42] Some one of the professors with whom Stevenson studied law in 1874-5.

LXVII

VOLUNTARY

Here in the quiet eve
My thankful eyes receive
   The quiet light.
I see the trees stand fair
Against the faded air,
And star by star prepare
   The perfect night.

And in my bosom, lo!
Content and quiet grow
   Toward perfect peace.
And now when day is done,
Brief day of wind and sun,
The pure stars, one by one,
   Their troop increase.

Keen pleasure and keen grief
Give place to great relief:
   Farewell my tears!
Still sounds toward me float;
I hear the bird's small note,
Sheep from the far sheepcote,
   And lowing steers.

For lo! the war is done,
Lo, now the battle won,
   The trumpets still.
The shepherd's slender strain,
The country sounds again
Awake in wood and plain,
   On haugh and hill.

Loud wars and loud loves cease.
I welcome my release;
   And hail once more
Free foot and way world-wide.
And oft at eventide
Light love to talk beside
   The hostel door.

LXVIII

O now, although the year be done,
Now, although the love be dead,
   Dead and gone;
Hear me, O loved and cherished one,
Give me still the hand that led,
   Led me on.

LXIX

AD SE IPSUM

Dear sir, good-morrow! Five years back,
When you first girded for this arduous track,
And under various whimsical pretexts
Endowed another with your damned defects,
Could you have dreamed in your despondent vein
That the kind God would make your path so plain?
Non nobis, domine! O, may He still
Support my stumbling footsteps on the hill!

LXX

In the green and gallant Spring,
Love and the lyre I thought to sing,
And kisses sweet to give and take
By the flowery hawthorn brake.

Now is russet Autumn here,
Death and the grave and winter drear,
And I must ponder here aloof
While the rain is on the roof.

LXXI

Death, to the dead for evermore
A King, a God, the last, the best of friends—
Whene'er this mortal journey ends
Death, like a host, comes smiling to the door;
Smiling, he greets us, on that tranquil shore
Where neither piping bird nor peeping dawn
Disturbs the eternal sleep,
But in the stillness far withdrawn
Our dreamless rest for evermore we keep.

For as from open windows forth we peep
Upon the night-time star beset
And with dews for ever wet;
So from this garish life the spirit peers;
And lo! as a sleeping city death outspread,
Where breathe the sleepers evenly; and lo!
After the loud wars, triumphs, trumpets, tears
And clamour of man's passion, Death appears,
And we must rise and go.

Soon are eyes tired with sunshine; soon the ears
Weary of utterance, seeing all is said;
Soon, racked by hopes and fears,
The all-pondering, all-contriving head,
Weary with all things, wearies of the years;
And our sad spirits turn toward the dead;
And the tired child, the body, longs for bed.

LXXII

TO CHARLES BAXTER

On the death of their common friend, Mr. John Adam, Clerk of Court.

Our Johnie's deid. The mair's the pity!
He's deid, an' deid o' Aqua-vitae.
O Embro', you're a shrunken city,
    Noo Johnie's deid!
Tak hands, an' sing a burial ditty
    Ower Johnie's heid.

To see him was baith drink an' meat,
Gaun linkin' glegly up the street.
He but to rin or tak a seat,
    The wee bit body!
Bein' aye unsicken on his feet
    Wi' whusky toddy.

To be aye tosh was Johnie's whim,
There's nane was better tent than him,
Though whiles his gravit-knot wad clim'
    Ahint his ear,
An' whiles he'd buttons oot or in
    The less or mair.

His hair a' lank about his bree,
His tap-lip lang by inches three—
A slockened sort 'mon,' to pree
    A' sensuality—
A drouthy glint was in his e'e
    An' personality.

An' day an' nicht, frae daw to daw,
Dink an' perjink an' doucely braw,
Wi' a kind o' Gospel ower a',
    May or October,
Like Peden, followin' the Law
    An' no that sober.

Whusky an' he were pack thegether.
Whate'er the hour, whate'er the weather,
John kept himsel' wi' mistened leather
   An' kindled spunk.
Wi' him, there was nae askin' whether—
   John was aye drunk.

The auncient heroes gash an' bauld
In the uncanny days of auld,
The task ance fo[u]nd to which th'were called,
   Stack stenchly to it.
His life sic noble lives recalled,
   Little's he knew it.

Single an' straucht, he went his way.
He kept the faith an' played the play.
Whusky an' he were man an' may
   Whate'er betided.
Bonny in life—in death—this twae
   Were no' divided.

An' wow! but John was unco sport.
Whiles he wad smile about the Court
Malvolio-like—whiles snore an' snort
   Was heard afar.
The idle winter lads' resort
   Was aye John's bar.

What's merely humorous or bonny
The Worl' regairds wi' cauld astony.
Drunk men tak' aye mair place than ony;
   An' sae, ye see,
The gate was aye ower thrang for Johnie—
   Or you an' me.

John micht hae jingled cap an' bells,
Been a braw fule in silks an' pells,
In ane o' the auld worl's canty hells
   Paris or Sodom.
I wadna had him naething else
   But Johnie Adam.

He suffered—as have a' that wan
Eternal memory frae man,
Since e'er the weary worl' began—
   Mister or Madam,
Keats or Scots Burns, the Spanish Don
   Or Johnie Adam.

We leuch, an' Johnie deid. An' fegs!
Hoo he had keept his stoiterin' legs
Sae lang's he did, 's a fact that begs
   An explanation.
He stachers fifty years—syne plegs
   To's destination.

LXXIII

The look of Death is both severe and mild,
And all the words of Death are grave and sweet;
He holds ajar the door of his retreat;
The hermitage of life, it may be styled;

He pardons sinners, cleanses the defiled,
And comfortably welcomes weary feet.
The look of Death is both severe and mild,
And all the words of Death are grave and sweet.

And you that have been loving pleasure wild,
Long known the sins and sorrows of the street,
Lift up your eyes and see, Death waits to greet,
As a kind parent a repentant child.

The bugle sounds the muster roll,
The blacksmith blows the roaring coal;
The look of Death is both severe and mild,
And all the words of Death are grave and sweet.

LXXIV

Her name is as a word of old romance
That thrills a careless reader out of sleep.
Love and old art, and all things pure and deep
Attend on her to honour her advance,—
The brave old wars where bearded heroes prance,
The courtly mien that private virtues keep,—
Her name is as a word of old romance.
Peer has she none in England or in France,
So well she knows to rouse dull souls [from sleep]

So deftly can she comfort those who weep
And put kind thought and comfort in a glance.
Her name is as a [word of old romance.]

LXXV

In Autumn when the woods are red
And skies are grey and clear,
The sportsmen seek the wild fowls' bed
Or follow down the deer;
And Cupid hunts by haugh and head,
By riverside and mere.
I walk, not seeing where I tread
And keep my heart with fear,
Sir, have an eye, on where you tread,
And keep your heart with fear,
For something lingers here;
A touch of April not yet dead,
In Autumn when the woods are red
And skies are grey and clear.

LXXVI

Light as my heart was long ago,
Now it is heavy enough;
Now that the weather is rough,
Now that the loud winds come and go
Winter is here with hail and snow,
Winter is sorry and gruff.
Light as last year's snow,
Where is my love? I do not know;
Life is a pitiful stuff,
Out with it—out with the snuff!
This is the sum of all I know,
Light as my heart was long ago.

LXXVII

GATHER ye roses while ye may,
Old time is still a-flying;
A world where beauty fleets away
   Is no world for denying.
Come lads and lasses, fall to play
   Lose no more time in sighing.

The very flowers you pluck to-day
To-morrow will be dying;
   And all the flowers are crying,
And all the leaves have tongues to say,—
   Gather ye roses while ye may.

LXXVIII

POEM FOR A CLASS RE-UNION

Whether we like it, or don't
   There's a sort of bond in the fact
That we all by one master [43] were taught,
   By one master were bullied and whackt.
And now all the more when we see
   Our class in so shrunken a state
And we, who were seventy-two,
   Diminished to seven or eight.

[43] Mr. D'Arcy Wentworth Thompson, whose private school in Edinburgh Stevenson attended, 1864-1867.

One has been married, and one
   Has taken to letters for bread;
Several are over the seas;
   And some I imagine are dead.
And that is the reason, you see,
   Why, as I have the honour to state,
We, who were seventy-two,
   Are now only seven or eight.

One took to heretical views,
   And one, they inform me, to drink;
Some construct fortunes in trade,
   Some starve in professions, I think.
But one way or other, alas!
   Through the culpable action of Fate
We, who were seventy-two,
   Are now shrunken to seven or eight.

So, whether we like it or not,
  Let us own there's a bond in the past,
And, since we were playmates at school,
  Continue good friends to the last.
The roll-book is closed in the room,
  The clackan is gone with the slate,
We, who were seventy-two,
  Are now only seven or eight.

We shall never, our books on our back,
  Trudge off in the morning again,
To the slide at the janitor's door,
  By the ambush of rods in the lane.
We shall never be sent for the tawse,
  Nor lose places for coming too late;
We shall never be seventy-two,
  Who are now but seven or eight!

We shall never have pennies for lunch,
  We shall never be strapped by Maclean,
We shall never take gentlemen down,
  Nor ever be schoolboys again.
But still for the sake of the past,
  For the love of the days of lang syne
The remnant of seventy-two
  Shall rally together to dine.

LXXIX

I saw red evening through the rain
Lower above the steaming plain;
I heard the hour strike small and still,
From the black belfry on the hill.

Thought is driven out of doors to-night
By bitter memory of delight;
The sharp constraint of finger tips,
Or the shuddering touch of lips.

I heard the hour strike small and still,
From the black belfry on the hill.
Behind me I could still look down
On the outspread monstrous town.

The sharp constraint of finger tips,
Or the shuddering touch of lips,
And all old memories of delight
Crowd upon my soul to-night.

Behind me I could still look down
On the outspread feverish town;
But before me, still and grey,
And lonely was the forward way.

LXXX

Last night we had a thunderstorm in style.
The wild lightning streaked the airs,
As though my God fell down a pair of stairs.
The thunder boomed and bounded all the while;
All cried and sat by water-side and stile,—
To mop our brow had been our chief of cares.
I lay in bed with a Voltairean smile,
The terror of good, simple guilty pairs,
And made this rondeau in ironic style,
Last night we had a thunderstorm in style.

Our God the Father fell down-stairs,
The stark blue lightning went its flight the
The very rain you might have heard a mile,—
The strenuous faithful buckled to their prayers.

LXXXI

O Lady fair and sweet
Arise and let us go
Where comes not rain or snow,
Excess of cold or heat,
To find a still retreat
By willowy valleys low
Where silent rivers flow.
There let us turn our feet
O lady fair and sweet,—
Far from the noisy street,
The doleful city row,
Far from the grimy street,
Where in the evening glow
The summer swallows meet,
The quiet mowers mow.
Arise and let us go,
O lady fair and sweet,

For here the loud winds blow,
Here drifts the blinding sleet.

LXXXII

If I had wings, my lady, like a dove
   I should not linger here,
But through the winter air toward my love,
   Fly swift toward my love, my fair,
If I had wings, my lady, like a dove.

If I had wings, my lady, like a dove,
   And knew the secrets of the air,
I should be gone, my lady, to my love,
   To kiss the sweet disparting of her hair,
If I had wings, my lady, like a dove.

If I had wings, my lady, like a dove,
   This hour should see my soul at rest,
Should see me safe, my lady, with my love,
   To kiss the sweet division of her breast,
If I had wings, my lady, like a dove.

For all is sweet, my lady, in my love;
   Sweet hair, sweet breast and sweeter eyes
That draw my soul, my lady, like a dove
   Drawn southward by the shining of the skies;
For all is sweet, my lady, in my love.

If I could die, my lady, with my love,
   Die, mouth to mouth, a splendid death,
I should take wing, my lady, like a dove,
   To spend upon her lips my all of breath,
If I could die, my lady, with my love.

LXXXIII

RONDELS

1

Far have you come, my lady, [44] from the town,
And far from all your sorrows, if you please,
To smell the good sea-winds and hear the seas,
And in green meadows lay your body down.

[44] Mrs. Stilwell afterwards became the wife of Sidney Colvin.

To find your pale face grow from pale to brown,
Your sad eyes growing brighter by degrees;
Far have you come, my lady, from the town,
And far from all your sorrows, if you please.

Here in this seaboard land of old renown,
In meadow grass go wading to the knees;
Bathe your whole soul a while in simple ease;
There is no sorrow but the sea can drown;
Far have you come, my lady, from the town.

2

Nous n'irons plus au bois

We'll walk the woods no more,
But stay beside the fire,
To weep for old desire
And things that are no more.
   The woods are spoiled and hoar,
The ways are full of mire;
We'll walk the woods no more,
But stay beside the fire.
   We loved, in days of yore,
Love, laughter, and the lyre.
Ah God, but death is dire,
And death is at the door—
We'll walk the woods no more.

3

Since I am sworn to live my life
And not to keep an easy heart,
Some men may sit and drink apart,
I bear a banner in the strife.

Some can take quiet thought to wife,
I am all day at *tierce* and *carte*,
Since I am sworn to live my life
And not to keep an easy heart.

I follow gaily to the fife,
Leave Wisdom bowed above a chart,
And Prudence brawling in the mart,
And dare Misfortune to the knife,
Since I am sworn to live my life.

LXXXIV

Eh, man Henley, you're a Don!
Man, but you're a devil at it!
This ye made an hour agone—
Tht!—like that—as tho' ye'd spat it,—
Eh, man Henley.

Better days will come anon
When you'll have your shoulders pattit,
And the whole round world, odd rat it!
Will cry out to cheer you on;
Eh, man Henley, you're a Don!

LXXXV

All night through, raves or broods
The fitful wind among the woods;
All night through, hark! the rain
Beats upon the window pane.

And still my heart is far away,
Still dwells in many a bygone day,
And still follows hope with [rainbow wing]
Adown the golden ways of spring.

In many a wood my fancy strays,
In many unforgotten Mays,
And still I feel the wandering—

LXXXVI

The rain is over and done;
I am aweary, dear, of love;
I look below and look above,
On russet maiden, rustling dame,
And love's so slow and time so long,
And hearts and eyes so blindly wrong,
I am half weary of my love,
And pray that life were done.

LXXXVII

There where the land of love,
Grown about by fragrant bushes,
Sunken in a winding valley,
   Where the clear winds blow
   And the shadows come and go,
   And the cattle stand and low
And the sheep bells and linnets
   Sing and tinkle musically.
Between the past and the future,
   Those two black infinities
     Between which our brief life
Flashes a moment and goes out.

LXXXVIII

Love is the very heart of spring;
   Flocks fall to loving on the lea
And wildfowl love upon the wing,
   When spring first enters like a sea.

When spring first enters like a sea
   Into the heart of everything,
Bestir yourselves religiously,
   Incense before love's altar bring.

Incense before love's altar bring,
   Flowers from the flowering hawthorn tree,
Flowers from the margin of the spring,
   For all the flowers are sweet to see.

Love is the very heart of spring;
   When spring first enters like a sea
Incense before love's altar bring,
   And flowers while flowers are sweet to see.

Bring flowers while flowers are sweet to see;
   Love is almighty, love's a King,
Incense before love's altar bring,
   Incense before love's altar bring.

Love's gifts are generous and free
   When spring first enters like a sea;
When spring first enters like a sea,
   The birds are all inspired to sing.

Love is the very heart of spring,
   The birds are all inspired to sing,
Love's gifts are generous and free;
   Love is almighty, love's a King.

LXXXIX

ON HIS PITIABLE TRANSFORMATION

I who was young so long,
   Young and alert and gay,
   Now that my hair is grey,
Begin to change my song.

Now I know right from wrong,
   Now I know *pay* and *pray*,
   I who was young so long,
Young and alert and gay.

Now I follow the throng,
Walk in the beaten way,
Hear what the elders say,
And own that I was wrong—
I who was young so long.

XC

   I who all the winter through,
Cherished other loves than you,
And kept hands with hoary policy in marriage-bed and pew;
   Now I know the false and true,
   For the earnest sun looks through,
And my old love comes to meet me in the dawning and the dew.

   Now the hedged meads renew
Rustic odour, smiling hue,
And the clean air shines and twinkles as the world goes wheeling through;
   And my heart springs up anew,
   Bright and confident and true,
And my old love comes to meet me in the dawning and the dew.

XCI

Love—what is love? A great and aching heart;
Wrung hands; and silence; and a long despair.
Life—what is life? Upon a moorland bare
To see love coming and see love depart.

XCII

Soon our friends perish,
Soon all we cherish
Fades as days darken—goes as flowers go.
   Soon in December
   Over an ember,
Lonely we hearken, as loud winds blow.

XCIII

As one who having wandered all night long
   In a perplexed forest, comes at length,
In the first hours, about the matin song,
   And when the sun uprises in his strength,
To the fringed margin of the wood, and sees,
   Gazing afar before him, many a mile
Of falling country, many fields and trees,
   And cities and bright streams and far-off Ocean's smile:—

I, O Melampus, halting, stand at gaze:
   I, liberated, look abroad on life,
Love, and distress, and dusty travelling ways,
   The steersman's helm, the surgeon's helpful knife,
On the lone ploughman's earth-upturning share,
   The revelry of cities and the sound
Of seas, and mountain-tops aloof in air,
   And of the circling earth the unsupported round:

I, looking, wonder: I, intent, adore;
   And, O Melampus, reaching forth my hands
In adoration, cry aloud and soar
   In spirit, high above the supine lands
And the low caves of mortal things, and flee
   To the last fields of the universe untrod,
Where is no man, nor any earth, nor sea,
   And the contented soul is all alone with God.

XCIV

Strange are the ways of men,
   And strange the ways of God!
We tread the mazy paths
   That all our fathers trod.

We tread them undismayed,
   And undismayed behold
The portents of the sky,
   The things that were of old.

The fiery stars pursue
   Their course in heav'n on high;
And round the 'leaguered town, [45]
   Crest-tossing heroes cry.

[45] Constantinople. In April 1877, Russia declared war on Turkey and within a year the Russian army was striking at Constantinople.

Crest-tossing heroes cry;
   And martial fifes declare
How small, to mortal minds,
   Is merely mortal care.

And to the clang of steel
   And cry of piercing flute
Upon the azure peaks
   A God shall plant his foot:

A God in arms shall stand,
   And seeing wide and far
The green and golden earth
   The killing tide of war,

He, with uplifted arm,
   Shall to the skies proclaim
The gleeful fate of man
   The noble road to fame!

XCV

   The Wind blew shrill and smart,
     And the wind awoke my heart
Again to go a-sailing o'er the sea,
     To hear the cordage moan
     And the straining timbers groan,
And to see the flying pennon lie a-lee.

O sailor of the fleet,
  It is time to stir the feet!
It's time to man the dingy and to row!
  It's lay your hand in mine
  And it's empty down the wine,
And it's drain a health to death before we go I

To death, my lads, we sail;
And it's death that blows the gale
And death that holds the tiller as we ride.
  For he's the king of all
  In the tempest and the squall,
And the ruler of the Ocean wild and wide!

XCVI

Man sails the deep a while;
  Loud runs the roaring tide;
  The seas are wild and wide;
O'er many a salt, o'er many a desert mile,
  The unchained breakers ride,
  The quivering stars beguile.

Hope bears the sole command;
  Hope, with unshaken eyes,
  Sees flaw and storm arise;
Hope, the good steersman, with unwearying hand,
  Steers, under changing skies,
  Unchanged toward the land.

O wind that bravely blows!
  O hope that sails with all
  Where stars and voices call!
O ship undaunted that for ever goes
  Where God, her admiral,
  His battle signal shows !

What though the seas and wind
  Far on the deep should whelm
  Colours and sails and helm?
There, too, you touch that port that you designed—
  There, in the mid-seas' realm,
  Shall you that haven find.

Well hast thou sailed: now die,
   To die is not to sleep.
   Still your true course you keep,
O sailor soul, still sailing for the sky;
   And fifty fathom deep
   Your colours still shall fly.

XCVII

The cock's clear voice into the clearer air
   Where westward far I roam, [46]
Mounts with a thrill of hope,
   Falls with a sigh of home.

[46] This poem was written on the train as Stevenson crossed America to join Mrs. Osborne whom he was soon to marry.

A rural sentry, he from farm and field
   The coming morn descries,
And, mankind's bugler, wakes
   The camp of enterprise.

He sings the morn upon the westward hills
   Strange and remote and wild;
He sings it in the land
   Where once I was a child.

He brings to me dear voices of the past
   The old land and the years:
My father calls for me,
   My weeping spirit hears.

Fife, fife, into the golden air, O bird,
   And sing the morning in;
For the old days are past
   And newer days begin.

XCVIII

Now when the number of my years [47]
Is all fulfilled, and I
From sedentary life
Shall rouse me up to die,
   Bury me low and let me lie
   Under the wide and starry sky.
   Joying to live, I joyed to die,
   Bury me low and let me lie.

[47] The earliest form (1879) of the famous poem, *Requiem*, published in 1887.

Clear was my soul, my deeds were free,
Honour was called my name,
I fell not back from fear
Nor followed after fame.
   Bury me low and let me lie
   Under the wide and starry sky.
   Joying to live, I joyed to die,
   Bury me low and let me lie.

Bury me low in valleys green
And where the milder breeze
Blows fresh along the stream,
Sings roundly in the trees—
   Bury me low and let me lie
   Under the wide and starry sky.
   Joying to live, I joyed to die,
   Bury me low and let me lie.

XCIX

What man may learn, what man may do,
Of right or wrong, of false or true,
While, skipper-like, his course he steers
Through nine and twenty mingled years,
Half misconceived and half forgot,
So much I know and practise not.

Old are the words of wisdom, old
The counsels of the wise and bold:
To close the ears, to check the tongue,
To keep the pining spirit young;
To act the right, to say the true,
And to be kind whate'er you do.

Thus we across the modern stage
Follow the wise of every age;
And, as oaks grow and rivers run
Unchanged in the unchanging sun,
So the eternal march of man
Goes forth on an eternal plan.

C

THE SUSQUEHANNA AND THE DELAWARE

TO SIDNEY COLVIN

  Of where or how, I nothing know;
    And why, I do not care;
    Enough if, even so,
  My travelling eyes, my travelling mind can go
By flood and field and hill, by wood and meadow fair,
Beside the Susquehanna and along the Delaware.

  I think, I hope, I dream no more
    The dreams of otherwhere,
    The cherished thoughts of yore;
  I have been changed from what I was before;
And drunk too deep perchance the lotus of the air,
Beside the Susquehanna and along the Delaware.

  Unweary, God me yet shall bring
    To lands of brighter air,
    Where I, now half a king,
  Shall with enfranchised spirit loudlier sing,
And wear a bolder front than that which now I wear
Beside the Susquehanna and along the Delaware.

CI

If I could arise and travel away
Over the plains of the night and the day,
I should arrive at a land at last
Where all of our sins and sorrows are past
And we're done with the Ten Commandments.

The name of the land I must not tell;
Green is the grass and cool the well:
Virtue is easy to find and to keep,
And the sinner may lie at his pleasure and sleep
By the side of the Ten Commandments.

Income and honour, and glory and gold
Grow on the bushes all over the wold;
And if ever a man has a touch of remorse,
He eats of the flower of the golden gorse,
And to hell with the Ten Commandments.

He goes to church in his Sunday's best;
He eats and drinks with perfect zest;
And whether he lives in heaven or hell
Is more than you or I can tell;
But he's DONE with the Ten Commandments.

CII

Good old ale, mild or pale,
India ale and Burton,
Give me a vat to swim a whale.
When far along the verdant dale
   The far-off spire appears,
The mind reverts to Burton's ale
And dreams of different beers.

CIII

Nay, but I fancy somehow, year by year
The hard road waxing easier to my feet;
   Nay, but I fancy as the seasons fleet
   I shall grow ever dearer to my dear.
Hope is so strong that it has conquered fear;
   Love follows, crowned and glad for fear's defeat.
   Down the long future I behold us, sweet,
Pass, and grow ever dearer and more near
Pass and go onward into the mild land
   Where the blond harvests slumber all the noon,
   And the pale sky bends downward to the sea;
Pass, and go forward, ever hand in hand,
   Till all the plain be quickened with the moon,
   And the lit windows beckon o'er the lea.

CIV

My wife and I, in one romantic cot,
The world forgetting, by the world forgot,
High as the gods upon Olympus dwell,
Pleased with the things we have, and pleased as well
To wait in hope for those which we have not.
She vows in ardour for a horse to trot;
I pledge my votive powers upon a yacht;
Which shall be first remembered, who can tell,—
   My wife or I?

Harvests of flowers o'er all our garden-plot,
She dreams; and I to enrich a darker spot,—
My unprovided cellar; both to swell
Our narrow cottage huge as a hotel,
That portly friends may come and share our lot—
   My wife and I.

CV

At morning on the garden seat
I dearly love to drink and eat;
To drink and eat, to drink and sing,
At morning in the time of spring.
In winter honest men retire
And sup their possets by the fire;
And when the spring comes round again, you see,
The garden breakfast pleases me.
The morning star that melts on high,
The fires that cleanse the changing sky,
The dew and perfumes all declare
It is the hour to banish care.
The air that smells so new and sweet,
All put me in the cue to eat,
   A pot at five, a crust at four,
   At half past six a pottle more.

CVI

Small is the trust when love is green
   In sap of early years;
A little thing steps in between
   And kisses turn to tears.

A while—and see how love be grown
   In loveliness and power!
A while, it loves the sweets alone,
   But next it loves the sour.

A little love is none at all
   That wanders or that fears;
A hearty love dwells still at call
   To kisses or to tears.

Such then be mine, my love, to give
   And such be yours to take:—
A faith to hold, a life to live,
   For loving kindness' sake:—

Should you be sad, should you be gay,
   Or should you prove unkind,
A love to hold the growing way
   And keep the helping mind:—

A love to turn the laugh on care
   When wrinkled care appears,
And, with an equal will, to share
   Your kisses and your tears.

CVII

Know you the river near to Grez,
   A river deep and clear?
Among the lilies all the way,
That ancient river runs to-day
   From snowy weir to weir.

Old as the Rhine of great renown,
   She hurries clear and fast,
She runs amain by field and town
From south to north, from up to down,
   To present on from past.

The love I hold was borne by her;
   And now, though far away,
My lonely spirit hears the stir
Of water round the starling spur
   Beside the bridge at Grez.

So may that love forever hold
   In life an equal pace;
So may that love grow never old,
But, clear and pure and fountain-cold,
    Go on from grace to grace.

CVIII

IT'S forth across the roaring foam, and on towards the west,
It's many a lonely league from home, o'er many a mountain crest,
From where the dogs of Scotland call the sheep around the fold,
To where the flags are flying beside the Gates of Gold.

Where all the deep-sea galleons ride that come to bring the corn,
Where falls the fog at eventide and blows the breeze at morn;
It's there that I was sick and sad, alone and poor and cold,
In yon distressful city beside the Gates of Gold.

I slept as one that nothing knows; but far along my way,
Before the morning God rose and planned the coming day;
Afar before me forth he went, as through the sands of old,
And chose the friends to help me beside the Gates of Gold.

I have been near, I have been far, my back's been at the wall,
Yet aye and ever shone the star to guide me through it all:
The love of God, the help of man, they both shall make me bold
Against the gates of darkness as beside the Gates of Gold.

CIX

DEDICATION [48]

Here, from the forelands of the tideless sea,
Behold and take my offering unadorned.
In the Pacific air it sprang; it grew
Among the silence of the Alpine air;
In Scottish heather blossomed; and at last
By that unshapen sapphire, in whose face
Spain, Italy, France, Algiers, and Tunis view
Their introverted mountains, came to fruit.
Back now, my Booklet! on the diving ship,
And posting on the rails, to home return,—
Home, and the friends whose honouring name you bear.

[48] On the fly-leaf of the copy of *The Silverado Squatters* sent to Virgil Williams and Dora Norton Williams, to whom it was dedicated.

CX

FAREWELL

Farewell, and when forth
I through the Golden Gates to Golden Isles
Steer without smiling, through the sea of smiles,
Isle upon isle, in the seas of the south,
Isle upon island, sea upon sea,
Why should I sail, why should the breeze?
I have been young, and I have counted friends.
A hopeless sail I spread, too late, too late.
Why should I from isle to isle
Sail, a hopeless sailor?

CXI

THE FINE PACIFIC ISLANDS

(HEARD IN A PUBLIC-HOUSE AT ROTHERHITHE)

The jolly English Yellowboy
   Is a 'ansome coin when new,
The Yankee Double-eagle
   Is large enough for two.
O, these may do for seaport towns,
   For cities these may do;
But the dibbs that takes the Hislands
   Are the dollars of Peru:
     O, the fine Pacific Hislands,
     O, the dollars of Peru!

It's there we buy the cocoanuts
   Mast 'eaded in the blue;
It's there we trap the lasses
   All waiting for the crew;
It's there we buy the trader's rum
   What bores a seaman through....
In the fine Pacific Hislands
   With the dollars of Peru:
     In the fine Pacific Hislands
     With the dollars of Peru!

Now, messmates, when my watch is up,
  And I am quite broached to,
I'll give a tip to 'Evving
  Of the 'ansome thing to do:
Let 'em just refit this sailor-man
  And launch him off anew
To cruise among the Hislands
  With the dollars of Peru:
    In the fine Pacific Hislands
    With the dollars of Peru!

CXII

TOPICAL SONG [49]

(TO THE TUNE OF "OLD BLACK JOE")

[49] Written during the cruise of the *Janet Nicholls* when Stevenson first met Jock Buckland, the original of "Tommy Haddon."

When, where, or how,
  It matters not a damn;
East, west, or south,
  Mariki or Apaman,
Land, only land, land me
  With my little pack,
Land on any mortal island,
  Poor Tin [50] Jack!

[50] "Tin" is "Mr." in Line Islands.

  Chorus

I'm landing, I'm landing,
  Landing with my little pack.
I hear your husky voices calling,
  Poor Tin Jack!

Much they may care
  For the dangers of my fate.
Martin's at home
  And the cow-tub's at the gate.
False nose on face
  Snowy wig on head and back.
Oh what a moving sight to see is
  Poor Tin Jack!

Bright rolls the sea
   On a hundred lovely shores.
Each'll do for me
   And my deteriorated stores.
Land, only land,
   Land me and my little pack,
And leave with Billy Jones's Cousin
   Poor Tin Jack!

Hear my last word
   Now when I'm about to land.
Drink wisdom in
   As we shake the parting hand.
No use to talk
   Or to argue for and back.
Approx-imacy forms the aim of
   Poor Tin Jack!

Long at your board
   'Mid the quibblers I was dumb.
Quaffing the wine,
   Laying on the little tum.
Now let your ship
   Square away along her track,
The flushed, fantastic quibblers leaving
   Poor Tin Jack!

CXIII

STUDENT SONG

They say that at the core of it
   This life is all regret;
But we've scarce yet learned the lore of it,
   We're only youngsters yet.
We only ask some more of it, some more of it,
   We only ask some more of it
—The less we're like to get!

Though ill may be the close of it,
   It's fair enough at morn;
And the manner to dispose of it
Is just to pluck the rose of it
   When first the rose is born.
Is first to pluck the rose of it, the rose of it, the rose of it,
   Is just to pluck the rose of it,
     The de'il may take the thorn!

The opinions of the old of it
    Depict a doleful land;
For the guide-books that are sold of it,
    The ill that we are told of it,
    Would make Columbus stand.
But come let's take a hold of it, a hold of it, a hold of it,
    But come let's take a hold of it
    With Alexander's hand.

When sages call the roll of it
    How sad their looks appear!
    But there's fire in every coal of it
    And hope is in the soul of it
    And never a word of fear.
So love we then the whole of it, the whole of it, the whole of it,
    So love we then the whole of it
    For as long as we are here.

CXIV

AN ENGLISH BREEZE

Up with the sun, the breeze arose,
Across the talking corn she goes,
And smooth she rustles far and wide
Through all the voiceful countryside.

Through all the land her tale she tells;
She spins, she tosses, she compels
The kites, the clouds, the windmill sails
And all the trees in all the dales.

God calls us, and the day prepares
With nimble, gay and gracious airs:
And from Penzance to Maidenhead
The roads last night He watered.

God calls us from inglorious ease,
Forth and to travel with the breeze
While, swift and singing, smooth and strong
She gallops by the fields along.

CXV

TO MISS CORNISH

They tell me, lady, that to-day
   On that unknown Australian strand—
Some time ago, so far away—
   Another lady joined the band.

She joined the company of those
   Lovelily dowered, nobly planned,
Who, smiling, still forgive their foes
   And keep their friends in close command.

She, lady, as I learn, was one
   Among the many rarely good;
And destined still to be a sun
   Through every dark and rainy mood;—

She, as they told me, far had come,
   By sea and land, o'er many a rood:—
Admired by all, beloved by some,
   She was yourself, I understood.

But, compliment apart and free
   From all constraint of verses, may
Goodness and honour, grace and glee,
   Attend you ever on your way—

Up to the measure of your will,
   Beyond all power of mine to say—
As she and I desire you still,
   Miss Cornish, on your natal day.

CXVI

TO ROSABELLE

When my young lady has grown great and staid,
And in long raiment wondrously arrayed,
She may take pleasure with a smile to know
How she delighted men-folk long ago.
For her long after, then, this tale I tell
Of the two fans and fairy Rosabelle.
Hot was the day; her weary sire and I
Sat in our chairs companionably nigh,
Each with a headache sat her sire and I.

Instant the hostess waked: she viewed the scene,
Divined the giants' languor by their mien,
And with hospitable care
Tackled at once an Atlantean chair.
Her pigmy stature scarce attained the seat—
She dragged it where she would, and with her feet
Surmounted; thence, a Phaeton launched, she crowned
The vast plateau of the piano, found
And culled a pair of fans; wherewith equipped,
Our mountaineer back to the level slipped;
And being landed, with considerate eyes,
Betwixt her elders dealt her double prize;
The small to me, the greater to her sire.
As painters now advance and now retire
Before the growing canvas, and anon
Once more approach and put the climax on:
So she awhile withdrew, her piece she viewed—
For half a moment half supposed it good—
Spied her mistake, nor sooner spied than ran
To remedy; and with the greater fan,
In gracious better thought, equipped the guest.

From ill to well, from better on to best,
Arts move; the homely, like the plastic kind;
And high ideals fired that infant mind.
Once more she backed, once more a space apart
Considered and reviewed her work of art:
Doubtful at first, and gravely yet awhile;
Till all her features blossomed in a smile.
And the child, waking at the call of bliss,
To each she ran, and took and gave a kiss.

CXVII

As in their flight the birds of song
Halt here and there in sweet and sunny dales,
But halt not overlong;
The time one rural song to sing
They pause; then following bounteous gales
Steer forward on the wing:
Sun-servers they, from first to last,
Upon the sun they wait
To ride the sailing blast.

So he awhile in our contested state,
Awhile abode, not longer—for his Sun—
Mother we say, no tenderer name we know—
With whose diviner glow
His early days had shone,
Now to withdraw her radiance had begun.
Or lest a wrong I say, not she withdrew,
But the loud stream of men day after day
And great dust columns of the common way
Between them grew and grew:
And he and she for evermore might yearn,
But to the spring the rivulets not return
Nor to the bosom comes the child again.

And he (O may we fancy so!),
He, feeling time forever flow
And flowing bear him forth and far away
From that dear ingle where his life began
And all his treasure lay—
He, waxing into man,
And ever farther, ever closer wound
In this obstreperous world's ignoble round,
From that poor prospect turned his face away.

CXVIII

PRAYER

I ask good things that I detest,
    With speeches fair;
Heed not, I pray Thee, Lord, my breast,
    But hear my prayer.

I say ill things I would not say—
    Things unaware:
Regard my breast, Lord, in Thy day,
    And not my prayer.

My heart is evil in Thy sight:
    My good thoughts flee:
O Lord, I cannot wish aright—
    Wish Thou for me.

O bend my words and acts to Thee,
    However ill,
That I, whate'er I say or be,
    May serve Thee still.

O let my thoughts abide in Thee
    Lest I should fall:
Show me Thyself in all I see,
    Thou Lord of all.

CXIX

THE PIPER

Again I hear you piping, for I know the tune so well,—
    You rouse the heart to wander and be free,
Tho' where you learned your music, not the God of song can tell,
    For you pipe the open highway and the sea.
O piper, lightly footing, lightly piping on your way,
    Tho' your music thrills and pierces far and near,
I tell you you had better pipe to someone else to-day,
    For you cannot pipe my fancy from my dear.

You sound the note of travel through the hamlet and the town;
    You would lure the holy angels from on high;
And not a man can hear you, but he throws the hammer down
    And is off to see the countries ere he die.
But now no more I wander, now unchanging here I stay;
    By my love, you find me safely sitting here:
And pipe you ne'er so sweetly, till you pipe the hills away,
    You can never pipe my fancy from my dear.

CXX

EPISTLE TO ALBERT DEW-SMITH

Figure me to yourself, I pray—
    A man of my peculiar cut—
Apart from dancing and deray, [51]
    Into an Alpine valley shut;

[51] "The whole front of the house was lighted, and there were pipes and fiddles, and as much dancing and deray within as used to be in Sir Robert's house at Pace and Yule, and such high seasons."—See *Wandering Willie's Tale* in *Redgauntlet*, borrowed perhaps from *Christ's Kirk of the Green*.

Shut in a kind of damned Hotel,
    Discountenanced by God and man;
The food?—Sir, you would do as well
    To cram your belly full of bran.

The company? Alas, the day
   That I should dwell with such a crew,
With devil anything to say,
   Nor any one to say it to!

The place? Although they call it Platz,
   I will be bold and state my view;
It's not a place at all—and that's
   The bottom verity, my Dew.

There are, as I will not deny,
   Innumerable inns; a road;
Several Alps indifferent high;
   The snow's inviolable abode;

Eleven English parsons, all
   Entirely inoffensive; four
True human beings—what I call
   Human—the deuce a cipher more;

A climate of surprising worth;
   Innumerable dogs that bark;
Some air, some weather, and some earth;
   A native race—God save the mark!—

A race that works, yet cannot work,
   Yodels, but cannot yodel right,
Such as, unhelp'd, with rusty dirk,
   I vow that I could wholly smite.

A river that from morn to night
   Down all the valley plays the fool;
Not once she pauses in her flight,
   Nor knows the comfort of a pool;

But still keeps up, by straight or bend,
   The selfsame pace she hath begun—
Still hurry, hurry, to the end—
   Good God, is that the way to run?

If I a river were, I hope
   That I should better realise
The opportunities and scope
   Of that romantic enterprise.

I should not ape the merely strange,
   But aim besides at the divine;
And continuity and change
   I still should labour to combine.

Here should I gallop down the race,
   Here charge the sterling like a bull;
There, as a man might wipe his face,
   Lie, pleased and panting, in a pool.

But what, my Dew, in idle mood,
   What prate I, minding not my debt?
What do I talk of bad or good?
   The best is still a cigarette.

Me whether evil fate assault,
   Or smiling providences crown—
Whether on high the eternal vault
   Be blue, or crash with thunder down—

I judge the best, whate'er befall,
   Is still to sit on one's behind,
And, having duly moistened all,
   Smoke with an unperturbed mind.

CXXI

Of schooners, Islands and Maroons,
   And Buccaneers and Buried Gold,
And torches red and rising moons,
   If all the old romance retold
Exactly in the ancient way,
   Can please, as me they pleased of old,
The wiser youngster of to-day—
So be it, and fall on! If not,—
   If all the boys on better things
Have set their spirits and forgot—
So be it, and fall on! If not,—
   If all the boys on solid food
Have set their fancies, and forgot
   Kingston and Ballantyne the brave
And Cooper of the land and wave,
   So be it also; and may I
And my late-born piratic brood
   Unread beside the ancients lie!
So be it and fall on! If not,—
   If studied youth no longer crave,—

Their ancients' appetites forgot,—
   Kingston and Ballantyne the brave
For Cooper of the sea and wood—
   So be it also; and may I
And all my pirates share the grave
   Where these and their creations lie.

CXXII

TO MRS. MACMARLAND

IN *Schnee der Alpen*—so it runs
   To those divine accords—and here
We dwell in Alpine snows and suns,
   A motley crew, for half the year:
A motley crew, we dwell to taste—
   A shivering band in hope and fear—
That sun upon the snowy waste,
   That Alpine ether cold and clear.

Up from the laboured plains, and up
   From low sea-levels, we arise
To drink of that diviner cup
   The rarer air, the clearer skies;
For, as the great, old, godly King
   From mankind's turbid valley cries,
So all we mountain-lovers sing:
   I to the hills will lift mine eyes.

The bells that ring, the peaks that climb,
   The frozen snow's unbroken curd
Might yet revindicate in rhyme
   The pauseless stream, the absent bird.
In vain—for to the deeps of life
   You, lady, you my heart have stirred;
And since you say you love my life,
   Be sure I love you for the word.

Of kindness, here I nothing say—
   Such loveless kindnesses there are
In that grimacing, common way,
   That old, unhonoured social war.
Love but my dog and love my love,
   Adore with me a common star—
I value not the rest above
   The ashes of a bad cigar.

CXXIII

Yes, I remember, and still remember wailing
Wind in the clouds and rainy sea-horizon,
Empty and lit with low, nocturnal glimmer;
How in the strong, deep-plunging, transatlantic
Emigrant ship we sang our songs in chorus.
Piping, the gull flew by, the roaring billows
Yawned and resounded round the mighty vessel;
Infinite uproar, endless contradiction;
Yet over all our chorus rose reminding
Wanderers here at sea of unforgotten
Homes and undying, old, memorial loves.

Here in the strong, deep-plunging transatlantic
Emigrant ship the waves arose gigantic;
Piping the gull flew by, the roaring billows
Rose and appeared before the eye like pillows.
Piping the gull flew by, the roaring waves,
Rose and appeared from subter-ocean caves,
And as across the smoothing sea we roam,
Still and anon we sang our songs of home.

Brown in his haste demanded this from me;
I in my leisure made the present verse.

CXXIV

TALES OF ARABIA

YES, friend, I own these tales of Arabia
Smile not, as smiled their flawless originals,
Age-old but yet untamed, for ages
Pass and the magic is undiminished.

Thus, friend, the tales of the old Camaralzaman,
Ayoub, the Slave of Love, or the Calendars,
   Blind-eyed and ill-starred royal scions,
    Charm us in age as they charmed in childhood.

Fair ones, beyond all numerability,
Beam from the palace, beam on humanity,
   Bright-eyed, in truth, yet soul-less houris
    Offering pleasure and only pleasure.

Thus they, the venal Muses Arabian,
Unlike, indeed, the nobler divinities,
   Greek Gods or old time-honoured muses,
   Easily proffer unloved caresses.

Lost, lost, the man who mindeth the minstrelsy;
Since still, in sandy, glittering pleasances,
   Cold, stony fruits, gem-like but quite in-
   Edible, flatter and wholly starve him.

CXXV

Behold, as goblins dark of mien
   And portly tyrants dyed with crime
Change, in the transformation scene,
   At Christmas, in the pantomime,

Instanter, at the prompter's cough,
   The fairy bonnets them, and they
Throw their abhorred carbuncles off
   And blossom like the flowers in May.

—So mankind, to angelic eyes,
   So, through the scenes of life below,
In life's ironical disguise,
   A travesty of man, ye go:

But fear not: ere the curtain fall,
   Death in the transformation scene
Steps forward from her pedestal,
   Apparent, as the fairy Queen;

And coming, frees you in a trice
   From all your lendings—lust of fame,
Ungainly virtue, ugly vice,
   Terror and tyranny and shame.

So each, at last himself, for good
   In that dear country lays him down,
At last beloved and understood
   And pure in feature and renown.

CXXVI

Still I love to rhyme, and still more, rhyming, to wander
   Far from the commoner way;
Old-time trills and falls by the brook-side still do I ponder,
   Dreaming to-morrow to-day.

Come here, come, revive me, Sun-God, teach me, Apollo,
   Measures descanted before;
Since I ancient verses, I emulous follow,
   Prints in the marbles of yore.

Still strange, strange, they sound in old-young raiment invested,
   Songs for the brain to forget—
Young song-birds elate to grave old temples benested
   Piping and chirruping yet.

Thoughts? No thought has yet unskilled attempted to flutter
   Trammelled so vilely in verse;
He who writes but aims at fame and his bread and his butter,
   Won with a groan and a curse.

CXXVII

Long time I lay in little ease
   Where, placed by the Turanian,
Marseilles, the many-masted, sees
   The blue Mediterranean.

Now songful in the hour of sport,
   Now riotous for wages,
She camps around her ancient port,
   As ancient of the ages.

Algerian airs through all the place
   Unconquerably sally;
Incomparable women pace
   The shadows of the alley.

And high o'er dark and graving yard
   And where the sky is paler,
The golden virgin of the guard
   Shines, beckoning the sailor.

She hears the city roar on high,
   Thief, prostitute, and banker;
She sees the masted vessels lie
   Immovably at anchor.

She sees the snowy islets dot
   The sea's immortal azure,
And If, that castellated spot,
   Tower, turret, and embrasure.

Here Dantés [52] pined; and here to-day
   Behold me his successor:
For here imprisoned long I lay
   In pledge for a professor.

[52] *Dantès* and *Château d'If* refer to the *Monte Cristo* of the elder Dumas.

CXXVIII

Flower god, god of the spring, beautiful, bountiful,
Cold-dyed shield in the sky, lover of versicles,
   Here I wander in April
   Cold, grey-headed; and still to my
Heart, Spring comes with a bound, Spring the deliverer,
Spring, song-leader in woods, chorally resonant;
   Spring, flower-planter in meadows,
   Child-conductor in willowy
Fields deep dotted with bloom, daisies and crocuses:
Here that child from his heart drinks of eternity:
   O child, happy are children!
   She still smiles on their innocence,
She, dear mother in God, fostering violets,
Fills earth full of her scents, voices and violins:
   Thus one cunning in music
   Wakes old chords in the memory:
Thus fair earth in the Spring leads her performances.
One more touch of the bow, smell of the virginal
   Green—one more, and my bosom
   Feels new life with an ecstasy.

CXXIX

Come, my beloved, hear from me
Tales of the woods or open sea.
Let our aspiring fancy rise
A wren's flight higher toward the skies;
Or far from cities, brown and bare,

Play at the least in open air.
In all the tales men hear us tell
Still let the unfathomed ocean swell,
Or shallower forest sound abroad
Below the lonely stars of God;
In all, let something still be done,
Still in a corner shine the sun,
Slim-ankled maids be fleet of foot,
Nor man disown the rural flute.
Still let the hero from the start
In honest sweat and beats of heart
Push on along the untrodden road
For some inviolate abode.
Still, O beloved, let me hear
The great bell beating far and near—
The odd, unknown, enchanted gong
That on the road hales men along,
That from the mountain calls afar,
That lures a vessel from a star,
And with a still, aerial sound
Makes all the earth enchanted ground.
Love, and the love of life and act
Dance, live and sing through all our furrowed tract;
Till the great God enamoured gives
To him who reads, to him who lives,
That rare and fair romantic strain
That whoso hears must hear again.

CXXX

Since years ago for evermore
My cedar ship I drew to shore;
And to the road and riverbed
And the green, nodding reeds, I said
Mine ignorant and last farewell:
Now with content at home I dwell,
And now divide my sluggish life
Betwixt my verses and my wife:
In vain; for when the lamp is lit
And by the laughing fire I sit,
Still with the tattered atlas spread
Interminable roads I tread.

CXXXI

FOR RICHMOND'S GARDEN WALL

When Thomas [53] set this tablet here,
Time laughed at the vain chanticleer;
And ere the moss had dimmed the stone,
Time had defaced that garrison.
Now I in turn keep watch and ward
In my red house, in my walled yard
Of sunflowers, sitting here at ease
With friends and my bright canvases.
But hark, and you may hear quite plain
Time's chuckled laughter in the lane.

[53] Identity not known.

CXXXII

HERE LIES EROTION

Mother and sire, to you do I commend
Tiny Erotion, who must now descend,
A child, among the shadows, and appear
Before hell's bandog and hell's gondolier.
Of six hoar winters she had felt the cold,
But lacked six days of being six years old.
Now she must come, all playful, to that place
Where the great ancients sit with reverend face;
Now lisping, as she used, of whence she came,
Perchance she names and stumbles at my name.
O'er these so fragile bones, let there be laid
A plaything for a turf; and for that maid
That ran so lightly footed in her mirth
Upon thy breast—lie lightly, mother earth!

CXXXIII

TO PRIAPUS

Lo, in thy green enclosure here,
Let not the ugly or the old appear,
Divine Priapus; but with leaping tread
The schoolboy, and the golden head
Of the slim filly twelve years old—
Let these to enter and to steal be bold!

CXXXIV

Aye, mon, it's true; I'm no' that weel,
  Close prisoner to my lord the de'il;
As weak's a bit o' aipple peel,
  Or ingan parin',
Packed like a codfish in a creel,
  I lie disparin'.

Mon, it's a cur-ous thing to think
How bodies sleep and eat and drink;
I'm no' that weel, but micht be waur
An' doubt na mony bodies are.

CXXV

Hail, [54] guest, and enter freely! All you see
Is, for your momentary visit, yours; and we
Who welcome you are but the guests of God,
And know not our departure.

[54] These verses and the next are proposed inscriptions for Stevenson's new house, "Skerryvore," presented to him and his wife by his father.

CXXXVI

Lo, now, my guest, if aught amiss were said,
Forgive it and dismiss it from your head.
For me, for you, for all, to close the date,
Pass now the ev'ning sponge across the slate;
And to that spirit of forgiveness keep
Which is the parent and the child of sleep.

CXXXVII

So live, so love, so use that fragile hour,
That when the dark hand of the shining power
Shall one from other, wife or husband, take,
The poor survivor may not weep and wake.

CXXXVIII

Before this little gift was come
The little owner had made haste for home;
And from the door of where the eternal dwell,
Looked back on human things and smiled farewell.
O may this grief remain the only one!
O may our house be still a garrison
Of smiling children, and for evermore
The tune of little feet be heard along the floor!

CXXXIX

Go, little book—the ancient phrase
And still the daintiest—go your ways,
My Otto, over sea and land,
Till you shall come to Nelly's [55] hand.

[55] To Nelly Sanchez, his sister-in-law, Stevenson dedicated *Prince Otto*. He sent a copy of the book to her and with it these verses.

How shall I your Nelly know?
By her blue eyes and her black brow,
By her fierce and slender look,
And by her goodness, little book!

What shall I say when I come there?
You shall speak her soft and fair:
See—you shall say—the love they send
To greet their unforgotten friend!

Giant Adulpho you shall sing
The next, and then the cradled king:
And the four corners of the roof
Then kindly bless; and to your perch aloof,
Where Balzac all in yellow dressed
And the dear Webster of the west
Encircle the prepotent throne
Of Shakespeare and of Calderon,
Shall climb an upstart.

                    There with these,
You shall give ear to breaking seas
And windmills turning in the breeze,
A distant undetermined din
Without; and you shall hear within
The blazing and the bickering logs,
The crowing child, the yawning dogs,
And ever agile, high and low,
Our Nelly going to and fro.

There shall you all silent sit,
Till, when perchance the lamp is lit
And the day's labour done, she takes
Poor Otto down, and, warming for our sakes,
Perchance beholds, alive and near,
Our distant faces reappear.

CXL

My love was warm; for that I crossed
   The mountains and the sea,
Nor counted that endeavour lost
   That gave my love to me.

If that indeed were love at all,
   As still, my love, I trow,
By what dear name am I to call
   The bond that holds me now

CXLI

Come, my little children, here are songs for you;
Some are short and some are long, and all, all are new.
You must learn to sing them very small and clear,
Very true to time and tune and pleasing to the ear.

Mark the note that rises, mark the notes that fall,
Mark the time when broken, and the swing of it all.
So when night is come, and you have gone to bed,
All the songs you love to sing shall echo in your head.

CXLII

Home from the daisied meadows, where you linger yet—
Home, golden-headed playmate, ere the sun is set;
For the dews are falling fast
And the night has come at last.
Home with you, home and lay your little head at rest,
Safe, safe, my little darling, on your mother's breast.
Lullaby, darling; your mother is watching you;
she'll be your guardian and shield.
Lullaby, slumber, my darling, till morning be
bright upon mountain and field.
Long, long the shadows fall.
All white and smooth at home your little bed is laid.
All round your head be angels.

CXLIII

Early in the morning I hear on your piano
You (at least, I guess it's you) proceed to learn to play.
Worthy little minds should take and tackle their piano,
While the birds are singing in the morning of the day.

CXLIV

FAIR Isle at Sea [56]—thy lovely name
Soft in my ear like music came.
That sea I loved, and once or twice
I touched at isles of Paradise.

[56] Samoa.

CXLV

Loud and low in the chimney
    The squalls suspire;
Then like an answer dwindles
    And glows the fire,
And the chamber reddens and darkens
    In time like taken breath.
Near by the sounding chimney
    The youth apart
Hearkens with changing colour
    And leaping heart,
And hears in the coil of the tempest
    The voice of love and death. [57]
Love on high in the flute-like

And tender notes
Sounds as from April meadows
  And hillside cotes;
But the deep wood wind in the chimney
  Utters the slogan of death.

[57] The war among the Samoa tribes.

CXLVI

1

I love to be warm by the red fireside,
  I love to be wet with rain:
I love to be welcome at lamplit doors,
  And leave the doors again.

2

At last she comes, O never more
In this dear patience of my pain
To leave me lonely as before,
Or leave my soul alone again.

CXLVII

Mine eyes were swift to know thee, [58] and my heart
As swift to love. I did become at once
Thine wholly, thine unalterably, thine
In honourable service, pure intent,
Steadfast excess of love and laughing care:
And as she was, so am, and so shall be.
I knew thee helpful, knew thee true, knew thee
And Pity bedfellows: I heard thy talk
With answerable throbbings. On the stream,
Deep, swift, and clear, the lilies floated; fish
Through the shadows ran. There, thou and I
Read Kindness in our eyes and closed the match.

[58] His wife.

CXLVIII

Fixed is the doom; and to the last of years
Teacher and taught, friend, lover, parent, child,
Each walks, though near, yet separate; each beholds
His dear ones shine beyond him like the stars.
We also, love, forever dwell apart;
With cries approach, with cries behold the gulph,
The Unvaulted; as two great eagles that do wheel in air
Above a mountain, and with screams confer,
Far heard athwart the cedars.

                Yet the years
Shall bring us ever nearer; day by day
Endearing, week by week, till death at last
Dissolve that long divorce. By faith we love,
Not knowledge; and by faith, though far removed,
Dwell as in perfect nearness, heart to heart.

                We but excuse
Those things we merely are; and to our souls
A brave deception cherish.
So from unhappy war a man returns
Unfearing, or the seaman from the deep;
So from cool night and woodlands to a feast
May someone enter, and still breathe of dews,
And in her eyes still wear the dusky night.

CXLIX

Men are Heaven's piers; they evermore
Unwearying bear the skyey floor;
Man's theatre they bear with ease,
Unfrowning cariatides!
I, for my wife, the sun uphold,
Or, dozing, strike the seasons cold.
She, on her side, in fairy-wise
Deals in diviner mysteries,
By spells to make the fuel burn
And keep the parlour warm, to turn
Water to wine, and stones to bread,
By her unconquered hero-head.
A naked Adam, naked Eve,
Alone the primal bower we weave;
Sequestered in the seas of life,
A Crusoe couple, man and wife,
With all our good, with all our will,

Our unfrequented isle we fill;
And victor in day's petty wars,
Each for the other lights the stars.
Come then, my Eve, and to and fro
Let us about our garden go;
And, grateful-hearted, hand in hand
Revisit all our tillage land,
And marvel at our strange estate,
For hooded ruin at the gate
Sits watchful, and the angels fear
To see us tread so boldly here.
Meanwhile, my Eve, with flower and grass
Our perishable days we pass;
Far more the thorn observe—and see
How our enormous sins go free—
Nor less admire, beside the rose,
How far a little virtue goes.

CL

SPRING CAROL

When loud by landside streamlets gush,
And clear in the greenwood quires the thrush,
With sun on the meadows
And songs in the shadows
  Comes again to me
    The gift of the tongues of the lea,
The gift of the tongues of meadows.

Straightway my olden heart returns
And dances with the dancing burns;
  It sings with the sparrows;
  To the rain and the (grimy) barrows
    Sings my heart aloud—
    To the silver-bellied cloud,
To the silver rainy arrows.

It bears the song of the skylark down,
And it hears the singing of the town;
  And youth on the highways
  And lovers in byways
    Follows and sees:
    And hearkens the song of the leas
And sings the songs of the highways.

So when the earth is alive with gods,
And the lusty ploughman breaks the sod,
   And the grass sings in the meadows,
   And the flowers smile in the shadows,
     Sits my heart at ease,
     Hearing the song of the leas,
Singing the songs of the meadows.

CLI

To what shall I compare her,
   That is as fair as she?
For she is fairer—fairer
   Than the sea.
What shall be likened to her,
   The sainted of my youth?
For she is truer—truer
   Than the truth.

As the stars are from the sleeper,
   Her heart is hid from me;
For she is deeper—deeper
   Than the sea.
Yet in my dreams I view her
   Flush rosy with new ruth—
Dreams! Ah, may these prove truer
   Than the truth.

CLII

When the sun comes after rain
   And the bird is in the blue,
The girls go down the lane
   Two by two.

When the sun comes after shadow
   And the singing of the showers,
The girls go up the meadow,
   Fair as flowers.

When the eve comes dusky red
   And the moon succeeds the sun,
The girls go home to bed
   One by one.

And when life draws to its even
   And the day of man is past,
They shall all go home to heaven,
   Home at last.

CLIII

Late, O miller,
The birds are silent,
The darkness falls.
In the house the lights are lighted.
See, in the valley they twinkle,
The lights of home.
Late, O lovers,
The night is at hand;
Silence and darkness
Clothe the land.

CLIV

To friends at home, the lone, the admired, the lost
The gracious old, the lovely young, to May
   The fair, December the beloved,
These from my blue horizon and green isles,
These from this pinnacle of distances I,
   The unforgetful, dedicate. [59]

[59] Doubtless expressing Stevenson's intention of putting together his verses in a volume.

CLV

I, whom Apollo sometime visited,
Or feigned to visit, now, my day being done,
Do slumber wholly; nor shall know at all
The weariness of changes; nor perceive
Immeasurable sands of centuries
Drink of the blanching ink, or the loud sound
Of generations beat the music down.

CLVI

THE FAR-FARERS

The broad sun,
   The bright day,
White sails
   On the blue bay:—
The far-farers
   Draw away.

Light the Fires
   And close the door.
To the old homes,
   To the loved shore,
The far-farers
   Return no more.

CLVII

Far over seas an island is
   Whereon when day is done
A grove of tossing palms
   Are printed on the sun.
And all about the reefy shore
   Blue breakers flash and fall.
There shall I go, methinks,
   When I am done with all.

Have I no castle then in Spain,
   No island of the mind,
Where I can turn and go again
   When life shall prove unkind?
Up, sluggard soul! and far from here
   Our mountain forest seek;
Or nigh enchanted island, steer
   Down the desired creek.

CLVIII

On the gorgeous hills of morning
A sudden piping of birds,
A piping of all the forest, high and merry and clear,
I lay in my tent and listened;
I lay and heard them long,
In the dark of the moonlit morning,
The birds of the night at song.

I lay and listened and heard them
Sing ere the day was begun;
Sing and sink into
Silence one by one.
I lay in my bed and looked—
Paler than starlight or lightning
A glimmer ...

In the highlands in the country places
Where the old plain men have rosy faces,
And the young fair lasses
Quiet eyes,
Light and heat begin, begin and strengthen,
And the shadows turn and shrink and lengthen,
As the great sun passes in the skies.
Life and death go by with heedful faces—
Mock with silent steps these empty places.

CLIX

Rivers and winds among the twisted hills,
Hears, and his hearing slowly fills,
And hearkens, and his face is lit,
Life facing, Death pursuing it.
As with heaped bees at hiving time
The boughs are clotted, as (ere prime)
Heaven swarms with stars, or the city street
Pullulates with passing feet;
So swarmed my senses once, that now
Repose behind my tranquil brow,
Unsealed, asleep, quiescent, clear;
Now only the vast shapes I hear—
Hear—and my hearing slowly fills—
Rivers and winds among the twisting hills,
And hearken—and my face is lit—
Life facing, Death pursuing it.

CLX

Tempest tossed and sore afflicted, sin defiled and care oppressed,
Come to me, all ye that labour; come, and I will give ye rest.
Fear no more, O doubting hearted; weep no more, O weeping eye!
Lo, the voice of your redeemer; lo, the songful morning near.
Here one hour you toil and combat, sin and suffer, bleed and die;
In my father's quiet mansion soon to lay your burden by.
Bear a moment, heavy laden, weary hand and weeping eye.
Lo, the feet of your deliverer; lo, the hour of freedom here.

CLXI

I now, O friend, whom noiselessly the snows
, Settle around; and whose small chamber grows
Dusk as the sloping window takes its load:

* * * * *

The kindly hill, as to complete our hap,
Has ta'en us in the shelter of her lap;
Well sheltered in our slender grove of trees
And ring of walls, we sit between her knees;
A disused quarry, paved with rose plots, hung
With clematis, the barren womb whence sprung
The crow-stepped house itself, that now far seen
Stands, like a bather, to the neck in green.
A disused quarry, furnished with a seat
Sacred to pipes and meditation meet
For such a sunny and retired nook.
There in the clear, warm mornings many a book
Has vied with the fair prospect of the hills
That, vale on vale, rough brae on brae, upfills
Halfway to the zenith all the vacant sky
To keep my loose attention. . . .
Horace has sat with me whole mornings through:
And Montaigne gossiped, fairly false and true;
And chattering Pepys, and a few beside
That suit the easy vein, the quiet tide,
The calm and certain stay of garden-life,
Far sunk from all the thunderous roar of strife.
There is about the small secluded place
A garnish of old times; a certain grace
Of pensive memories lays about the braes:
The old chestnuts gossip tales of bygone days.
Here, where some wandering preacher, blest Lazil, [60]
Perhaps, or Peden, on the middle hill
Had made his secret church, in rain or snow,
He cheers the chosen residue from woe.
All night the doors stood open, come who might,
The hounded kebbock mat the mud all night.
Nor are there wanting later tales; of how
Prince Charlie's Highlanders . . .

* * * * *

[60] "Lazil" should read "Cargil."

I have had talents, too. In life's first hour
God crowned with benefits my childish head.
Flower after flower, I plucked them; flower by flower
Cast them behind me, ruined, withered, dead.
Full many a shining godhead disappeared.
From the bright rank that once adorned her brow
The old child's Olympus—

* * * * *

Gone are the fair old dreams, and one by one,
As, one by one, the means to reach them went,
As, one by one, the stars in riot and disgrace,
I squandered what . . .

There shut the door, alas! on many a hope
Too many;
My face is set to the autumnal slope,
Where the loud winds shall . . .

There shut the door, alas! on many a hope,
And yet some hopes remain that shall decide
My rest of years and down the autumnal slope.

* * * * *

Gone are the quiet twilight dreams that I
Loved, as all men have loved them; gone!
I have great dreams, and still they stir my soul on high—
Dreams of the knight's stout heart and tempered will.
Not in Elysian lands they take their way;
Not as of yore across the gay champaign,
Towards some dream city, towered . . .
and my . . .
The path winds forth before me, sweet and plain,
Not now; but though beneath a stone-grey sky
November's russet woodlands toss and wail,
Still the white road goes thro' them, still may I,
Strong in new purpose, God, may still prevail.

* * * * *

I and my like, improvident sailors!

* * * * *

At whose light fall awaking, all my heart
Grew populous with gracious, favoured thought,
And all night long thereafter, hour by hour,
The pageant of dead love before my eyes
Went proudly, and old hopes with downcast head
Followed like Kings, subdued in Rome's imperial hour,
Followed the car; and I . . .

CLXII

Since thou hast given me this good hope, O God,
That while my footsteps tread the flowery sod
And the great woods embower me, and white dawn
And purple even sweetly lead me on
From day to day, and night to night, O God,
My life shall no wise miss the light of love;
But ever climbing, climb above
Man's one poor star, man's supine lands,
Into the azure steadfastness of death,
My life shall no wise lack the light of love,
My hands not lack the loving touch of hands;
But day by day, while yet I draw my breath,
And day by day, unto my last of years,
I shall be one that has a perfect friend.
Her heart shall taste my laughter and my tears,
And her kind eyes shall lead me to the end.

CLXIII

God gave to me a child in part,
Yet wholly gave the father's heart:—
Child of my soul, O whither now,
Unborn, unmothered, goest thou?

You came, you went, and no man wist;
Hapless, my child, no breast you kist;
On no dear knees, a privileged babbler, clomb,
Nor knew the kindly feel of home.

My voice may reach you, O my dear—
A father's voice perhaps the child may hear;
And, pitying, you may turn your view
On that poor father whom you never knew.

Alas! alone he sits, who then,
Immortal among mortal men,
Sat hand in hand with love, and all day through
With your dear mother wondered over you.

CLXIV

Over the land is April,
Over my heart a rose;
Over the high, brown mountain
The sound of singing goes.
Say, love, do you hear me,
Hear my sonnets ring?
Over the high, brown mountain,
Love, do you hear me sing?

By highway, love, and byway
The snows succeed the rose.
Over the high, brown mountain
The wind of winter blows.
Say, love, do you hear me,
Hear my sonnets ring?
Over the high, brown mountain
I sound the song of spring,
I throw the flowers of spring.
Do you hear the song of spring?
Hear you the songs of spring?

CLXV

Light as the linnet on my way I start,
For all my pack I bear a chartered heart.
Forth on the world without a guide or chart,
Content to know, through all man's varying fates,
The eternal woman by the wayside waits.

CLXVI

Come, here is adieu to the city
   And hurrah for the country again.
The broad road lies before me
   Watered with last night's rain.
The timbered country woos me
   With many a high and bough;
And again in the shining fallows
   The ploughman follows the plough.

The whole year's sweat and study,
    And the whole year's sowing time,
Comes now to the perfect harvest,
    And ripens now into rhyme.
For we that sow in the Autumn,
    We reap our grain in the Spring,
And we that go sowing and weeping
    Return to reap and sing.

CLXVII

It blows a snowing gale in the winter of the year;
The boats are on the sea and the crews are on the pier.
The needle of the vane, it is veering to and fro,
A flash of sun is on the veering of the vane.
    Autumn leaves and rain,
    The passion of the gale.

CLXVIII

NE SIT ANCILLAE TIBI AMOR PUDORI

There's just a twinkle in your eye
That seems to say I *might*, if I
Were only bold enough to try
    An arm about your waist.
I hear, too, as you come and go,
That pretty nervous laugh, you know;
And then your cap is always so
    Coquettishly displaced.

Your cap! the word's profanely said.
That little top-knot, white and red,
That quaintly crowns your graceful head,
    No bigger than a flower,
Is set with such a witching art,
Is so provocatively smart,
I'd like to wear it on my heart,
    An order for an hour!

O graceful housemaid, tall and fair,
I love your shy imperial air,
And always loiter on the stair
    When you are going by.
A strict reserve the fates demand;
But, when to let you pass I stand,
Sometimes by chance I touch your hand
    And sometimes catch your eye.

CLXIX

To all that love the far and blue:
    Whether, from dawn to eve, on foot
The fleeing corners ye pursue,
    Nor weary of the vain pursuit;
Or whether down the singing stream,
    Paddle in hand, jocund ye shoot,
To splash beside the splashing bream
    Or anchor by the willow root:

Or, bolder, from the narrow shore
    Put forth, that cedar ark to steer,
Among the seabirds and the roar
    Of the great sea, profound and clear;
Or, lastly if in heart ye roam,
    Not caring to do else, and hear,
Safe sitting by the fire at home,
    Footfalls in Utah or Pamere:

Though long the way, though hard to bear
    The sun and rain, the dust and dew;
Though still attainment and despair
    Inter the old, despoil the new;
There shall at length, be sure, O friends,
    Howe'er ye steer, whate'er ye do—
At length, and at the end of ends,
    The golden city come in view.

CLXX

Now bare to the beholder's eye
Your late denuded bindings lie,
Subsiding slowly where they fell,
A disinvested citadel;
The obdurate corset, Cupid's foe,
The Dutchman's breeches frilled below.
Those that the lover notes to note,
And white and crackling petticoat.

From these, that on the ground repose,
Their lady lately re-arose;
And laying by the lady's name,
A living woman re-became.
Of her, that from the public eye
They do enclose and fortify,
Now, lying scattered as they fell,

An indiscreeter tale they tell:
Of that more soft and secret her
Whose daylong fortresses they were,
By fading warmth, by lingering print,
These now discarded scabbards hint.

A twofold change the ladies know:
First, in the morn the bugles blow,
And they, with floral hues and scents,
Man their beribboned battlements.
But let the stars appear, and they
Shed inhumanities away;
And from the changeling fashion see,
Through comic and through sweet degree,
In nature's toilet unsurpassed,
Forth leaps the laughing girl at last.

CLXXI

THE BOUR-TREE DEN

Clinkum-clank in the rain they ride,
Down by the braes and the grey sea-side;
Clinkum-clank by stane and cairn:
Weary fa' their horse-shoe-airn!

Loud on the causey, saft on the sand,
Round they rade by the tail of the land,
Round and up by the Bour-Tree Den:
Weary fa' the red-coat men!

Aft hae I gane where they hae rade
   And straigled in the gowden brooms—
Aft hae I gane, a saikless maid,
   And O! sae bonny as the bour-tree blooms!

Wi' swords and guns they wanton there,
   Wi' red, red coats and braw, braw plumes.
But I gaed wi' my gowden hair,
   And O! sae bonny as the bour-tree blooms!

I ran, a little hempie lass,
In the sand and the bent grass,
Or took and kilted my small coats
To play in the beached fisher-boats.
I waded deep and I ran fast,
I was as lean as a lugger's mast,
I was as brown as a fisher's creel,
And I liked my life unco weel.

They blew a trumpet at the cross,
Some forty men, both foot and horse,
A'body cam to hear and see,
And wha, among the rest, but me.
My lips were saut wi' the saut air,
My face was brown, my feet were bare
The wind had ravelled my tautit hair,
And I thought shame to be standing there.

Ae man there in the thick of the throng,
Sat in his saddle, straight and strong.
I looked at him and he at me,
And he was a master-man to see.
—And who is this yin? and who is yon
That has the bonny lendings on?
That sits and looks sae braw and crouse?
—Mister Frank o' the Big House!

I gaed my lane beside the sea;
The wind it blew in bush and tree,
The wind blew in bush and bent:
Muckle I saw, and muckle kent!
Between the beach and the sea-hill,
I sat my lane and grat my fill—
I was sae clarty and hard and dark,
And like the kye in the cow park!

There fell a battle far in the north;
The evil news gaed back and forth,
And back and forth by brae and bent
Hider and hunter cam and went:
The hunter clattered horse-shoe-airn
By causey-crest and hill-top cairn;
The hider, in by shag and sheuch,
Crept on his wame and little leuch?

The eastland wind blew shrill and snell,
The stars arose, the gloaming fell,
The firelight shone in window and door
When Mr. Frank cam here to shore.
He hirpled up by the links and the lane,
And chappit laigh in the back-door-stane.
My faither gaed, and up wi' his han'!
—*Is this Mr. Frank, or a beggarman?*

I have mistrysted sair, he said,
But let me into fire and bed,
Let me in, for auld lang syne,
And give me a dram of the brandy wine.

They hid him in the Bour-Tree Den,
And I thought it strange to gang my lane.
I thought it strange, I thought it sweet,
To gang there on my naked feet,

In the mirk night, when the boats were at sea,
I passed the burn abune the knee.
In the mirk night, when the folks were asleep,
I had a tryst in the den to keep.

Late and air', when the folks were asleep,
I had a tryst, a tryst to keep,
I had a lad that lippened to me,
And bour-tree blossom is fair to see!

O' the bour-tree leaves I busked his bed,
The mune was siller, the dawn was red:
Was nae man there but him and me—
And bour-tree blossom is fair to see!

Unco weather hae we been through,
The mune glowered, and the wind blew,
And the rain it rained on him and me,
And bour-tree blossom is fair to see!

Dwelling his lane but house or hauld,
Aft he was wet and aft was cauld;
I warmed him wi' my briest and knee—
And bour-tree blossom is fair to see!

There was nae voice of beast ae man,
But the tree soughed and the burn ran,
And we heard the ae voice of the sea:
Bour-tree blossom is fair to see!

CLXXII

SONNETS

1

TO THE SEA

Thy God permits thee, but with dreadful hand,
   Canst churn great boulders into little sand,
On fruitless tasks to waste they summer ease,
   In tide washed seaweeds find a childish joy.
Or—harnessing the unruly force of sea
   To lick smooth stone into a fretted toy—
From thy great page, turn forth knick-knacks to please
   A Lilliputian fancy—yea produce
Such nice laborious fritters as could these
   Old chinamen whose life, by slow degrees,
Frayed four twenty peachstones into lace.
   Hence know that in our smallest work God sees
Some service to himself, or some good use,
   From us yet hidden and our blinded race.

2

A golden service, most loveworthy yoke,
   Thou, O my pipe, imposes, when thy bowl
   Alternate dusks and quickens like a coal
At every inhalation of sweet smoke.
   Thou, thrifty farmer of the mind o'erbraced,
Dost clear a stage for fancy's puppet folk,
   And giv'st rich fallow seasons to the soul,
   Moods soft as sleep that me could wake to taste.
Therefore to these the incense do I pour
   Of one white volley, that around my head
     Weaves fragrant circlets ere it spreads to nought:
This service do I pay thee, thus adore
   The healing power in thy soft office shed
     To dull old griefs and ease harassing thought.

3

The roadside lined with ragweed, the sharp hills
    Standing against the glow of eve, the patch
      Of rough white oats mongst darkling granite knolls,
   The ferny coverts where the adders hatch,
The hollow that the northern sea upfills,
   The seagull wheeling by with strange, sad calls,
All these, this evening, weary me. Full fain
   Would I turn up the little elm tree way
And under the last elm tree, once again
    Stretch myself with my head among the grass;
So lying, tyne the memories of day
    And let my loosed, insatiate being pass
Into the blackbird's song of summer ease,
Or, with the white moon, rise in spirit from the trees.

4

SIR ALAN M'LEANS EFFIGY, ON INCH KENNETH

Hard by the ruined kirk above the sound
    Among worn headstones, old Sir Alan lies:
   ?—of rich grapes buries him around;
    And thou mays't see the birds withouten fear
    Trip on his face and treble in his ear,
And round his senseless head buzzy summer flies.
   Close by from out a trumpet comes a scroll,
    Between a skull and crossbones carven deep,
And on the scroll, these words—"The dead shall rise."
Till when whoever, under summer skies
Shall see the place that guards his quiet sleep,
   From—— for a bed so held at rest
    Amongst the lap of mountains, shall suggest
'Tis better with his body than his soul.

5

Nor judge me light, tho' light at times I seem
And lightly in the stress of fortune bear
The innumerable flaws of changeful care—
Nor judge me light for this, nor rashly deem
(Office forbid to mortals, kept supreme
And separate the prerogative of God!)
That seaman idle who is borne abroad
To the far haven by the favouring stream.
Not he alone that to contrarious seas

Opposes, all night long, the unwearied oar,
Not he alone, by high success endeared,
Shall reach the Port; but, winged, with some light breeze
Shall they, with upright keels, pass in before
Whom easy Taste, the golden pilot, steered.

6

So shall this book wax like unto a well,
Fairy with mirrored flowers about the brim,
Or like some tarn that wailing curlews skim,
Glassing the sallow uplands or brown fell;
And so, as men go down into a dell
(Weary with noon) to find relief and shade,
When on the uneasy sick-bed we are laid,
We shall go down into thy book, and tell
The leaves, once blank, to build again for us
Old summer dead and ruined, and the time
Of later autumn with the corn in stook.
So shalt thou stint the meagre winter thus
Of his projected triumph, and the rime
Shall melt before the sunshine in thy book.

7

I have a hoard of treasure in my breast;
The grange of memory steams against the door,
Full of my bygone lifetime's garnered store,
Old pleasures crowned with sorrow for a zest,
Old sorrow grown a joy, old penance blest,
Chastened remembrance of the sins of yore
That, like a new evangel, more and more
Supports our halting will toward the best.
Ah! what to us the barren after years
May bring of joy or sorrow, who can tell?
O, knowing not, who cares? It may be well
That we shall find old pleasures and old fears,
And our remembered childhood seen thro' tears
The best of Heaven and the worst of Hell.

8

As starts the absent dreamer when a train,
Suddenly disengulphed below his feet
Roars forth into the sunlight, to its seat
My soul was shaken with immediate pain
Intolerable as the scanty breath
Of that one word blew utterly away

The fragile mist of fair deceit that lay
O'er the bleak years that severed me from death.
Yes, at the sight I quailed; but, not unwise
Or not, O God, without some nervous thread
Of that best valour, Patience, bowed my head
And with firm bosom and most steadfast eyes,
Strong in all high resolve, prepared to tread
The unlovely path that leads me toward the skies.

9

Not undelightful, friend, our rustic ease
To grateful hearts; for by especial hap,
Deep nested in the hill's enormous lap
With its own ring of walls and grove of trees
Sits, in deep shelter, our small cottage—nor
Far-off is seen, rose carpeted and hung
With clematis, the quarry whence she sprung,
O mater pulchra filia pulchrior,
Whither in early spring, unharnessed folk,
We join the pairing swallows, glad to stay
Where, loosened in the hills, remote, unseen,
From its tall trees, it breathes a slender smoke
To heaven, and in the noon of sultry day
Stands, coolly buried, to the neck in green.

10

As in the hostel by the bridge I sate
Nailed with indifference fondly deemed complete
And (O strange chance, more sorrowful than sweet)
The counterfeit of her that was my fate,
Dressed in like vesture, graceful and sedate,
Went quietly up the vacant village street,
The still small sound of her most dainty feet
Shook, like a trumpet blast, my soul's estate.
Instant revolt ran riot through my brain;
And all night long, thereafter, hour by hour,
The pageant of dead love before my eyes
Went proudly; and old hopes, broke loose again
From the restraint of wisely temperate power,
With ineffectual ardour sought to rise.

11

The strong man's hand, the snow-cool head of age,
The certain-footed sympathies of youth—
These, and that lofty passion after truth,
Hunger unsatisfied in priest or sage
Or the great men of former years, he needs
That not unworthily would dare to sing
(Hard task!) black care's inevitable ring
Settling with years upon the heart that feeds
Incessantly on glory. Year by year
The narrowing toil grows closer round his feet;
With disenchanting touch rude-handed time
The unlovely web discloses, and strange fear
Leads him at last to eld's inclement seat,
The bitter north of life—a frozen clime.

12

As Daniel, bird-alone, in that far land,
Kneeling in fervent prayer, with heart-sick eyes
Turned thro' the casement toward the westering skies;
Or as untamed Elijah, that red brand
Among the starry prophets; or that band
And company of Faithful sanctities,
Who in all times, when persecutions rise,
Cherish forgotten creeds with fostering hand;
Such do ye seem to me, light-hearted crew,
O turned to friendly arts with all your will,
That keep a little chapel sacred still,
One rood of Holy-land in this bleak earth
Sequestered still (our homage surely due!)
To the twin Gods of mirthful wine and mirth.

CLXXIII

THE FAMILY

1

MOTHER AND DAUGHTER.

High as my heart! the quip be mine
That draws their stature to a line,
My pair of fairies plump and dark,
The dryads of my cattle park.
Here by my window close I sit,
And watch (and my heart laughs at it)
How these my dragon-lilies are
Alike and yet dissimilar.
From European womankind
They are divided and defined
By the free limb and wider mind,
The nobler gait, the little foot,
The indiscreeter petticoat;
And show, by each endearing cause,
More like what Eve in Eden was—
Buxom and free, flowing and fine,
In every limb, in every line,
Inimitably feminine.
Like ripe fruit on the espaliers
Their sun-bepainted hue appears,
And the white lace (when lace they wear)
Shows on their golden breast more fair.
So far the same they seem, and yet
One apes the shrew, one the coquette—
A sybil or a truant child
One runs—with a crop halo—wild;
And one more sedulous to please,
Her long dark hair, deep as her knees,
And thrid with living silver, sees.
What need have I of wealth or fame,
A club, an often-printed name?
It more contents my heart to know
Them going simply to and fro;
To see the dear pair pause and pass
Girded, among the drenching grass,
In the resplendent sun, or hear,
When the huge moon delays to appear,
Their kindred voices sounding near
In the veranda twilight.

So Sound ever; so, forever go
And come upon your small brown feet,
Twin honors to my country seat,
And its too happy master lent:
My solace and its ornament.

2

THE DAUGHTER, TEUILA, HER NATIVE NAME THE DECORATOR.

Man, child or woman, none from her
The insatiable embellisher, Escapes!
She leaves, where'er she goes,
A wreath, a ribbon, or a rose;
A bow or else a button changed,
Two hairs coquettishly deranged,
Some vital trifle, takes the eye,
And shows the adorner has been by.
Is fortune more obdurate grown?
And does she leave my dear alone
With none to adorn, none to caress?
Straight on her proper loveliness
She broods and lingers, cuts and carves,
With combs and brushes, rings and scarves;
The treasure of her hair she takes
Therewith a new presentment makes,
Babe, Goddess, Naiad of the grot,
And weeps if any like it not!
Oft clustered by her bended knees
(Smiling himself) the gazer sees,
Compact as flowers in garden beds,
The smiling faces and shaved heads
Of the brown island babes: with whom
She exults to decorate her room,
To dress them, cheer them when they cry,
And still to pet and prettify.
Or see, as in a looking-glass,
Her graceful, dimpled person pass,
Nought great therein but eyes and hair,
On her true business here and there:
Her huge, half-naked Staff, intent,
See her review and regiment,
An ant with elephants, and how
A smiling mouth, a clouded brow,
Satire and turmoil, quips and tears,
She deals among her grenadiers!
Her pantry and her kitchen squad,
Six-footers all, obey her nod,

Incline to her their martial chests,
With school-boy laughter hail her jests,
And do her in her kilted dress
Obsequious obeisances.
So, dear, may you be never done
Your pretty busy round to run.
And show with changing frocks and scents,
Your ever-varying lineaments :
Your saucy step, your languid grace,
Your sullen and your smiling face,
Sound sense, true valor, baby fears,
And bright unreasonable tears :
The Hebe of our aging tribe :
Matron and child, my friend and scribe.

3

About my fields, in the broad sun
And blaze of noon, there goeth one, [61]
Barefoot and robed in blue, to scan
With the hard eye of the husbandman
My harvests and my cattle. Her,
When even puts the birds astir
And day has set in the great woods,
We seek, among her garden roods,
With bells and cries in vain: the while
Lamps, plate, and the decanter smile
On the forgotten board. But she,
Deaf, blind, and prone on face and knee,
Forgets time, family and feast
And digs like a demented beast.

[61] Mrs. Stevenson.

4

Tall [62] as a guardsman, pale as the east at dawn,
Who strides in strange apparel on the lawn?
Rails for his breakfast? routs his vassals out
(Like boys escaped from school) with song and shout?
Kind and unkind, his Maker's final freak,
Part we deride the child, part deride the antique!
See where his gang, like frogs, among the dew
Crouch at their duty, an unquiet crew;
Adjust their staring kilts; and their swift eyes
Turn still to him who sits to supervise.
He in the midst, perched on a fallen tree
Eyes them at labour; and, guitar on knee,

Now ministers alarm, now scatters joy,
Now twangs a halting chord—now tweaks a boy.
Thorough in all, my resolute vizier,
Plays both the despot and the volunteer,
Exacts with fines obedience to my laws,
—And for his music, too, exacts applause.

[62] Lloyd Osbourne.

5

The Adorner [63] *of the uncomely*—Those
Amidst whose tall battalions goes
Her pretty person out and in
All day with an endearing din,
Of censure and encouragement;
And when all else is tried in vain
See her sit down and weep again.
She weeps to conquer;
She varies on her grenadiers
From satire up to girlish tears!
Or rather to behold her when
She plies for me the unresting pen,
And when the loud assault of squalls
Resounds upon the roof and walls,
And the low thunder growls and I
Raise my dictating voice on high.

[63] Mrs. Strong's daughter, Mrs. Stevenson's grandaughter.

6

What glory for a boy of ten, [64]
Who now must three gigantic men,
And two enormous, dapple grey
New Zealand pack-horses, array
And lead, and wisely resolute
Our day-long business execute
In the far shore-side town. His soul
Glows in his bosom like a coal;
His innocent eyes glitter again,
And his hand trembles on the rein.
Once he reviews his whole command
And chivalrously planting hand
On hip—a borrowed attitude—
Rides off downhill into the wood.

[64] Mrs. Strong's son, Austin, Mrs. Stevenson's grandson.

7

The old lady [65] (so they say) but I
Admire your young vitality.
Still brisk of foot, still busy and keen
In and about and up and down.

[65] Stevenson's mother.

I hear you pass with bustling feet
The long verandahs round, and beat
Your bell, and 'Lotu! Lotu!' cry;
Thus calling our queer company
In morning or in evening dim,
To prayers and the oft mangled hymn.

All day you watch across the sky
The silent, shining cloudlands ply,
That, huge as countries, swift as birds,
Beshade the isles by halves and thirds;
Till each with battlemented crest
Stands anchored in the ensanguined west,
An Alp enchanted. All the day
You hear the exuberant wind at play,
In vast, unbroken voice uplift
In roaring tree, round whistling clift.

8

I meanwhile in the populous house apart
Sit, snugly chambered, and my silent art
Uninterrupted, unremitting ply
Before the dawn, by morning lamplight, by
The glow of smelting noon, and when the sun
Dips past my westering hill and day is done;
So, bending still over my trade of words,
I hear the morning and the evening birds,
The morning and the evening stars behold;—
So there apart I sit as once of old
Napier in wizard Merchiston; and my
Brown innocent aides in home and husbandry,
Wonder askance, *What ails the boss? they ask,*
Him, richest of the rich, an endless task
Before the earliest birds or servants stir
Calls and detains him daylong prisoner?
He, whose innumerable dollars hewed
This cleft in the boar—and devil-haunted wood,

And bade therein, far seen to seas and skies,
His many-windowed, painted palace rise
Red-roofed, blue-walled, a rainbow on the hill,
A wonder in the forest glade: he still
Unthinkable Aladdin, dawn and dark,
Scribbles and scribbles, like a German clerk.
We see the fact, but tell, O tell us why?
My reverend washman and wise butler cry.
And from their lips the unanswered questions drop.
How can he live that does not keep a shop?
And why does he, being acclaimed so rich,
Not dwell with other gentry on the beach?
But harbour, impiously brave,
In the cold, uncanny wood, haunt of the fleeing slave?
The sun and the loud rain here alternate:
Here, in the unfathomable bush, the great
Voice of the wind makes a magnanimous sound.
Here, too, no doubt, the shouting doves abound
To be a dainty; here in the twilight stream
That brawls adown the forest, frequent gleam
The jewel-eyes of crawfish. These be good:
Grant them! and can the thing be understood?
That this white chief, whom no distress compels,
Far from all compeers in the mountain dwells?
And finds a manner of living to his wish
Apart from high society and sea fish?
Meanwhile at times the manifold
Imperishable perfumes of the past
And coloured pictures rise on me thick and fast
And I remember the white rime, the loud
Lamplitten city, shops and the changing crowd
And I remember home and the old time,
The winding river, the white morning rime,
The autumn robin by the riverside,
That pipes in the grey eve.

9

These rings, [66] O my beloved pair,
For me on your brown fingers wear:
Each, a perpetual caress
To tell you of my tenderness.

[66] Stevenson had three topaz rings made, topaz being the stone of his birth month, November. His initials were inscribed inside two of the rings, and these he gave to Mrs. Stevenson and her daughter.

Let—when at morning as ye rise
The golden topaz takes your eyes—
To each her emblem whisper sure
Love was awake an hour before.

Ah yes! an hour before ye woke
Low to my heart *my* emblem spoke,
And grave, as to renew an oath,
It I have kissed and blessed you both.

CLXXIV

AIR OF DIABELLI'S [67]

[67] Diabelli, an Austrian composer who died in 1858.

Call it to mind, O my love.
Dear were your eyes as the day,
Bright as the day and the sky;
Like the stream of gold and the sky above,
Dear were your eyes in the grey.
We have lived, my love, O, we have lived, my love!
Now along the silent river, azure
Through the sky's inverted image,
Softly swam the boat that bore our love,
Swiftly ran the shallow of our love
Through the heaven's inverted image,
In the reedy mazes round the river.
See along the silent river,

See of old the lover's shallop steer.
Berried brake and reedy island,
Heaven below and only heaven above.
Through the sky's inverted image
Swiftly swam the boat that bore our love.
Berried brake and reedy island,
Mirrored flower and shallop gliding by.
All the earth and all the sky were ours,
Silent sat the wafted lovers,
Bound with grain and watched by all the sky,
Hand to hand and eye to eye.

Days of April, airs of Eden,
Call to mind how bright the vanished angel hours,
Golden hours of evening,
When our boat drew homeward filled with flowers.
O darling, call them to mind; love the past, my love.
Days of April, airs of Eden.
How the glory died through golden hours,
And the shining moon arising;
How the boat drew homeward filled with flowers.
Age and winter close us slowly in.

Level river, cloudless heaven,
Islanded reed mazes, silver weirs;
How the silent boat with silver
Threads the inverted forest as she goes,
Broke the trembling green of mirrored trees.
O, remember, and remember
How the berries hung in garlands.

Still in the river see the shallop floats.
Hark! Chimes the falling oar.
Still in the mind
Hark to the song of the past!
Dream, and they pass in their dreams.

Those that loved of yore, O those that loved of yore!
Hark through the stillness, O darling, hark!
Through it all the ear of the mind

Knows the boat of love. Hark!
Chimes the falling oar.

O half in vain they grew old.
Now the halcyon days are over,
Age and winter close us slowly round,
And these sounds at fall of even
Dim the sight and muffle all the sound.
And at the married fireside, sleep of soul and sleep of fancy,
Joan and Darby.
Silence of the world without a sound;
And beside the winter faggot
Joan and Darby sit and dose and dream and wake—
Dream they hear the flowing, singing river,
See the berries in the island brake;
Dream they hear the weir,
See the gliding shallop mar the stream.
Hark! in your dreams do you hear?

Snow has filled the drifted forest;
Ice has bound the . . . stream.
Frost has bound our flowing river;
Snow has whitened all our island brake.

Berried brake and reedy island,
Heaven below and only heaven above azure
Through the sky's inverted image
Safely swam the boat that bore our love.
Dear were your eyes as the day,
Bright ran the stream, bright hung the sky above.
Days of April, airs of Eden.
How the glory died through golden hours,
And the shining moon arising,
How the boat drew homeward filled with flowers.
Bright were your eyes in the night:
We have lived, my love;
O, we have loved, my love.
Now the . . . days are over,
Age and winter close us slowly round.

Vainly time departs, and vainly
Age and winter come and close us round.

Hark the river's long continuous sound.
Hear the river ripples in the reeds.

Lo, in dreams they see their shallop
Run the lilies down and drown the weeds
Mid the sound of crackling faggots.
So in dreams the new created
Happy past returns, to-day recedes,
And they hear once more,
From the old years,
Yesterday returns, to-day recedes,
And they hear with aged hearing warbles

Love's own river ripple in the weeds.
And again the lover's shallop;
Lo, the shallop sheds the streaming weeds;
And afar in foreign countries
In the ears of aged lovers.

And again in winter evens
Starred with lilies . . . with stirring weeds.
In these ears of aged lovers
Love's own river ripples in the reeds.

CLXXV

DE EROTIO PUELLA

This girl was sweeter than the song of swans,
And daintier than the lamb upon the lawns
Or Lucrine oyster. She, the flower of girls,
Outshone the light of Erythræan pearls;
The teeth of India that with polish glow,
The untouched lilies or the morning snow.
Her tresses did gold-dust outshine
And fair hair of women of the Rhine.
Compared to her the peacock seemed not fair,
The squirrel lively, or the phoenix rare;
Her on whose pyre the smoke still hovering waits;
Her whom the greedy and unequal fates
On the sixth dawning of her natal day,
My child-love and my playmate—snatcht away.

CLXXVI

I look across the ocean,
   And kneel upon the shore,
I look out seaward—westward,
   My heart swells more and more.

I see the great new nation,
   New spirit and new scope
Rise there from the sea's round shoulder,—
   A splendid sun of hope!

I see it and I tremble—
   My voice is full of tears—
America tread softly,
   You bear the fruit of years.

Tread softly—you are pregnant
   And growing near your time—

CLXXVII

I am a hunchback, yellow faced,—
   A hateful sight to see,—
'Tis all that other men can do
   To pass and let me be.

I am a woman,—my hair is white—
    I was a drunkard's lass;
The gin dances in my head,—
    I stumble as I pass.

I am a man that God made at first,
    And teachers tried to harm;
Here hunchback, take my friendly hand,
    Good woman, take my arm.

CLXXVIII

SONG

Light foot and tight foot,
    And green grass spread,
Early in the morning,
    But hope is on ahead.

Brief day and bright day,
    And sunset red,
Early in the evening,
    The stars are overhead.

CLXXIX

THE NEW HOUSE

IS the house not homely yet?
There let pleasant thoughts be set:
With bright eyes and hurried feet,
There let severed friendships meet,
There let sorrow learn to smile,
And sweet talk the nights beguile.

Thus shall each, a friendly elf,
Leave you something of himself,
Something dear and kind and true,
That will stay and talk with you.

They shall go, but one and all
Leave their faces on the wall,
Leave brave words of hope and love
Legendwise inscribed above.

CLXXX

Men marvel at the works of man
   And with unstinted praises sing
   The greatness of some worldly thing
Encompassed during one life's span;
   An empire built, kingdom born.
   And straightway men sound man's own horn.

The human brain's a wondrous work,
So chant the sages and the deans—
Those thought and labour go-betweens,
Who ever life's deep mysteries shirk.
   A steel ribbed ship, an engine new—
   Ah, mighty things strong man doth do!

Man rears great piles of chiselled stone,
   And builds across the roaring streams,
   And tunnels mountains while he dreams
Of sterner tasks to do alone.
   'Tis I, he says, these things have wrought—
   Through darkness to the heights I've fought.

But comes a time when in his might
   The man of sceptre or of gold
   Is laid upon the marble cold,
And soul within takes hurried flight.
   The wondrous man is but a clod
   As lowly as the earth he trod.

Far in the realm of the unknown
   A little light has found its way
   A flicker in the newer day
That hallows round a Godly throne;
   Once housed in the Eternal Land
   The light perceives the Master Hand.

CLXXXI

TO MASTER ANDREW LANG

ON HIS RE-EDITING OF "CUPID AND PSYCHE."

You, that are much a fisher in the pool
Of things forgotten, and from thence bring up
Gold of old song, and diamonds of dead speech,
The scholar, and the angler, and the friend
Of the pale past, this unremembered tale
Restore, and this dead author re-inspire;
And lo, Oblivion the iniquitous
Remembers, and the stone is rolled away.
And he, the long asleep, sees once again
The busy bookshop, once again is read.
Brave as at first, in his new garb of print,
Shines forth the Elizabethan. But when Death,
The unforgettable shepherd, shall have come
And numbered us with these, the numberless,
The inheritors of slumber and neglect—
O correspondent of the immortal dead,
Shall any pious hand re-edit us?

CLXXXII

TO THE STORMY PETREL

TO HIS WIFE, ON HER BIRTHDAY.

Ever perilous
And precious, like an ember from the fire
Or gem from a volcano, we to-day
When the drums of war reverberate in the land
And every face is for the battle blacked—
No less the sky, that over sodden woods
Menaces now in the disconsolate calm
The hurly-burly of the hurricane,
Do now most fitly celebrate your day.

Yet amid turmoil keep for me, my dear,
The kind domestic faggot. Let the hearth
Shine ever as (I praise my honest gods)
In peace and tempest it has ever shone.

CLXXXIII

The indefensible impulse of my blood [68]
Surround me sleeping in this isle; and I
Behold rain falling and the rainbow dawn
On Lammermuir; and hearkening heard again,
In my precipitous city, beaten bells
Winnow the keen sea wind. So this I wrote
Of my own race and place: which being done,
Take thou the writing. True it is, for who
Burnished the sword, breathed on the damp coal,
Held still the target higher, chary of praise
And prodigal of censure—who but thou?
So here in the end, if this in the least be well,
If any deed be done, if any fire
Live in the imperfect page, the praise be thine!

[68] These lines are found in the manuscript of *Weir of Hermiston*. They suggest a projected dedication of the book to Mrs. Stevenson.

CLXXXIV

Who would think, herein to look,
That from these exiguous bounds,
I have dug a printed book
And a cheque for twenty pounds?
Thus do those who trust the Lord
Go rejoicing on their way
And receive a great reward
For having been so kind as lay.

Had the fun of the voyage
   Had the sport of the boats
Who could have hoped in addition
   The pleasure of fing'ring the notes?

Yes, sir, I wrote the book; I own the fact;
It was perhaps, sir, an unworthy act.
Have you perused it, sir?—You have?—indeed!
Then between you and me there no debate is.
I did a silly act, but I was fee'd;
You did a sillier, and you did it gratis!

CLXXXV

EPISTLE TO CHARLES BAXTER

Noo lyart leaves blaw ower the green,
Red are the bonny woods o' Dean,
An' here we're back in Embro, freen',
   To pass the winter.
Whilk noo, wi' frosts afore, draws in,
   An' snaws ahint her.

I've seen's hae days to fricht us a',
The Pentlands poothered weel wi' snaw,
The ways half-smoored wi' liquid thaw,
   An' half-congealin',
The snell an' scowtherin' norther blaw
   Frae blae Brunteelan'.

I've seen's been unco sweir to sally,
And at the door-cheeks daff an' dally,
Seen's daidle thus an' shilly-shally
   For near a minute—
Sae cauld the wind blew up the valley,
   The deil was in it!—

Syne spread the silk an' tak the gate,
In blast an' blaudin', rain, deil hae't!
The hale toon glintin', stane an' slate,
   Wi' cauld an' weet,
An' to the Court, gin we 'se be late,
   Bicker oor feet.

And at the Court, tae, aft I saw
Whaur Advocates by twa an' twa
Gang gesterin' end to end the ha'
   In weeg an' goon,
To crack o' what ye wull but Law
   The hale forenoon.

That muckle ha', maist like a kirk,
I've kent at braid mid-day sae mirk
Ye'd seen white weegs an' faces lurk
   Like ghaists frae Hell,
But whether Christian ghaists or Turk,
   Deil ane could tell.

The three fires hinted in the gloom,
The wind blew like the blast o' doom,
The rain upo' the roof abune
   Played Peter Dick—
Ye wad nae'd licht enough i' the room
   Your teeth to pick!

But, freend, ye ken how me an' you,
The ling-lang lanely winter through,
Keep'd a guid speerit up, an' true
   To lore Horatian,
We aye the ither bottle drew
   To inclination.

Sae let us in the comin' days
Stand sicker on our auncient ways—
The strauchtest road in a' the maze
   Since Eve ate apples;
An' let the winter weet our cla'es—
   We'll weet oor thrapples.

EDINBURGH, OCTOBER 1875.

CLXXXVI

AD MARTIALEM

God knows, my Martial, if we two could be
To enjoy our days set wholly free;
To the true life together bend our mind,
And take a furlough from the falser kind.
No rich saloon, nor palace of the great,
Nor suit at law should trouble our estate;
On no vainglorious statues should we look,
But of a walk, a talk, a little book,
Baths, wells and meads, and the veranda shade,
Let all our travels and our toils be made.
Now neither lives unto himself, alas!
And the good suns we see, that flash and pass
And perish; and the bell that knells them cries:
"Another gone: O when will ye arise?"

CLXXXVII

DE M. ANTONIO

Now Antoninus, in a smiling age,
Counts of his life the fifteenth finished stage.
The rounded days and the safe years he sees,
Nor fears death's water mounting round his knees.
To him remembering not one day is sad,
Not one but that its memory makes him glad.
So good men lengthen life; and to recall
The past is to have twice enjoyed it all.

CLXXXVIII

Not roses to the rose, I trow,
    The thistle sends, nor to the bee
Do wasps bring honey. Wherefore now
    Should Locker ask a verse from me?

Martial, perchance,—but he is dead,
    And Herrick now must rhyme no more;
Still burning with the muse, they tread
    (And arm in arm) the shadowy shore.

They, if they lived, with dainty hand,
    To music as of mountain brooks,
Might bring you worthy words to stand
    Unshamed, dear Locker, in your books.

But tho' these fathers of your race
    Be gone before, yourself a sire,
To-day you see before your face
    Your stalwart youngsters touch the lyre.

On these—on Lang, or Dobson—call,
Long leaders of the songful feast.
They lend a verse your laughing fall—
A verse they owe you at the least.

CLXXXIX

TO A LITTLE GIRL [69]

All on a day of gold and blue,
Hearken the children calling you!
All on a day of blue and gold,
Here for your baby hands to hold,
Flower and fruit and fairy bread
Under the breathing trees are spread.
Here are kind paths for little feet:
Follow them, darling!

[69] Written on the fly-leaf of *A Child's Garden of Verses*.

CXC

TO MISS RAWLINSON

Of the many flowers you brought me,
   Only some were meant to stay,
And the flower I thought the sweetest
   Was the flower that went away.

Of the many flowers you brought me,
   All were fair and fresh and gay,
But the flower I thought the sweetest
   Was the blossom of the May.

CXCI

The pleasant river gushes
   Among the meadows green;
At home the author tushes;
   For him it flows unseen.

The Birds among the Bushes
   May wanton on the spray;
But vain for him who tushes
   The brightness of the day!

The frog among the rushes
   Sits singing in the blue.
By 'r la'kin ! but these tushes
   Are wearisome to do!

The task entirely crushes
   The spirit of the bard :
God pity him who tushes—
   His task is very hard.

The filthy gutter slushes,
   The clouds are full of rain,
But doomed is he who tushes
   To tush and tush again.

At morn with his hair-brushes,
   Still "tush" he says, and—weeps;
At night again he tushes,
   And tushes till he sleeps.

And when at length he pushes
   Beyond the river dark—
'Las, to the man who tushes,
   "Tush" shall be God's remark!

CXCII

TO H. F. BROWN

Brave lads in olden musical centuries
Sang, night by night, adorable choruses,
   Sat late by alehouse doors in April
   Chaunting in song as the moon was rising:

Moon-seen and merry, under the trellises,
Flush-faced they played with old polysyllables;
   Spring scents inspired, old wine diluted,
   Love and Apollo were there to chorus.

Now these, the songs, remain to eternity,
Those, only those, the bountiful choristers
   Gone—those are gone, those unremembered
   Sleep and are silent in earth for ever.

So man himself appears and evanishes,
So smiles and goes; as wanderers halting at
   Some green-embowered house, play their music,
   Play and are gone on the windy highway;

Yet dwells the strain enshrined in the memory
Long after they departed eternally,
   Forth-faring tow'rd far mountain summits,
   Cities of men on the sounding Ocean.

Youth sang the song in years immemorial;
Brave chanticleer, he sang and was beautiful;
   Bird-haunted, green tree-tops in spring-time
   Heard and were pleased by the voice of singing;

Youth goes, and leaves behind him a prodigy—
Songs sent from thee afar from Venetian
   Sea-grey lagunas, sea-paven highways,
   Dear to me here in my Alpine exile.

CXCIII

TO W. E. HENLEY

Dear Henley, with a pig's snout on
I am starting for London,
Where I likely shall arrive,
On Saturday, if still alive:
Perhaps your pirate doctor might
See me on Sunday? If all's right,
I should then lunch with you and with she
Who's dearer to you than you are to me.
I shall remain but little time
In London, as a wretched clime,
But not so wretched (for none are)
As that of beastly old Braemar.
My doctor sends me skipping. I
Have many facts to meet your eye.
My pig's snout now upon my face:
And I inhale with fishy grace,
My gills outflapping right and left,
Ol. pin. sylvest. [70] I am bereft
Of a great deal of charm by this—
Not quite the bull's eye for a kiss—
But like the gnome of olden time
Or bogey in a pantomime.
For ladies' love I once was fit,
But now am rather out of it.
Where'er I go, revolted curs
Snap round my military spurs;
The children all retire in fits
And scream their bellowses to bits.

Little I care: the worst's been done:
Now let the cold impoverished sun
Drop frozen from his orbit; let
Fury and fire, cold, wind, and wet,
And cataclysmal mad reverses
Rage through the federate universes;
Let Lawson triumph, cakes and ale,
Whiskey and hock and claret fail;—
Tobacco, love, and letters perish,
With all that any man could cherish:
You it may touch, not me. I dwell
Too deep already—deep in hell;
And nothing can befall, O damn!
To make me uglier than I am.

[70] *Ol. Pin. Sylvest.* This refers to an ori-nasal respirator for the inhalation of pine-wood oil, *oleum pini sylvestris.*

CXCIV

O Henley, in my hours of ease
You may say anything you please,
But when I join the Muses' revel,
Begad, I wish you at the devil!
In vain my verse I plane and bevel,
Like Banville's rhyming devotees;
In vain by many an artful swivel
Lug in my meaning by degrees;
I'm sure to hear my Henley cavil;
And grovelling prostrate on my knees,
Devote his body to the seas,
His correspondence to the devil!

CXCV

All things on earth and sea,
All that the white stars see,
Turns about you and me.

And where we two are not,
Is darkness like a blot
And life and love forgot.

But when we pass that way,
The night breaks into day,
The year breaks into May.

The earth through all her bowers
Carols and breathes and flowers
About this love of ours.

CXCVI

ON SOME GHOSTLY COMPANIONS AT A SPA

I had an evil day when I
To Strathpeffer drew anigh,
For there I found no human soul,
But ogres occupied the whole.
They had at first a human air
In coats and flannel underwear.
They rose and walked upon their feet
And filled their bellies full of meat,
Then wiped their lips when they had done—
But they were ogres every one.
Each issuing from his secret bower
I marked them in the morning hour.
By limp and totter, lisp and droop
I singled each one from the group.
Detected ogres, from my sight
Depart to your congenial night
From these fair vales: from this fair day
Fleet, spectres, on your downward way,
Like changing figures in a dream
To Muttonhole and Pittenweem!
Or, as by harmony divine
The devils quartered in the swine,
If any baser place exist
In God's great registration list—
Some den with wallow and a trough—
Find it, ye ogres, and be off!

CXCVII

TO CHARLES BAXTER

Blame me not that this
　Is the first you have from me.
　　Idleness has held me fettered,
　　　But at last the times are bettered
And once more I wet my whistle
　Here in France, beside the sea.

All the green and idle weather
   I have had in sun and shower
      Such an easy warm subsistence,
      Such an indolent existence
I should find it hard to sever
   Day from day and hour from hour.

Many a tract-provided ranter
   May upbraid me, dark and sour,
      Many a bland Utilitarian
      Or excited Millenarian,
—"Pereunt et imputantur
   You must speak to every hour."

But the very term's deceptive,
   You, at least, my friend, will see,
      That in sunny grassy meadows
      Trailed across by moving shadows
To be actively receptive
   Is as much as man can be.

He that all the winter grapples
   Difficulties, thrust and ward—
      Needs to cheer him thro' his duty
      Memories of sun and beauty
Orchards with the russet apples
   Lying scattered on the sward.

Many such I keep in prison,
   Keep them here at heart unseen,
      Till my muse again rehearses
      Long years hence, and in my verses
You shall meet them re-arisen
   Ever comely, ever green.

You know how they never perish,
   How, in time of later art,
      Memories consecrate and sweeten
      These defaced and tempest-beaten
Flowers of former years we cherish,
   Half a life, against our heart.

Most, those love-fruits withered greenly,
   Those frail, sickly amourettes,
     How they brighten with the distance
     Take new strength and new existence
Till we see them sitting queenly
   Crowned and courted by regrets!

All that loveliest and best is,
   Aureole-fashion round their heads,
     They that looked in life but plainly,
     How they stir our spirits vainly
When they come to us Alcest-
Like, returning from the dead!

Not the old love but another,
   Bright she comes at Memory's call
     Our forgotten vows reviving
     To a newer, livelier living,
As the dead child to the mother
   Seems the fairest child of all.

Thus our Goethe, sacred master,
   Travelling backward thro' his youth,
     Surely wandered wrong in trying
     To renew the old, undying
Loves that cling in memory faster
   Than they ever lived in truth.

CXCVIII

TO HENRY JAMES

Adela, Adela, Adela Chart,
What have you done to my elderly heart?
Of all the ladies of paper and ink
I count you the paragon, call you the pink.
The word of your brother depicts you in part:
"You raving maniac I" Adela Chart:
But in all the asylums that cumber the ground,
So delightful a maniac was ne'er to be found.
I pore on you, dote on you, clasp you to heart,
I laud, love, and laugh at you, Adela Chart,
And thank my dear Maker the while I admire
That I can be neither your husband nor sire.
Your husband's, your sire's were a difficult part;
You're a byway to suicide, Adela Chart;
But to read of, depicted by exquisite James,
O, sure you're the flower and quintessence of dames.

Eructavit cor meum.

Though oft I've been touched by the volatile dart
To none have I grovelled but Adela Chart.
There are passable ladies, no question, in art—
But where is the marrow of Adela Chart?
I dreamed that to Tyburn I passed in the cart—
 I dreamed I was married to Adela Chart:
From the first I awoke with a palpable start,
The second dumbfoundered me, Adela Chart!

CXCIX

HERE you rest among the valleys, maiden known to but a few,
Here you sleep unsighing, but how oft of yore you sighed!
And how oft your feet elastic trod a measure in the dew
On a green beside the river ere you died!

Where are now the country lovers whom you trembled to be near—
Who, with shy advances, in the falling eventide,
Grasped thee tighter at your fingers, whispered lowlier in your ear,
On a green beside the river ere you died?

All the sweet old country dancers who went round with you in tune,
Dancing, flushed and silent, in the silent eventide,
All departed by enchantment at the rising of the moon
From the green beside the river when you died.

CC

AND thorns, but did the sculptor spare
Sharp steel upon the marble, ere,
After long vigils and much care
And cruel discipline of blows,
From the dead stone the statue rose?

Think you I grudge the seed, who see
Broad armed the consummated tree?
Or would go back if it might be
To some old geologic time
With Saurians wallowing in fat slime,

Before the rivers and the rains
Had fashioned, and made fair with Plains
And shadowy places fresh with flowers,
This green and quiet world of ours.

Where, as the grass in Springtime heals
The furrow of the winter's wheels,
Serene maturity conceals
All memory on the perfect earth
Of the bygone tempestuous birth.

CCI

My brain swims empty and light
Like a nut on a sea of oil;
And an atmosphere of quiet
Wraps me about from the turmoil and clamour of life.
I stand apart from living,
Apart and holy I stand,
In my new-gained growth of idleness, I stand,
As stood the Shekinah of yore in the holy of holies.

I walk the streets smoking my pipe
And I love the dallying shop-girl
That leans with rounded stern to look at the fashions;
And I hate the bustling citizen,
The eager and hurrying man of affairs I hate,
Because he bears his intolerance writ on his face
And every movement and word of him tells me how much he hates me.

I love night in the city,
The lighted streets and the swinging gait of harlots.
I love cool pale morning,
In the empty bye-streets,
With only here and there a female figure,
A slavey with lifted dress and the key in her hand,
A girl or two at play in a corner of waste-land
Tumbling and showing their legs and crying out to me loosely.

CCII

1

THE LIGTH-KEEPER

The brilliant kernel of the night,
    The flaming lightroom circles me:
I sit within a blaze of light
    Held high above the dusky sea.
Far off the surf doth break and roar
Along bleak miles of moonlit shore,
    Where through the tides the tumbling wave
Falls in an avalanche of foam
And drives its churned waters home
    Up many an undercliff and cave.

The clear bell chimes: the clockworks strain:
    The turning lenses flash and pass,
Frame turning within glittering frame
    With frosty gleam of moving glass:
Unseen by me, each dusky hour
    The sea-waves welter up the tower
Or in the ebb subside again;
    And ever and anon all night,
Drawn from afar by charm of light,
    A sea-bird beats against the pane.

And lastly when dawn ends the night
    And belts the semi-orb of sea,
The tall, pale pharos in the light
    Looks white and spectral as may be.
The early ebb is out: the green
    Straight belt of sea-weed now is seen,
That round the basement of the tower
    Marks out the interspace of tide;
And watching men are heavy-eyed,
    And sleepless lips are dry and sour.

The night is over like a dream:
   The sea-birds cry and dip themselves;
And in the early sunlight, steam
   The newly-bared and dripping shelves,
Around whose verge the glassy wave
   With lisping wash is heard to lave;
While, on the white tower lifted high,
   With yellow light in faded glass
The circling lenses flash and pass,
   And sickly shine against the sky.

2

As the steady lenses circle
With a frosty gleam of glass;
And the clear bell chimes,
And the oil brims over the lip of the burner,
Quiet and still at his desk,
The lonely light-keeper
Holds his vigil.

Lured from far,
The bewildered seagull beats
Dully against the lantern;
Yet he stirs not, lifts not his head
From the desk where he reads,
Lifts not his eyes to see
The chill blind circle of night
Watching him through the panes.
This is his country's guardian,
The outmost sentry of peace.
This is the man
Who gives up that is lovely in living
For the means to live.
Poetry cunningly gilds
The life of the light-keeper,
Held on high in the blackness
In the burning kernel of night,
The seaman sees and blesses him.
The Poet, deep in a sonnet,
Numbers his inky fingers
Fitly to praise him.
Only we behold him,
Sitting, patient and stolid
Martyr to a salary.

1870.

CCIII

THE DAUGHTER OF HERODIAS

Three yellow slaves were set to swing
   The doorway curtain to and fro,
With rustle of light folds and ring
   Of little bells that hung below;
The still, hot night was tempered so.

And ever, from the carven bed,
   She watched the labour of the men;
And saw the band of moonlight spread,
   Leap up upon her feet and then
Leap down upon the floor again;

And ever, vexed with heat and doubt,
   Below the burthen of their shawls,
The still grey olives saw without
   And glimmer of white garden walls,
Between the alternate curtain falls.

What ailed the dainty lady then,
   The dainty lady, fair and sweet?
Unseen of these three silent men,
   A something lay upon her feet,
Not comely for such eyes to meet.

She saw a golden salver there
   And, laid upon it, on the bed,
The white teeth showing keen and bare
   Between the sundered lips, a head
Sallow and horrible and dead.

She saw upon the sallow cheek
   Rust-coloured blood-stains; and the eye
Her frightened glances seemed to seek
   Half-lifting its blue lid on high,
Watching her, horrible and sly.

Thus spake she: "Once again that head!
   "I ate too much pilau to-night,
"My mother and the eunuchs said.
   "Well, I can take a hint aright—
   "To-morrow's supper shall be light."

CCIV

THE CRUEL MISTRESS

Here let me rest, here nurse the uneasy qualm
That yearns within me;
And to the heaped-up sea,
Sun-spangled in the quiet afternoon,
Sing my devotions.

In the sun, at the edge of the down,
The whin-pods cackle
In desultory volleys;
And the bank breathes in my face
Its hot sweet breath—
Breath that stirs and kindles,
Lights that suggest, not satisfy—
Is there never in life or nature
An opiate for desire?
Has everything here a voice,
Saying "I am not the goal;
Nature is not to be looked at alone;
Her breath, like the breath of a mistress,
Her breath also,
Parches the spirit with longing
Sick and enervating longing."

Well, let the matter rest.
I rise and brush the windle-straws
Off my clothes; and lighting another pipe
Stretch myself over the down.
Get thee behind me, nature!
I turn my back on the sun
And face from the grey new town at the foot of the bay.
I know an amber lady
Who has her abode
At the lips of the street
In prisons of coloured glass.
I had rather die of her love
Than sicken for you, O Nature!
Better be drunk and merry
Than dreaming awake!
Better be Falstaff than Obermann!

CCV

STORM

The narrow lanes are vacant and wet;
The rough wind bullies and blusters about the township.
And spins the vane on the tower
And chases the scurrying leaves,
And the straw in the damp innyard.
See—a girl passes
Tripping gingerly over the pools,
And under her lifted dress
I catch the gleam of a comely, stockinged leg.
Pah! the room stifles me,
Reeking of stale tobacco—
With the four black mealy horrible prints
After Landseer's pictures.
I will go out.

Here the free wind comes with a fuller circle,
Sings, like an angry wasp, in the straining grass
Sings and whistles;
And the hurried flow of rain
Scourges my face and passes.
Behind me, clustered together, the rain-wet roofs of the town
Shine, and the light vane shines as it veers
In the long pale finger of sun that hurries across them to me.
The fresh salt air is keen in my nostrils,
And far down the shining sand
Foam and thunder
And take the shape of the bay in eager mirth
The white-head hungry billows.
The earth shakes
As the semicircle of waters
Stoops and casts itself down;
And far outside in the open,
Wandering gleams of sunshine
Show us the ordered horde that hurries to follow.

Ei! merry companions,
Your madness infects me.
My whole soul rises and falls and leaps and tumbles with you!
I shout aloud and incite you, O white-headed merry companions.
The sight of you alone is better than drinking.
The brazen band is loosened from off my forehead;
My breast and my brain are moistened and cool;
And still I yell in answer

To your hoarse inarticulate voices,
O big, strong, bullying, boisterous waves,
That are of all things in nature the nearest thoughts to human,
Because you are wicked and foolish,
Mad and destructive.

CCVI

STORMY NIGHTS

I cry out war to those who spend their utmost,
Trying to substitute a vain regret
For childhood's vanished moods,
Instead of a full manly satisfaction
In new development.
Their words are vain as the lost shouts,
The wasted breath of solitary hunters
That are far buried in primeval woods—
Clamour that dies in silence,
Cries that bring back no answer
But the great voice of the wind-shaken forest,
Mocking despair.

No—they will get no answer;
For I too recollect,
I recollect and love my perished childhood,
Perfectly love and keenly recollect;
I too remember; and if it could be
Would not recall it.

Do I not know, how, nightly, on my bed
The palpable close darkness shutting round me,
How my small heart went forth to evil things,
How all the possibilities of sin
That were yet present to my innocence
Bound me too narrowly,
And how my spirit beat
The cage of its compulsive purity:
How—my eyes fixed,
My shot lip tremulous between my fingers
I fashioned for myself new modes of crime,
Created for myself with pain and labour
The evil that the cobwebs of society,
The comely secrecies of education,
Had made an itching mystery to me ward.

Do I not know again,
When the great winds broke loose and went abroad
At night in the lighted town—
Ah! then it was different—
Then, when I seemed to hear
The storm go by me like a cloak-wrapt horseman
Stooping over the saddle—
Go by, and come again and yet again,
Like some one riding with a pardon,
And ever baffled, ever shut from passage:—
Then when the house shook and a horde of noises
Came out and clattered over me all night,—
Then, would my heart stand still,
My hair creep fearfully upon my head
And, with my tear-wet face
Buried among the bed-clothes,
Long and bitterly would I pray and wrestle
Till gentle sleep
Threw her great mantle over me,
And my hard breathing gradually ceased.

I was then the Indian,
Well and happy and full of glee and pleasure,
Both hands full of life.
And not without divine impulses
Shot into me by the untried non-ego;
But, like the Indian, too,
Not yet exempt from feverish questionings
And on my bed of leaves,
Writhing terribly in grasp of terror,
As when the still stars and the great white moon
Watch me athwart black foliage,
Trembling before the interminable vista,
The widening wells of space
In which my thought flags like a wearied bird
In the mid ocean of his autumn flight—
Prostrate before the indefinite great spirit
That the external warder
Plunged like a dagger
Into my bosom.

Now, I am a Greek
White-robed among the sunshine and the statues
And the fair porticos of carven marble—
Fond of olives and dry sherry,
Good tobacco and clever talk with my fellows,
Free from inordinate cravings.

Why would you hurry me, O evangelist,
You with the bands and the shilling packet of tracts
Greatly reduced when taken for distribution?
Why do you taunt my progress,
O green-spectacled Wordsworth! in beautiful verses,
You, the elderly poet? So I shall travel forward
Step by step with the rest of my race,
In time, if death should spare me,
I shall come on to a farther stage.
And show you St. Francis of Assisi.

CCVII

SONG AT DAWN

I see the dawn creep round the world,
Here damm'd a moment backward by great hills,
There racing o'er the sea.
Down at the round equator,
It leaps forth straight and rapid,
Driving with firm sharp edge the night before it.

Here gradually it floods
The wooded valleys and the weeds
And the still smokeless cities.
The cocks crow up at the farms;
The sick man's spirit is glad;
The watch treads brisker about the dew-wet deck;
The light-keeper locks his desk,
As the lenses turn,
Faded and yellow.

The girl with the embroidered shift
Rises and leans on the sill,
And her full bosom heaves
Drinking deep of the silentness.
I too rise and watch
The healing fingers of dawn—
I too drink from its eyes
The unaccountable peace—
I too drink and am satisfied as with food.
Fain would I go
Down by the winding crossroad by the trees,
Where at the corner of wet wood,
The blackbird in the early grey and stillness
Wakes his first song.

Peace who can make verses clink,
Find ictus following surely after ictus
At such an hour as this, the heart
Lies steeped and silent.
O dreaming, leaning girl.
Already are the sovereign hill-tops ruddy,
Already the grey passes, the white-streak
Brightens above dark wood-lands, Day begins.

CCVIII

Sole scholar of your college I appear, [71]
Plenipotential for the party here
Assembled, elegant to present
Their salutations and my compliment

[71] Written upon Mrs. Thomas Stevenson's birthday, to be recited by Austin Strong.

A while ago, when to your hand I came
I tripped on commas, stumbled at a name.
Browsed, like the sheep of some ungenerous breeder
On that lean pasture-land, a First Reader.

Since when, by you presented, early and late,
I sit and feast with all the good and great.
And pass the flagon round, and praise my lot,
With Burns and Byron, Addison and Scott.

Since when, a practiced knight, fear laid aside,
Through verbal Alps, unfaltering I ride.
With polysyllables prove a passed practitioner,
And need not blush before a Land Commissioner.

For which good gifts, they choose me (choosing right),
To grace with speech the ritual of the night;
Deliver his rough verse with easy mien
And make my bow before our lady Dean.

CCIX

DARK WOMEN

I must not cease from singing
   And leave their praise unsung,
The praise of swarthy women
   I have loved since I was young;
That shine like coloured pictures
   In the pale book of my life;
The gem of meditation,
   The dear reward of strife.

To you, let snow and roses
   And golden locks belong.
These are the world's enslavers,
   Let these delight the throng.
For her of duskier lustre
   Whose favour still I wear,
The snow be in her kirtle,
   The rose be in her hair!

The hue of highland rivers
   That's flowing, full and cool,
From sable on to garden,
   From rapid onto pool.
The hue of heather honey bees,
   The hue of honey bees,
Shall tinge her golden shoulder,
   Shall gild her tawny knees.

There shines in her glowing favour
   A gem of darker look,
The eye of coral and topaz,
   The pool of the mountain brook.
And strands of brown and sunshine,
   And threads of silver and snow
In her dusky treasure of tresses
   Twinkle and shine and glow.

I have been young and am old
    And trodden various ways.
Now I behold from a window
    The wonder of bygone days.
The mingling of many colours,
    The crossing of many threads,
The dear and smiling faces,
    The dark and graceful heads.

The defeats and the successes,
    The strife, the race, the goal,
And the touch of a dusky woman
    Was Fairly worth the whole.
And sun and moon and morning,
    With glory I recall,
But the clasp of a dusky woman
    Outweighed them one and all.

CCX

A VALENTINE

WRITTEN FOR TEUILA

I, that was silent long, at last
    May praise with a good grace—
Your morning smile, your gallant heart
    Your honest eyes and face.

Go on, go down your radiant years,
    Fulfill your destined part,
But then as now, ah! keep for me
    That corner of your heart.

Loyal and kind you were at first
    And will be to the end:
Keep ever, what your youth has earned
    A loyal woman friend!

CCXI

TO A MIDSHIPMAN [72]

[72] Unfinished fragment written in answer to a present of some chocolate from the officers of H. M. S. *Curaçoa.* Vailima, 1894.

Off on the daring Curaçoa,
When on a journey,
I had been asked about the hour of four
By Admiral Burney;
I had been asked by him, and he
Had led me, right unwilling to a sea-collation,
When by the bits, by lantern light, there waited
A bowl of chocolate; and we, unsated,
Fell to the meal with gallant emulation.
And not unequally mated
Did glorious justice to that chocolation.

Soon an ungrateful country spurned my service,
And I, though bold as Admiral Hurd,
And adamant as Admiral Jervis,
Was, for that country's good,
Without the least emolument or justification,
Returned to a shore station.

Where oft, awaking ere the day,
Before the earliest lightening in the east,
Murmuring, I lay,
Mourning that absent feast
And the rich dish,
In memory dear but far beyond a wish.

Then Woodward rose, Woodward beneficient.
   Stern purser he, the eloquent diarist
Of that unparalleled voyage; and he sent
   Up through the arduous forest, by the mist
And constant dash
   Of sounding waterfalls,
And that chaotic hash
   I have the impudence to call a road,
A welcome load,
   Being two sticks,
Each of the pleasing hue of clay
   And both the consistency of bricks.

Sail on, my Woodward! Sail for aye
   To acclamation!
Whether in your ears the hostile cannon bang,
   Or, on some more pacific station
Respected, there adown the stage
   Of speculation,
Still may this humble testimonial hang
   In chateau Woodward for an age!
There may no irritant Soldier circumvent
   In angry disputation,
Nor unexpected Warren hit aslant
   With an interrogation—

CCXII

The faces and the forms of yore.
   Again recall, again recast ;
Let your fine fingers [73] raise once more
   The curtains of the quiet past;

[73] A postscript to a letter to Mrs. Richmond Thackeray.

And there, beside the English fires
   That sung and sparkled long ago.
The sires of your departed sires,
   The mothers of our mothers, show.

CCXIII

THE CONSECRATION OF BRAILLE
TO MRS. A. BAKER

I was a barren tree before,
   I blew a quenchèd coal,
I could not, on their midnight shore,
   The lonely blind console.

A moment, lend your hand, I bring
   My sheaf for you to bind,
And you can teach my words to sing
   In the darkness of the blind.

CCXIV

BURLESQUE SONNET
TO ÆNEAS WILLIAM MACKINTOSH

Thee, Mackintosh, artificer of light,
Thee, the lone smoker hails! the student, thee;
   Thee, oft upon the ungovernable sea,
The seaman, conscious of approaching night;
Thou, with industrious fingers, hast outright
   Mastered that art, of other arts the key,
   That bids thick night before the morning flee,
And lingering day retains for mortal sight.
O Promethean workman, thee I hail,
   Thee hallowed, thee unparalleled, thee bold
   To affront the reign of sleep and darkness old,
     Thee William, thee Æneas, thee I sing;
Thee by the glimmering taper clear and pale,
     Of light, and light's purveyance, hail, the king.

CCXV

TO TEUILA

1

I have been far, I have been near,
   I have been young and old,
But one of your eyes is brown, my dear,
   And one is brown and gold.

Your pretty points you still renew
   And alter from of old.
For once I knew it brown and blue
  That now is brown and gold.

Ten thousand dames and twenty-two
   Compete to take the crown,
They cannot put their purpose through
   Against the gold and brown.

Ten thousand dames and fifty-five
   Alas! Must all go down.
For the shyest, kindest glance alive
   Shoots from the gold and brown.

2

My dear and fair, my kind and pretty,
    Why come and sue to me for praise?
Why come and tease me for a ditty?
    Who are, yourself, my song of days.

Yourself the goddess bright that lingers
    Anear—and sings and sanctifies.
The days go round between your fingers,
    And the house brightens with your eyes!

Yourself the poem and the poet,
    My dear and fair, my bright and sweet,
The days rhyme (though *you* don't know it)
    And the season's chime, dear, with your feet!

My bright light (and who could oppose you?)
    My inexhaustible fount of smiles,
You are the tune that the whole world goes to
    And the brightness of the passing miles!

The beauty and the song of water,
    The brightness and the blue of the air—
I can be happy, my friend and daughter,
    So long as you are kind and fair.

CCXVI

TO KO UNG

Upon the departure of A. S. for school. Vailima, September 15, 1892.

A little fellow, putting forth alone
Upon his first adventure, begs Ko Ung
To guard his little fortunes and bring back
Himself at last, a bigger and a better boy.

CCXVII

TO KO UNG, THE GODDESS

My fortune has been great, I grant.
You have spoiled me like a maiden aunt.
You gave, I own, as much as it was in you,
And all I crave you now is to continue.
Bless, bless my house and bless my books,
Keep all my people in good health, good looks,
And temper, too; let still my credit mount
And keep an eye upon my bank account.

CCXVIII

IN LUPUM

Beyond the gates thou gav'st a field to till;
I have a larger on my window-sill.
A farm, d'ye say? Is this a farm to you,
Where for all woods I spay one tuft of rue,
And that so rusty, and so small a thing,
One shrill cicada hides it with a wing;
Where one cucumber covers all the plain;
And where one serpent rings himself in vain
To enter wholly; and a single snail
Eats all and exit fasting to the pool?
Here shall my gardener be the dusty mole.
My only ploughman the . . . mole.
Here shall I wait in vain till figs be set,
And till the spring disclose the violet.
Through all my wilds a tameless mouse careers,
And in that narrow boundary appears,
Huge as the stalking lion of Algiers,
Huge as the fabled boar of Calydon.
And all my hay is at one swoop impresst
By one low-flying swallow for her nest,
Strip god Priapus of each attribute
Here finds he scarce a pedestal to foot.
The gathered harvest scarcely brims a spoon;
And all my vintage drips in a cocoon.
Generous are you, but I more generous still:
Take back your farm and stand me half a gill!

CCXIX

IN CHARIDEMUM

You, Charidemus, who my cradle swung,
And watched me all the days that I was young;
You, at whose step the laziest slaves awake,
And both the bailiff and the butler quake;
The barber's suds now blacken with my beard,
And my rough kisses make the maids afeared;
But with reproach your awful eyebrows twitch,
And for the cane, I see, your fingers itch.
If something daintily attired I go,
Straight you exclaim: "Your father did not so."
And fuming, count the bottles on the board
As though my cellar were your private hoard.
Enough, at last: I have done all I can,
And your own mistress hails me for a man.

CCXX

AD NEPOTEM

O Nepos, twice my neighbour (since at home
We're door by door, by Flora's temple dome;
And in the country, still conjoined by fate,
Behold our villas standing gate by gate),
Thou hast a daughter, dearer far than life—
Thy image and the image of thy wife.
Thy image and thy wife's, and be it so!
But why for her, O Nepos, leave the can
And lose the prime of thy Falernian?
Hoard casks of money, if to hoard be thine;
But let thy daughter drink a younger wine!
Let her go rich and wise, in silk and fur;
Lay down a bin that shall grow old with her;
But thou, meantime, the while the batch is sound,
With pleased companions pass the bowl around;
Nor let the childless only taste delights,
For Fathers also may enjoy their nights.

CCXXI

EPITAPHIUM EROTII

Here lies Erotion, whom at six years old
Fate pilfered. Stranger (when I too am cold,
Who shall succeed me in my rural field),
To this small spirit annual honours yield!
Bright be thy hearth, hale be thy babes, I crave
And this, in thy green farm, the only grave.

CCXXII

AD QUINTILIANUM

O chief director of the growing race,
Of Rome the glory and of Rome the grace,
Me, O Quintilian, may you not forgive
Before from labour I make haste to live?
Some burn to gather wealth, lay hands on rule,
Or with white statues fill the atrium full.
The talking hearth, the rafters sweet with smoke,
Live fountains and rough grass, my line invoke:
A sturdy slave, not too learned wife,
Nights filled with slumber, and a quiet life.

CCXXIII

DE HORTIS JULII MARTIALIS

My Martial owns a garden, famed to please,
Beyond the glades of the Hesperides;
Along Janiculum lies the chosen block
Where the cool grottos trench the hanging rock.
The moderate summit, something plain and bare,
Tastes overhead of a serener air;
And while the clouds besiege the vales below,
Keeps the clear heaven and doth with sunshine glow.
To the June stars that circle in the skies
The dainty roofs of that tall villa rise.
Hence do the seven imperial hills appear;
And you may view the whole of Rome from here;
Beyond, the Alban and the Tuscan hills;
And the cool groves and the cool falling rills,
Rubre Fidenæ, and with virgin blood
Anointed once Perenna's orchard wood.
Thence the Flaminian, the Salarian way,

Stretch far broad below the dome of day;
And lo! the traveller toiling towards his home;
And all unheard, the chariot speeds to Rome!
For here no whisper of the wheels; and tho'
The Mulvian Bridge, above the Tiber's flow,
Hangs all in sight, and down the sacred stream
The sliding barges vanish like a dream,
The seaman's shrilling pipe not enters here,
Nor the rude cries of porters on the pier.
And if so rare the house, how rarer far
The welcome and the weal that therein are!
So free the access, the doors so widely thrown,
You half imagine all to be your own.

CCXXIV

IN MAXIMUM

Wouldst thou be free? I think it not, indeed;
But if thou wouldst, attend this simple rede:
When quite contented thou canst dine at home
And drink a small wine of the march of Rome;
When thou canst see unmoved thy neighbour's plate,
And wear my threadbare toga in the gate;
When thou hast learned to love a small abode,
And not to choose a mistress *à la mode*:
When thus contained and bridled thou shalt be,
Then, Maximus, then first shalt thou be free.

CCXXV

AD OLUM

Call me not rebel, though in what I sing
If I no longer hail thee Lord and King
I have redeemed myself with all I had,
And now possess my fortunes poor but glad.
With all I had I have redeemed myself,
And escaped at once from slavery and pelf.
The unruly wishes must a ruler take,
Our high desires do our low fortunes make:
Those only who desire palatial things
Do bear the fetters and the frowns of Kings;
Set free thy slave; thou settest free thyself.

CCXXVI

DE CŒNATIONE MICAE

Look round: You see a little supper room;
But from my window, lo! great Caesar's tomb!
And the great dead themselves, with jovial breath
Bid you be merry and remember death.

CCXXVII

AD PISCATOREM

For these are sacred fishes all
Who know that lord that is the lord of all;
Come to the brim and nose the friendly hand
That sways and can beshadow all the land.
Nor only so, but have their names, and come
When they are summoned by the Lord of Rome.
Here once his line an impious Lybian threw;
And as with tremulous reed his prey he drew,
Straight, the light failed him.
He groped, nor found the prey that he had ta'en.
Now as a warning to the fisher clan
Beside the lake he sits, a beggarman.
Thou, then, while still thine innocence is pure,
Flee swiftly, nor presume to set thy lure;
Respect these fishes, for their friends are great;
And in the waters empty all thy bait.

THE END